Bad Money

Brendan Brown · Philippe Simonnot

Bad Money

Inflation Mongers in War, Pandemic, and Recession

palgrave
macmillan

Brendan Brown
London, UK

Philippe Simonnot
Paris, France

ISBN 978-3-031-95424-5 ISBN 978-3-031-95425-2 (eBook)
https://doi.org/10.1007/978-3-031-95425-2

This Palgrave Macmillan imprint is published by the registered company Springer Nature Switzerland AG
The registered company address is: Gewerbestrasse 11, 6330 Cham, Switzerland

To my late mother, Irene Brown

The original version of the book has been revised. A correction to this book can be found at https://doi.org/10.1007/978-3-031-95425-2_19

Acknowledgements Robert Pringle has been a great inspiration to the ideas and their development in this book. As co-author of a previous work—A Guide to Good Money—he nurtured putting the case forward for over-turning the present deeply flawed monetary regime. He has read the whole manuscript, and his feedback triggered several important changes both in content and overall structure.

Neil Behrmann has graciously given expert advice on both writing and organization of the material.

Tula Weis, the editor both of this and our previous joint work, and long-time editor of Brendan Brown's books, has kept the project alive by quiet patience, confidence, and inspirational insights both at inception and through the writing process.

The Mises Institute continues to provide much appreciated intellectual and publishing support and in particular Brendan Brown acknowledges the encouragement at key stages from Professor Joe Salerno and Senior Editor Ryan McMaken.

The Hudson Institute has granted Brendan Brown much privilege to advance his ideas on sound money both in the form of research papers and public meetings. Alex Pollock joined in as co-speaker at the Hudson events. Our friendship and dialogue over many years—much longer than the present great inflation—have been essential to the development of ideas here as well as to fostering conviction and enthusiasm.

Competing Interests The authors have no competing interests to declare that are relevant to the content of this manuscript.

Intro: Blame A Corrupt Monetary Regime

The virulence of inflation in the US and Europe during the early years of this decade (the 2020s) and its continuation beyond are not inevitable consequences of pandemic, recession and war. Rather, we should view the Great Pandemic Inflation as a crescendo in malfunctioning of the actual monetary regime—the so-called 2 per cent inflation standard—in which the hegemon is the US dollar. The regime had gained and consolidated power in the US, Europe and Japan during the previous quarter century.

The fateful steps in the founding of that flawed regime occurred in the "Decade of the Lost Peace", the 1990s. There had been a clearing of the monetary skies in the early 1990s following the Volcker-Greenspan monetary inflation of 1985-8/9 and its aftermath of crisis through 1990–92. The inflation had got a jump-start with the Plaza Accord (Autumn 1985), when the Volcker Fed joined in the dollar devaluation policy, abandoning fully (partial abandonment already evident in 1983) the monetarist experiment of the early 1980s (see Brown and Pringle 2022). That Volcker-Greenspan inflation featured goods and services inflation and asset inflation—the latter most extreme in the case of Japan. Both symptoms of monetary inflation faded during the recession of 1990 (July)–91 (March) and its immediate aftermath. There was then an opportunity for the US to found a better monetary regime. Pre-construction work would have included crucially learning from the monetarist experiment how to better anchor the monetary system so that supply shocks would not be a catalyst to aggravated monetary inflation.

Instead, the US then took fateful steps towards a 2 per cent inflation standard—a bizarre development as by then (from the early-mid 1990s) the IT revolution was at a stage of powering rapid productivity growth and a spurt in globalization was occurring alongside. Under a good monetary regime these developments would have meant goods and services prices falling as a trend. Instead, the Federal Reserve—and the newly created ECB alongside—used the opportunity of downward pressure on prices to quixotically "combat deflation", fuelling thereby asset and credit inflation.

To understand why the US as global monetary hegemon took that fork in the road rather than the one which would have led to a sound money system we should take note of dominant political currents. The concept of dollar hegemony and the hazards of the US failing to couple this with sound money was the main theme of an earlier dialogue between the authors, (see Brown and Simonnot 2022). The second Reagan Administration (1985–8) and the George HW Bush Administration (1989–92) were not inclined to pioneer sound money reform. Difficult elections had to be won; according to the view from on top (including powerful Cabinet officials nominated by the President alongside political advisers) sufficient progress had been made in overcoming high inflation albeit the Fed should be on its guard against allowing this to return. Neo-Keynesian economic advisers held sway on both sides of the aisle.

Yes, there was the populist challenge on the Right (then in 1992 presidential candidate Ross Perrot), but this did not feature a sound money agenda. President Clinton had won the 1992 election on the theme that "it's the economy stupid", promising that "economic management" as in Europe would bring better results. Fed Chair Greenspan, albeit with an early history of mixing in the Ayn Rand circle and writing about the advantages of gold, had keen political antennae as necessary to his survival at the top (see Mallaby 2016). The Reagan-Baker White House nominated him for Chair in Summer 1987. The choice presumably reflected a view that Alan Greenspan was more likely than incumbent Paul Volcker (who in early 1987 was getting cold feet about the consequences of the monetary inflation which had followed the Plaza devaluation of the dollar) to run a policy which would help win the November 1988 election after the setback of the 1986 mid-terms.

We should rank this dismal outcome on the monetary front as part of a more general failure of Washington in the 1990s to build on the rare opportunities for peace, freedom and prosperity which had emerged.

The fall of the Berlin Wall and then of the Soviet Empire, the IT revolution, had created much potential for progress. Democracy and freedom in Russia and China were the prizes which skilful US policy might well have fostered. Instead, there were the missteps of first, the "special relationship of Bill Clinton with Boris Yeltsin". And second, the admission of China into the WTO, all despite the status quo of Beijing's repression evident in the shock events of Tiananmen Square (1989) and accompanied by a vast apparatus of state industrial control including subsidization. This extensive control, suppression of market forces, and financial coupled with political repression, had a corollary in massive savings surpluses in China which in turn matched equal size trade surpluses. All this meant that China's entry into a global free trade arrangement (WTO) would not be a win-win for all as simple trade textbooks might suggest. Instead, the gainers might be the totalitarian regime (including its elites) in China and monopolists/oligopolists in the US with crony links in Washington and Beijing; and the loser—laissez-faire liberalism.

There is a question which follows on from these considerations—hard yet to answer given huge unknowns about what lies ahead. Should we rank the blunders of US strategy regarding Russia and China in the 1990s with those of the Lost Peace in the mid-late 1920s (1924–1929)? Then the emergence of brief economic miracles in the US and Germany raised hopes of long-lasting prosperity and global peace. War-repelled citizens celebrated the apparent détente between France and Germany and the signing by 15 countries (including France, Germany, the US, Italy, Great Britain) of the Kellog-Briand pact (the US Secretary of State and French foreign minister respectively) of 1928 (coming into legal effect in 1929) renouncing war. All was for nought. Monetary malfunctioning—symptomized by vast asset inflation in the US hegemon and the Weimar Republic (on the dollar standard effectively from 1924)—played a key role in rendering ultimate disappointment.

Fast forward to the 2020s. As we shall show in this book under a good money regime the Great Pandemic would have featured most likely some modest rise in prices of goods and services overall followed by a decline in its aftermath. There would have been no negative implications for general confidence in money sustaining its purchasing power over the long run. There would have been no episodes of virulent asset inflation followed eventually by bust. And there would not have been the giant levies on citizens in the form of monetary taxation.

Defenders of the status quo might argue that any such ideal monetary regime as hypothesized in our book is “impractical”. They might argue that in any case the actual regime of the 2 per cent inflation standard has had much success—the great “age of moderation” from the mid-1990s to the mid-2000s, and again the years of low unemployment and low inflation from the early/mid 2010s to the end of that decade. The claim that the monetary system worked fine except for the unfortunate interruptions of the Great Financial Crisis, the Great European Debt Crisis, then the Great Pandemic, and now (though not inevitably) a US-China economic war, is bogus even in terms of its highly restricted reference periods.

We identify serious costs of the monetary regime during its 30-year existence to date including those long periods which went well according to the official narrative. Stimulatory monetary policies aimed at accelerating recovery from recession or averting the feared onset of recession may have had some superficial success as viewed by contemporaries. But there was a heavy toll of after-effects.

These ill consequences included cumulative mal-investment and a build-up of monopoly capitalism. And there was a giant increase in Big Government enabled by cheap monetary funding. Think in the US of the vast tax cuts and increases in discretionary government spending under the Bush Administration (some explained by war on terror but much beyond this), then the Obama Administration stimulus programs of 2009–11, on to Obamacare; and then the unfunded tax cuts under the first Trump Administration with no reigning back of public spending and then the mega outlays during the pandemic. The denouement was the splurge of public spending—social, environmental, infrastructure, war-related - under the Biden Administration. Sound money would have put a powerful brake on all of this—via the need to sustain the government’s solvency when stripped of access to monetary financing including inflation tax revenue.

Towards demonstrating how the Great Pandemic inflation emanated from a rotten monetary system it is essential to demonstrate the counterfactual workings of a good monetary system under similar circumstances––including the proxy war between NATO and Russia which followed the pandemic. This demonstration cannot by its nature substantiate on its own a guilty verdict meeting the test of “beyond reasonable doubt” test. Yet it can provide strong evidence. Counterfactual analysis concerning how a good money system would have worked including its restraining influence on the inflation mongers and ultimately warmongers was a recurring topic for discussion between the authors.

What is the essence of a good money system? This should have at its base a core of assets which have extreme moneyness of the highest quality whether as store of value or medium of exchange. The system has a solid anchor which operates such as to keep the supply of the base tightly constrained in a way that prevents "money getting out of control"––meaning no sustained emergence of serious monetary inflation which in turn gives rise to troublesome symptoms in goods and asset markets. A solid anchor requires for its functioning that the demand for base money, wholly non-interest-bearing, is broad and strong.

Supply shocks such as pandemic in a good money system do not trigger a perilous journey into an unchartered range of inflation. Instead, there is widespread and justifiable confidence in no triggering of monetary inflation. Any overall rise in prices on impact corresponding to the disruptions and shortages will be modest only and eventually reversed at least to a substantial degree.

In developing these ideas about how good money would have performed so differently and so much better than the actual monetary system during pandemic, war, and recession, the authors had a written dialogue with each other. Philippe asked the question, Brendan tried to answer, then Phillippe would pose a follow-up question. The death of Philippe Simonnot ended the written dialogue, but not his huge inspiration and founding contribution to the writing of this book. Previous dialogues between us go all the way back to 2015 when Philippe wrote to Brendan expressing his keen wish to understand his perspectives and relay them to a French language audience. Our first book under joint authorship came out in 2020—*Europe's Century of Crises under Dollar Hegemony*—and included large parts of our dialogue in question-and-answer form. This present work is not a dialogue book—but at various key stages in the argument the insights from the founding dialogue are highlighted.

Bibliography

Brown B and Pringle R "A Guide to Good Money" Palgrave 2022

Brown B and Simonnot P, "Europe's Century of Crisis under Dollar Hegemony" Palgrave 2020

Mallaby, Sebastian "The Man Who Knew: the Life and Times of Alan Greenspan" Penguin 2016

Thomas, Graham "Why the Russian Democratic Transition Failed" Council of Foreign Relations June 2024

Contents

PART I

Monetary Status Quo on Eve of Pandemic

CHAPTER 1

A Brutal Repression of Declining Prices

An ugly characteristic of fiat money regimes led by the US has been their repression of any periodic tendency for prices to fall. Repression has been brutal under the actual regime—the 2 per cent inflation standard. Potential catalysts to episodes of lower prices include spurts in productivity growth and in globalization or sudden resource abundance following famine. The Federal Reserve, in always acting to prevent overall price declines, most recently in the aftermath of the COVID-19 pandemic, has afflicted the US and indeed the whole world with the scourge of monetary inflation.

In the long history of US-led monetary inflations (say from 1921 onwards), we observe variable lags between the onset of malaise and the emergence of symptoms, whether in goods and services markets or in asset markets. Non-monetary forces pressing down on prices can camouflage inflation in goods markets for a considerable time. Inflation symptoms might emerge sooner in asset markets, but their diagnosis could be subject to some dispute. A chorus of commentators might claim that current market exuberance is rational and low long-term interest rates are natural. Diagnosis of symptoms is especially difficult if there can be no precise or timely measurement of overall monetary inflation. In any case, asset inflation does not incite the same type of general political opposition that we observe for a run-up of consumer prices.

Some definitions here (see Brown and Pringle 2022):

B. Brown and P. Simonnot, *Bad Money*,
https://doi.org/10.1007/978-3-031-95425-2_1

Monetary inflation is where the supply of money is veering persistently ahead of demand. Ideally, this definition applies to base money where even at the margin of holding it renders intense monetary services both as medium of exchange and store of value. Otherwise, the concept of monetary inflation becomes harder to operationalize. Improvisations based on the gap between the actual key policy rate and the so-called neutral rate are highly flawed.

Goods and services inflation is where prices are pursuing a path which is cumulatively diverging further in an upward direction from the path which would be followed in the absence of monetary inflation. It can be hard to detect this symptom as mentioned in a period when non-monetary forces (from the "supply side") are pressing down on prices.

Asset inflation is where monetary inflation has induced mal signalling by capital market prices, including crucially the long-term interest rate. Features of asset inflation include widespread irrational exuberance and more generally impairment of rational thought in ways identified by behavioural finance theorists, a boom in financial engineering which disguises leverage to produce apparently higher returns, and the spread of highly speculative narratives which investors in rational mood would treat with considerable scepticism.

In a good money system on average over time, there would be lengthy episodes of price falls and of price rises which stochastically tend to offset each other—consistent with money sustaining its purchasing power over the very long run. Such offsets, however, and their timing are uncertain. A good monetary system should have a structure which guides money's purchasing power so as to meet that long-run condition even if no offsets. The episodes of price declines would coincide with strong non-monetary disinflationary forces emanating from business cycle downturns, spurts in productivity growth, great new discoveries of natural resources, or abundance after famine; episodes of price rises would relate to the converse—business cycle booms, sharp slowdowns in productivity growth (including adverse terms of trade changes), famine. The monetary accompaniment to all this would be a very slow and largely steady growth in the supply of monetary base, which enjoys a broad and strong demand. In good money systems this base pays no interest.

So, for example, during a business cycle downturn, demand for monetary base would likely rise above trend in line with increased uncertainty. Individuals and businesses would seek to build up their "precautionary balances", made up of monetary instruments with a very high backing of base money. The resulting potential shortage of intense monetary services as rendered by base money is relieved by a contemporaneous fall in prices and wages, which reflects poor business conditions and related sales promotions.

During a famine or any other type of supply shock a rise in prices (as occurs at first through businesses boosting prices for items in short supply) is consistent with a decrease in demand for monetary base in real terms at such a time. This weaker demand reflects real hardship (and diminished real incomes). There is no offset as in the case of recession from an increase in precautionary holdings related to uncertainty and danger; in fact, there may be general optimism about better times soon after the temporary shock).

Productivity growth surges mean a big increase in the real demand for money, which is facilitated (given the steady low growth in nominal supply of base money) by the fall in prices. This fall occurs naturally on impact at a micro-level, as in competitive conditions, businesses cut prices in line with cost reductions, which occur due to the productivity boost.

This pattern of price swings as described across different types of departure from the normal (whether in the form of abnormally bad or good economic conditions) is consistent with efficient intertemporal allocation of expenditures. For example, during the business cycle downturn, recognition at large that prices are now depressed compared to where they will be in the long run means that individuals (and businesses) will bring forward spending into the present from the future. Alternatively, during the famine/supply shock, the present high prices compared to lower prices later encourage individuals and businesses to delay consumption. In the example of productivity growth swings, the realization that prices are falling means that individuals and businesses delay spending and increase present spending. Accordingly, savings increase to finance a likely capital spending boom.

A monetary regime, which represses the natural rhythm of prices as described (fluctuations in overall prices driven by powerful non-monetary forces) consistent with intertemporal allocation of expenditures, weighs on economic performance. Readers might question whether the repressive regime could induce a pattern of interest rate fluctuations which substitutes for the lack of natural rhythm of prices in inducing intertemporal allocation of spending.

The short answer is no. Now for the long answer.

Take the example of a famine followed by resumption of supplies. If all individuals expected prices overall to be stable throughout, then in principle interest rates could rise to a high level during the famine and then to a much lower level during the post-famine resumption of supplies. But that engineering would require monetary stringency during the famine and monetary looseness through the post-famine sequel. In any case, why create a shortage of monetary services during the famine and add to the woes at that time? Similarly, why create a surplus (of monetary services) further ahead? Surely it is better to have neither shortage nor surplus.

Take the example of business cycle fluctuation. Suppose the authorities seek to stabilize prices and repress any tendency of prices to fall during the recession. Then they could seek to compensate for the lack of stimulus which would have stemmed from a present fall in prices matched by expectations of higher prices in the future by lowering interest rates to very low levels now (during the recession). They could then aim to tighten monetary conditions at an especially rapid pace once the subsequent expansion is established so as to prevent overheating then. But how to produce this exceptional monetary stimulus during the recession period? The low or even negative rates during the recession and no price falls could mean a shrinking of real money balances or no growth in these at that time; that is the opposite of how a good money system which would stimulate spending via some windfall increase for each individual in the amount of super-money services which they enjoy (via a fall in prices).

Then finally turn to the example of the productivity surge. Towards repressing the price fall in the present, the authorities would have to engineer monetary stimulus. But that runs counter to the operation of natural rhythm, which would stimulate increased savings in the present (consumption delayed in anticipation of lower prices further ahead as costs fall with increased productivity). So, there is no way to suppress the natural rhythm of prices downwards without monetary inflation which in turn spawns the diseases of asset inflation and camouflaged (but still present) inflation in goods and services markets.

The monetary suppression of the natural rhythm of prices was an important factor in the persistence of asset inflation during the now roughly 30-year history of the 2% inflation regime. First, there was the so-called miracle period of the IT revolution from the mid-1990s to the mid-2000s, during which there was a sustained spurt in productivity growth. Simultaneously, there was an increase in the supply of resources (becoming more abundant), especially skilled labour, as the collapse of the Berlin Wall and the access of China to the WTO and the launch of NAFTA pushed back previous constraints on output. But the Fed, followed by the ECB, abstained from policies which would have meant inflation falling substantially below "target" even to zero or less. Such policies would surely have meant the end of the asset inflation, characterised by a general state of "irrational exuberance".

Hence, we had the build-up of asset inflation culminating first in the NASDAQ and related telecommunications bubble of the end 1990s (in fact matched by the onset of an at most a very mild US recession in 2001 which has now faded from the historical record due to data revisions). Second, there followed the reinvigorated and even more powerful lap of the Great Asset Inflation during 2002–7 leading on to the Great Recession. There were echoes of the great asset bubble of the mid/late 1920s, when the Fed was pulling out all the stops to prevent price deflation in the midst of the second industrial revolution (mass electrification, the auto assembly line, radio) accompanied by a huge surplus of commodities especially agricultural (resulting from the excesses of the First World War), culminating in the Great Crash and Depression. The origins, however, of the monetary disinflation which triggered the respective crashes were different. In 1928, it was the determination of the Fed, working in tune with powerful forces in the political arena—including the Treasury Secretary and President to be Herbert Hoover—to crush the apparently mad speculation on Wall Street.

In 2006–7, the basis of the Fed's continuing with high interest rates (Fed funds stuck at a high of 5.25% from Summer 2006 to Summer 2007 which turned out to be powerfully contractionary in the monetary and credit system, where exposure to a real estate market already weakening was already a huge question for some) was to combat a rise of CPI inflation (above 4% p.a. as pushed higher by a sudden vast bubble in commodities including oil) to well above target (at around 2% p.a.). The new Fed Chair (from early 2006) Ben Bernanke was a strong advocate of inflation targeting and enjoyed the sponsorship of President Bush from his initial appointment to the Fed Board in 2002 (the appeal being his writings and speeches in favour of powerful anti-recessionary policies—even though now on closer examination his policy approach of inflation-targeting in its application threatened (unrealized by the President) recession and crash (see Brown, 2022).

In the aftermath of the Great Financial Crisis, the natural rhythm of prices was surely downwards. The uncertainty and risks spawned by the crisis, together with the "reform" to the US monetary system whereby interest was now paid on reserve deposits at the Fed, added to the demand for money. Yet the Fed was set on convincing all that despite those downward pressures on prices, it would achieve its 2% inflation target. This "convincing" involved some emperors' new clothes style tricks—including all the hype about quantitative easing, albeit that in a system where this paid interest now on reserves at the market rate, there were grounds for scepticism about its power (to bring about inflation in the future).

Even so, tricks or non-tricks, including all the paraphernalia of zero rate policy and forward rate, there were grounds for anxiety about whether big inflation mistakes might lie ahead (meaning bouts of inflation above target), and at first this was reflected in dollar weakness (until later the ECB made clear that it was on exactly the same page as the Fed in all these matters). Those expectations of future inflation shocks might have prompted some bringing forward of spending but in a much weaker form than what would have been triggered by a pro-cyclical fall in prices under a good money regime. Under the latter, there would not have been the offsetting concerns about an unstable path ahead of asset inflation boom and bust holding back a strong recovery of business spending. And there would have been the bonus stimulus from the present fall in prices during the recession boosting the real supply of money (in a system where at the margin base money yielded much sought after monetary services rather than this having been diluted to zero as under the QE regime).

We should note the influence the Fed's natural rhythm-suppressing policies (at this time aimed at preventing a fall in prices, misleadingly described as "deflation") had on Chinese policy and in turn fuelling a vast commodity boom and bubble through 2010–11/12, thereby shoring up the reported rate of US CPI inflation (see Brown 2024). The weak dollar and near zero US interest rates provided a great context for Beijing to engage in a massive monetary and fiscal stimulus without triggering either a great flight of capital (exchange restrictions not withstanding) or a collapse of the yuan. In turn, this action by Beijing meant a huge boom in global commodity prices including energy (some would say bubble), along with all the related mal investment (and boom meanwhile) in commodity extraction industries around the globe. That commodity boom may well have held back the economic/recovery expansion in the main commodity/energy importing countries; in the case of the US, it may have been somewhat positive for economic re-bound taking account of the boom which got underway in shale oil and gas production.

When the China boom cooled and the commodity bubble burst (along with a devaluation of the yuan) in 2013–16, US prices in general would have fallen under a good money regime. But again, the Fed swung into action, this time under the new Fed Chair Janet Yellen, to repress the decline in a phone fight against "deflation". Some would say the intent was at least partially to take the opportunity to impart a monetary reflation/inflation that would be politically well-timed given the approaching Presidential and Congressional Elections (November 2016). The Democrats had lost control of both the Senate and the House in the mid-terms of November 2014.

Whatever the political motivation of Fed Chair Yellen, the consequences were a new high tide for asset inflation after the brief and somewhat shallow pull-back of late 2014 and 2015. The Yellen Fed could continue its zero or near zero interest rate regime through 2016 and 2017 (and remember in that last year though Yellen was hoping for a new term as Fed Chair from the New President). In turn, that made it feasible for the Trump Administration to launch its big business tax cuts expanding thereby the Federal deficit to over 5% of GDP in a cyclical boom without apparently running into any debt or debt-servicing constraint. The new President cheered the rising stock market albeit that his luck was running out and asset inflation had started to cool from Spring 2018, partly related to an unexpected significant rise in policy rates implemented through that year by the new Fed Chair (Jay Powell). This also came as goods and services inflation (as reported by the CPI) had started to pick up (through late 2017 and 2018), though still not breaching the 2% target.

The Powell Fed, in response to a growth cycle downturn (a period of actual growth below estimated trend growth) which became apparent during Winter 2018–9)—in fact a global growth cycle downturn which had set in (with hindsight) somewhere in the second quarter of 2018—started to hint at a coming reversal of its rate rise policies. The Fed funds rate had got to a present peak of only 2.4%. It fell to just below 2% by end-2019. The Chair was under political pressure most ostensibly from the White House in the context of the 2020 elections looming and the Republicans having lost control of the House in the mid-terms. Without the COVID-19 pandemic erupting (in Winter 2019/20), perhaps inflation—with a combination of symptoms including goods/services inflation and asset inflation—would have gathered strength in the early 2020s. Like most counterfactual questions, the answer remains shrouded in mystery.

There is no mystery though about the acutely inflationary monetary conditions during the pandemic in 2020–1 nor about the extraordinarily brutal repression by the Fed of a sharply declining rhythm of prices into 2022–3/4 as a positive post-pandemic supply shock struck (supply disruptions receded). Some of that force behind the brutal repression came from a build-up of monetary inflation potential during the pandemic, which had not yet spent itself. A component of that potential was asset inflation—including widespread irrational exuberance. The Fed during the post-pandemic period had no intention of neutering that potential before it impacted the economy by a strategy of severe disinflation.

References

Brown, Brendan "Book Review: 21st Century Monetary Policy by Ben Bernanke (2022)" Quarterly Journal of Austrian Economics, Vol. 25 (2) September 2022

Brown, Brendan "How the Fed Helped Create the China Bubble and Bust" Mises Wire, May 21, 2024

Brown, Brendan and Pringle, Robert "A Guide to Good Money" Palgrave 2022

CHAPTER 2

The Regime's Toxic Toolbox

Under the 2% inflation standard, the lead central bankers, whether at the Federal Reserve, European Central Bank (ECB), or Bank of Japan (BoJ) boast about their box of non-conventional tools. They developed these in and beyond the Great financial crisis (as in 2007–12 for the Fed and ECB, and starting in the mid-1990s for the BoJ) to address the ills of credit and banking crisis, recession, and of course deflation of which they have a great phobia. In effect, "non-conventional" seems to describe radical management of the central bank's balance sheet and the explicit manipulation of interest rates, including crucially long-term interest rates.

It is an exaggeration and indeed a serious inaccuracy to claim that the modern central banker under the 2% inflation regime was an innovator from scratch in developing the toolbox. We can trace as far back as 1919 the Fed moving the short-term interest rate around in conjunction with open market operations, which expanded or contracted the monetary base to achieve specific policy aims. For example, in the decade from 1919, the Fed did that on several occasions, whether to rein back post-war price rises, or to prevent prices falling in the early/mid 1920s, or to provide support to Sterling and to the US stock market (see Meltzer, 2004). In general, the Fed limited the size of these discretionary changes in the supply of monetary base, and its long-run path was only modestly upward sloping (albeit too fast for monetary soundness—see Brown [2023]),

B. Brown and P. Simonnot, *Bad Money*,
https://doi.org/10.1007/978-3-031-95425-2_2

quite different from what occurred under contemporary "unconventional policy".

The variations in the US monetary base in the 1920s were ultimately constrained by the dollar being fully convertible into gold. That constraint, though, was quite weak given the breakdown of the international gold standard in 1914, the huge "excess" gold reserves which had accumulated in the US during the war, and the fact that many countries adopted a gold exchange standard during the course of the 1920s (mostly from 1924 onwards) rather than reverting to a full gold coin standard (see Brown and Simonnot 2020). The only modest pace of base money growth in the US was capable of spurring powerful monetary forces of inflation (see Brown and Pringle 2022). It is plausible that the supply of monetary base in the early and mid-1920s was well above a path consistent with no monetary inflation given that the demand for monetary base had shrunken in consequence of the Fed's creation, which imbued new confidence in the safety of bank deposits (As highlighted in the previous chapter this situation meant that the Fed was thwarting a downward rhythm of prices—and so monetary inflation was camouflaged in goods and services markets, but not in asset markets).

In the years following the US dollar's break with the gold standard (1933), there was a huge expansion of the monetary base, though this did not occur (in contrast to 2008 onwards) as a pre-meditated deliberate use of a novel monetary tool—so-called quantitative expansion (QE). Rather the increase occurred passively in response to huge gold inflows to the US through 1934, 1935, and the first half of 1936, the Treasury buying gold to prevent its price falling below the new floor set in Washington of $35 per ounce.

Fast forward to the re-activation of monetary policy in the early 1950s—with the so-called "Accord" between the Treasury and the Fed—and through to the late 1970s. The Fed operated monetary policy by boosting or contracting the growth of monetary base, with no repeat of the big discontinuous and cumulative changes which occurred in the immediate aftermath of the Great Depression or during World War Two. Yes, Fed officials doubtless thought of themselves as "varying the policy interest rate", but they implemented this by instructing the New York Fed to add to or reduce the pressure on the supply of monetary base. And until the late 1960s, the obligations of the US as regards keeping the "gold window open" and joining in joint international operations (the so-called Gold Pool) to prevent the dollar price of gold rising above

$35 per ounce in world markets) were a theoretical, though dubious practical constraint, on the Fed's freedom of action (see Meltzer 2014).

Under the "Volcker Monetarist Experiment" of 1979–82/3, the Fed focused (with an intermission in mid-1980) on strictly limiting the growth of monetary base: the sharp curtailment in supply caused overnight interest rates to rise to very high levels amidst huge volatility. The Fed was not piloting the policy rate directly to achieve a macro-economic objective but so as to rein in the growth of monetary base such as would be consistent with a new and better monetary regime no-longer deeply inflationary. After the abandonment of monetarism, the Fed still ostensibly piloted the policy rate in line with objectives for the path of the monetary base or a wider monetary aggregate. The connection, though, became much less precise, urgent or exacting.

Alongside the abandonment of monetarism, the Volcker Fed took steps which we can view now as the forerunner of non-conventional tools in the sense of "using its balance sheet". These occurred first in the context of the Latin American debt crisis of 1981–2/3 which enfeebled several large money centre US banks: Fed and Treasury support for the banks at that point went beyond the classical concept of lender of last resort function and related monetary accommodation. The essence of that concept was the central bank making limited emergency loans against strictly marketable collateral at a penal rate on the assumption that the bank was still solvent but facing a liquidity crisis. There would be a related transitory increase in the supply of monetary base so as to "match" a sudden increase in demand for this from banks and individuals at a time of financial uncertainty (without such an increase short-term rates could surge to extremely high levels). There was none of the explicit build-up of the central bank balance sheet which we were to see from the eve of the Great Financial Crisis onwards. Even so, this early version of "too big to fail" help to "systemically important banks" was an important step in further undermining what remained of any solid anchoring for the monetary system.

Again at the end of the 1980s, amidst the asset inflation and bust which was one symptom of the new monetary inflation which the Fed propagated as part of the Plaza Accord negotiated by the second Reagan Administration (Treasury Secretary Baker) to devalue the dollar, the Fed and Treasury alongside other agencies of the US government played a role in "containing the financial system damage" of the Savings and Loans debacle. As in the early 80s (discussed above), containing the damage to the financial system risk was to increase the damage to any residual anchor to the monetary system. With "too big to fail" making its way into the US (and indeed global) financial scene, the demand for monetary base became even less strong, less broad and less stable. So, when the decisions would come (or no decision by default) on how to modify the US monetary regime after the further inflation episode of the mid-late 1980s (and its accompaniment globally in asset inflation, including the Great Japan bubble economy), advocates of the 2% inflation standard could make the case that a monetarist alternative was just not feasible given lack of stability in demand for money.

The adoption of the 2% standard was to occur under the second Clinton Administration. Alan Greenspan as head of the Fed had renowned political antennae which were doubtless sensitive to the power of the neo-Keynesians in the Administration (Larry Summers, Stanley Fischer, to mention a few). And as an economic forecasting consultant ahead of his Fed appointment, Greenspan had built a reputation for analysis based on conventional macro-economic modelling. So, it was all par for the course that in the early/mid-1990s the Greenspan Fed had already de-emphasized money supply aggregates. Then came the notorious Fed meeting of 1996 when FOMC Governor Janet Yellen produced her policy paper on why with inflation now approaching (from above) 2 per cent there should be no further fall in this—a view endorsed, with some qualifications (in fact political—would Congress agree to this divergence from price stability as specified in Fed legislation) by the Chair (see Blinder 2023).

It was under the Bush Administration that the influence of neo-Keynesianism in the building of the new monetary regime reached a new climax. In the run-up to the Iraq War (early 2003), President Bush fired his free-market chief economic adviser Larry Lindsay replacing him with a Wall Street "heavyweight" (from top of Goldman Sachs). Earlier (Autumn 2022) he had nominated Princeton Professor Ben Bernanke (a neo-Keynesian economist renowned for his advocacy of inflation targeting and his embracing of aggressive policy to thwart onset of great depression) to the Federal Reserve as Governor. The President's apparent intent was that Bernanke would become the academic heavy weight at that institution to whom Chair Greenspan would defer as the monetary expert. In line with this, Chair Greenspan got his term extended (by the Bush Administration) to early 2006. And already we can see Bernanke's imprint in the forward guidance, which started to be given in 2003 onwards with respect to the policy rate. This novel guidance was a key component of the monetary policy, which accompanied the rapid recovery of the economy from the long growth recession of 2000–2.

The tightening of monetary policy through late 2004, 2005 and into early 2006 was according to a new playbook where the Fed indicated strongly to the market its intentions for the path of the policy rate over the next 1–2 years so as to extend its power to control medium-term interest rates. The Fed now broadcast its intention to make a long string of small rate rises which cumulatively would add up to a substantial change (in fact 450 bp rise in Fed funds from 2004 to 2006). In effect this was the brandishing of a new tool—designed to manipulate medium term and even long-term interest rates. Correspondingly, long-term rates became even less than previously an expression of any fundamental facts about the global economy, whether excess savings or investment opportunity.

How far these measured and discounted short-term rate rises—large cumulatively in nominal terms—amounted to a severe if any monetary disinflation was open to question in a monetary system where any anchoring tied to the monetary base had become largely but not yet totally dysfunctional. There was no simple thermometer for monetary inflation based on the monetary data. The severity of the asset market crash and recession suggest that there could well have been a substantial degree of monetary disinflation through 2006–7; and the range of manias (as discussed in Chapter 15) together with the rapid rise of the gold price in the years before (2003–6) are consistent with intense monetary inflation before the denouement. We should also acknowledge that it is possible in principle—though rare in practice if at all—for asset deflations and recessions to emerge after a sustained long period of monetary inflation (as from the mid-1990s to at least the early/mid 2000s) without some monetary disinflation as co-trigger to the process. This "immaculate asset deflation" could happen due to operation of endogenous forces, especially if they impact the banking and near banking systems, throwing them into crisis.

Total monetary dysfunctionality was to follow. That occurred with the big addition of toxic tools to the non-conventional box through the years 2008–12. First, there was the Congressional authority obtained by the Fed in the depth of the crisis to pay interest on reserves at the policy rate (as against as previously zero). This was in effect a revolutionary change, burying any potential to mend the already highly decrepit anchoring system of the monetary system. With interest now paid on reserves, individuals (indirectly) and bank would increase their holdings well beyond the point at which they delivered any intense monetary service. Hence, changes in the supply of monetary base or shifts in the real amount held corresponding to price changes would not spur expenditure changes; in effect base money would now be powerless (see Selgin, 2018)—no monkey wrench in the machine. Base money had just become a very close substitute for high-quality government short-term debt rather than in a class of its own. Welcome to the world of interest rate policy and the death of monetary policy. No one—including the neo-Keynesians—had any good way of predicting the relationship between the path of interest rates in a world where base money had been neutered and price/inflation outcomes, no matter how sophisticate their measurements of the neutral interest rate or of augmented Phillips curves.

The decision to pay interest on reserves played directly into further innovation for the toxic tool box—QE expansion and credit market intervention strategies. The greatly magnified demand for deposits at the central bank meant a big increase in its buying of assets to match (see Ireland, Peter N, 2019). Hence, it could now fund a large share (if not all) of big government debt issuance, whilst also dispensing favours (in effect by increasing availability of credit and reducing its costs) to a range of private sector borrowers, including notably mortgage borrowers. The central bank buying of bonds expanded the capacity of big government to borrow in two important respects. First it in effect converted vast amounts of long-term fixed rate government bonds into floating rate debt for which an enhanced appetite now existed (interest payment on reserve deposits at the Fed meant that these had become virtually floating rate debt of the government). The containment of the effective stock of fixed rate debt issuance would mean less risk premium on this (whether against default or inflation risk). Indeed, the central bank buying made it even less credible that in the future this institution would turn round and refuse to monetize government debt in any default-type crisis scenario.

Turning to the credit support programs, these went now far beyond any classical concept related to lender of last resort function as set out originally by the legendary Bagehot. These were now aimed at preventing any seize-up of credit markets during crisis, and some would say explicit subsidies to favoured categories of borrowers (including, for example, the private equity industry). During the early stages of the crisis itself, there was the emergence of the bogus "separation theorem", applied again as we will discover later in this volume during the US banking crisis in the pandemic aftermath (early Spring 2023). According to this during a crisis, the Fed (or any other central bank) should continue to steer the policy rate to achieve its inflation target whilst alongside it should use emergency balance sheet programs to keep the credit markets afloat.

The problem here is a crisis of credit should be viewed as part of monetary process—how asset inflation, one key symptom of monetary inflation, comes to an end as monetary inflation turns to monetary deflation. Separation of credit and monetary policy makes no sense when they are both intrinsic to how monetary conditions are evolving. Indeed. the eruption of crisis indicated that monetary conditions had already become deflationary and the lead question for the Federal Reserve should already have been how to respond to this new information about monetary conditions having become contractionary. Yes, it is the case that the demand for money or especially monetary base would increase during a credit crisis and amidst economic uncertainty. There may be arguments for temporarily increasing the supply of monetary base during the crisis, whilst not intending to suppress the natural rhythm of prices downwards in an ensuing recession. How could it make sense for the Fed to continue pegging the short-term rate at an elevated level alongside all this whilst also indicating that this high level would persist?

Then we come to three other "innovatory" instruments in the toxic non-conventional toolbox deployed by the Federal Reserve or foreign central banks in the aftermath of the crisis—forward guidance for the policy rate (already tried by the Fed as we have seen during 2003-5), negative interest rates, and yield curve control. The Fed applied the first in 2012 during the European Sovereign Debt Crisis (and a partly related threatened downturn in the US, which did not materialize); and then again during the pandemic. In the simplest type of forward guidance, the Fed announces that the policy rate will be held at a given very low level, for say, the next 2 years. In a somewhat more complicated form of forward guidance, the Fed may make known that gradual rate rises are to occur over an extended period giving its view about the terminal rate. Indeed, the latter procedure became commonplace in the years following the Great Financial Crisis and including the pandemic. A key purpose of all of this is to strongly manipulate the say 2-year interest rate and indeed going on from there, the longer-term rate. The central bank view is that such rate manipulation is a more effective tool in influencing demand in the economy than simply restricting policy operation to the overnight rate. Of course, none of this would even be a starter in a good money system where the solid anchor is attached to the monetary base and interest rates are freely determined.

We can view the strong case made by the theoreticians and senior officials of the 2% regime for "transparency" as a lamb in wolf's clothing. The transparency on offer is shallow, extending in the main to the central bank's intentions as regards the path of the policy rate. This transparency is in effect an exercise in propaganda whose purpose is to strengthen forward guidance or the equivalent and thereby the Fed's power to manipulate interest rates. The questions at the press briefings which are a vaunted part of transparency are never about fundamental issues but of the nature of under what conditions will the policy rate next change and where will be the so-called "terminal rate". Very rare critical questions are deflected by the presiding Chair sometimes in visible irritation (for example, "what exactly is your question"). A good monetary system with solid anchor does not require press briefings.

The next innovatory tool, negative interest rates, seems simple in concept (see Santiago Carbos Valverde 2021). If zero rates are not enough to stimulate the economy out of a recession, why not take interest rates into sub-zero territory. But on closer examination, the argument is full of holes. Negative interest rates can be created only in a regime where reserves at the central bank pay interest rates (in this case, negative). And if the rates are to become substantially negative (way beyond what we observed in recent years in Europe or Japan), the 1:1 convertibility of banknotes into cash must be suspended. This is all the antithesis of a solidly anchored monetary system. Beyond that, the negative interest rates in themselves mean a loss of income to savers in monetary assets and this might weigh on their consumption, even though "the substitution effect" of negative rates is to encourage the bringing forward of spending. Negative rates nonetheless had backers in the political arena. And big government has an obvious predilection for borrowing at negative rates and can promise more to its voters in consequence. All the groups in the economy, including the financial engineers, that do well out of asset inflation, which negative rates are likely to stimulate directly (for example via desperation for yield) may have good reason to back them.

We should note that a solidly anchored classical monetary system does have automatic access to an important stimulus made of natural ingredients (rather than policy-injected). In a period of business, depression prices of goods and services fall to a level below their long-run norm and expectations of price rises in the future (as present abnormally bad business conditions fade) encourage the bringing forward of spending now. The initial fall in prices means an increase in the real supply of money (especially monetary base) even though growing only near a long-run very slow pace. The increase in real supply might induce spending (how much depends on the simultaneous increase in the demand for real money balances given general uncertainty and risk aversion at such times). Unlike for negative policy rates, where the aim of monetary regime officials is that prices should rise during the depression ("combatting deflation"), there is no restraint on spending from the side of monetary developments (for negative rates, this restraint comes from income loss both nominal and real for savers).

Finally, we come to the innovatory toxic tool of yield curve control (see Kliesen and Bokun, 2020). The idea is that the central bank fixes directly the long-term interest rate by readiness to intervene as much as is necessary in the long-maturity government bond markets. Effectively, in the present corrupted monetary regime, the central bank would issue reserve deposits to buy bonds. In its ultimate yield curve control means steering the policy rate below the yield peg; the income advantage of the long-term rate over the policy rate and belief in the success/continuation of yield curve control stimulates the bond buying. But suppose it transpires that the policy rate has to be set on a path much higher than the present if indeed inflation is to be held down at the target as set under the inflation standard or any other standard. Continuation of yield curve control could then mean an accelerated rise in the rate of inflation. At any stage where such fears/presentiments emerge, there is likely to be huge exit from the long-term bond market. Ultimately keeping the long-term rate fixed would mean no long-term bonds left. All outstanding debt liabilities of the government would be in effectively floating rate form—now at the policy rate. A return to the 2% inflation standard or any aim for sustaining the purchasing power of money would mean a sudden large rise in the policy rate, with the cost of government borrowing up correspondingly. In the process, a large share of the present purchasing power of the money could have been wiped out.

The adoption of yield curve control (YCC) by the central bank of a given currency is not good news for its holders. Essentially, they are being tempted into long-term bonds by their income-appeal compared to the policy rate obtainable on short-term debt securities and money, alongside the fact that whilst YCC remains unchanged (with the peg unchanged) price volatility of the bonds is low. But the holders of this money and especially in bond form should realize that there is a future scenario where the pegged rate rises or is abandoned altogether, alongside a general rise (and freeing) of money market rates, and when this scenario approaches or rises in probability the holder may not get out in time, unless quick off the mark. And if he is too quick off the mark, he might lose considerable income. Moreover, there is a good likelihood that the whole apparatus of YCC increases the likelihood that there will be a serious inflation mistake further down the road, even if the central bank/government do not intend at the start of engineer an inflation outbreak (so as to levy inflation tax ultimately); and there is the risk that the government/central bank all along have it in mind to eventually unleash a big inflation tax collection and YCC allows them to raise more than otherwise (in that long-term rates are hold down by manipulation).

In fact, the tools of YCC and negative rates have not been forged in the US as yet. But they have been applied in Europe and Japan, subjects we return to later in this volume.

References

Blinder, Alan "Landings Soft and Hard: The Federal Reserve 1965–2022" Journal of Economic Perspectives, Vol. 37, No. 1 Winter 2023 pp. 101–120

Brown, Brendan "The Qualities of Monetary Base Essential to Sound Money: fiat and gold" Quarterly Journal of Austrian Economics, Vol. 26, No. 4 Winter 2023

Brown, Brendan and Simonnot, Philippe "Europe's Century of Crises under Dollar Hegemony", Palgrave 2020

Brown, Brendan and Pringle, Robert "A Guide to Good Money" Palgrave 2022

Ireland, Peter N "Interest on Reserves: History and Rationale, Complications and Risks" Cato Journal 39, No. 2 (Spring/Summer) 2019, pp. 327–37

Meltzer, Allan "A History of the Federal Reserve" Vol. 1, 1913–51 University of Chicago 2004

Meltzer, Allan "A History of the Federal Reserve" Vol. 2, 1951–69 University of Chicago 2014

Santiago Carbos Valverde "The Effects of Negative Interest Rates: a literature review" European Journal of Finance vol. 27 May 2021 Issue 18 pp. 908-38

CHAPTER 3

Bad Money-Induced Fragilities on the Eve of Pandemic

On the eve of the pandemic (say Winter 2019/20), there were two types of vulnerability which bad money over so many years had spawned.

The first was a monetary system without solid anchor. This absence meant that supply shocks (such as emitted for example by war—whether military or economic—and pandemic) or fiscal explosions could easily dislocate any of its in-built restraints against monetary inflation. As this emerged, there would be no swift and effective resistance in the essential form of a powerful monetary brake.

The second vulnerability was the damage already done by over a decade of inflationary monetary policy since the Great Financial Crisis. The damage included over-leverage in the industrial or financial sectors; the advance of monopoly capitalism—most obvious in the case of Big Tech and the "killer zones" around them to defend against new entrants; disappointingly slow growth in overall prosperity as due to pervasive mal-investment; and indeed geo-political fault lines as worsened by the scope for war and proxy war financing created by bad money.

A monetary system that has no solid anchor has no mechanism to prevent it being set adrift by storm—economic or otherwise—meaning the given money gets out of control. The fitting of a solid anchor requires that the monetary base enjoys strong and stable demand despite its components paying no interest. For this to be so, base money renders much sought after intense services—described as super-money

B. Brown and P. Simonnot, *Bad Money*,
https://doi.org/10.1007/978-3-031-95425-2_3

qualities in Brown and Pringle 2022 and Brown 2023—as store of value and medium of exchange. In the anchor-less system, there are no equilibrating forces which strengthen such as to prevent the disturbance causing the emergence of severe monetary inflation.

The monetary regime of the 2% inflation standard was firmly in power on the eve of the pandemic—in the US, in Europe and Japan. Why would any rational individual have thought that the stated intentions of central bank officials to achieve this objective would prevent the periodic emergence of severe monetary inflation with its symptoms of asset inflation and goods/services inflation? Fanning such doubts would be the fact that a key historically reliable parameter in making monetary diagnosis—the path of the monetary base (and some would also include broad money aggregates)—had lost meaning.

Moreover, the overhang of huge government debts and massive private indebtedness worked powerfully against the political system establishing and sustaining fierce or reliable watchdogs to warn about and prevent a bout of loss in money's purchasing power. Indeed, quite the opposite: powerful individuals in the executive and legislative branches of government and also in the central bank might well "go along" with benign and optimistic forecasts about inflation whilst downplaying the danger scenario. These individuals in their inner-most thoughts could find the danger of "inflation break-out" quite acceptable and even advantageous (see Chapter 7).

We now know the nature of one big combination of disturbances which occurred in reality—the COVID 19 pandemic, the accompanying vast public spending packages, then the Ukraine-Russia war and the post-pandemic public spending bonanza in the US ("Bidenomics"). All of this was in the context of the central banks led by the Federal Reserve administering an interest rate policy misleadingly described as monetary policy (no role for any money supply aggregate—and indeed in the corrupted actual monetary system, any such role was difficult if not impossible to determine). The interest rate policymakers were surely sensitive to implications for the immediate cost of public borrowing and the deficit (especially given the large overall share of the public debt now effectively in floating rate form). Any solid anchoring mechanism in the monetary system had long become dysfunctional.

Yes, there were unsolid anchors touted such as to strengthen "monetary control"—for example the Fed Chief's readiness to "pivot", promising to take so-called tough action at some point in the future as evidenced by hikes in the policy rate which would bring inflation back down to 2% and distributing hawkish propaganda about this commitment. Tough action meant piloting the policy rate along a path which would turn out to be substantially "restrictive". But no one, including the Fed chief could have any great conviction in the degree of restrictiveness (if at all) in a monetary system without a functional monetary base as already described in this book. There was no indication at all that the policy pivot was sufficient to combat forces of inflation which had strengthened under policy rate piloting to date.

In the inflation process, none of the big disturbances and their knock-on effects, whether economic or geo-political, have featured black swans. Thoughtful individuals could and some would say should have been able to imagine the possibility of pandemic, war (direct military, proxy and economic), or public spending bonanza, or some combination of these, all ahead of time. The clues and references were out there. And there were a range of other disturbances which could have occurred in the course of time.

Let's turn to the damage done by more than a decade of inflationary monetary policies prior to the pandemic and war crises of 2021–3. We have already commented in this book on how these had fanned mal-investment and growth of monopoly capitalism—alongside an extreme distribution of income and wealth which went far beyond what would be the case in a well-functioning competitive capitalist economy operating under a sound money regime. Unsound money, by fanning crony and monopoly capitalism, has been a critical factor in generating the extreme distribution.

Some illustrations help demonstrate monetary cause and effect. A decade or more of central banks led by the Fed manipulating down long-term interest rates (whether by QE operations, forward guidance/propaganda on the path of the policy interest rate, aiming for 2% inflation despite the natural rhythm of prices being strongly downwards) stoked a hunt for yield. In this, tech companies or any other companies with possible monopoly-type streams of rents in the future became a particularly attractive asset to yield-hungry investors. In the climate of asset inflation, various forms of "irrationality" become prevalent as have been identified by behavioural finance theorists.

For example, individuals shun a certain loss of amount X in favour of assuming a risky bet with actuarial negative value substantially larger than

X but which offers the possibility (low probability) of a substantial pay-out (but a larger probability of big loss) (see Kahneman 2011). Such behaviour would translate into investment behaviour under monetary inflation, which shuns certain negative real returns on money in favour of over-priced risky assets, albeit the over-pricing can last a long time and become more severe before correcting in the long-run. Moreover, especially under monetary inflation individuals are prone to self-delusion, believing far-fetched narratives which appear to make the risky bets seem less risky than they are.

There are types of irrational exuberance, which involve extrapolating continuing large capital gains from recent realized gains. And investors chase speculative narratives, which under sound money conditions they would treat with much scepticism. These enabled budding monopolists to proceed along a path where they could wipe out competitors including new entrants that threatened them. The means of destruction was the cheapness of their capital costs (including equity capital).

As regards malinvestment in general, highly popular speculative narratives about the colossal advantages of new technologies (beyond the issue of monopoly rent) have been intrinsic to the capital spending boom related to their implementation. In general, these narratives have sped the adoption of digitalization. Under the conditions of unsound money, there is no reliable guide for the invisible hands which would keep the pace of adoption of new technology to a path which would be optimal. The train of technological progress under the influence of monetary inflation might travel too fast into the forest of the unknown and also take some serous wrong turnings on the way. The subject is not new. Did asset inflation in the mid-nineteenth century cause an over-rapid and wasteful expansion of the railroad system and too rapid decline in the canal alternative? We can see that possible connection in the work of Fogel (1970), albeit that his focus is not directly on the role of monetary inflation and its key symptom of asset inflation in the process. (Incidentally the US railway "manias" occurred across periods where the gold standard had been suspended (as in the aftermath of the Civil War) or where the US government was heavily tinkering with the rules of the standard (see Rothbard, 2002).

A topic less reviewed/discussed in the literature of monetary inflation is how this can enfeeble international security or more blatantly work against world peace. Most important here is to realize the key role of monetary instability in the hegemon, the US. US led monetary inflation through the twenty-first century and indeed stretching back into the last decade of the twentieth century fits into this description. Let's start with the Greenspan Great Asset Inflation, which emerged in the mid-late 1990s when this Fed Chief considered around 2% inflation the optimal outcome despite a third industrial revolution in progress which was driving down costs (the IT revolution). So monetary inflation in goods and services markets was camouflaged, but not in asset markets. Fantastic credit growth internationally was part of the outcome, which played to the advantages at least for a time of the first post-Soviet regime in Russia, the government of Boris Yeltsin. Huge credit inflows backed by IMF lending arrangements bank-rolled a perversion of the de-communization process to the benefit of a new oligarchy amidst systemic corruption.

In Europe, the nascent monetary union (from 1997 onwards) followed US monetary policy having demolished what was remaining (not much) of German monetarism; rampant asset inflation got under way especially in the European financial and real estate sectors—and in the markets for high-yield government debt (whether risky sovereign debt or risky bank paper or real estate-backed paper). In Asia, the Chinese government beyond the massacre of Tiananmen Square (1989) derived from the situation of inflationary US money policy much scope to follow suit. Beijing administered monetary inflation and financial repression whilst becoming the destination of global capital flows whether in the form of direct investment or credit. The latter included huge offshore borrowing (including via Hong Kong) by Chinese financial and non-financial institutions, predominantly at first in dollar denomination.

The Great Financial Crisis of 2007–12 (the later finishing date is chosen to include the sequel of the European Sovereign Debt and Banking Crisis) in Europe left Germany bearing a key burden in holding European Monetary Union together, meaning a piling up of its contingent and actual liabilities, whether in the form of debt guarantees agencies shoring up weak sovereign and banks or as key participator in the mega expansion of the ECB balance sheet. The Merkel Government in Germany had leaned heavily on the Obama Administration and its fears of a second "Lehman Crisis" before the mid-term elections of 2014 to get the IMF committed to the bailing out of European sovereigns, with IMF capital in fact all used up for this purpose (see Brown 2014). Two direct consequences of US financial support and the strains on the German budget of shoring up European monetary union; Germany was not going to object strongly to the US policy of extending NATO eastwards; and it would go slow on any increase in military commitments to NATO, meaning that the military axis in NATO would shift from Washington-Berlin to Washington-Warsaw.

In Asia, the vast soft money experimentation of the Bernanke Fed following the GFC facilitated a mega monetary stimulus in China—again shoring up the communist regime there amidst a fantastic apparent economic boom albeit featuring a giant bubble in residential real estate construction. In Japan, the post-GFC US soft money policies played a key role in undermining the brief new hard yen experimentation under BoJ Governor Shirakawa. The climb of the yen—the dollar falling below 80 against the yen—was one final straw together with the ineptness of the DPJ government response to the Triple Disasters of 2011/12. The consequence was a victory for Shinzo Abe and the immediate coup at the Bank of Japan installing a soft money regime which would provide endless costless financing it seemed to Big Government. Hypothetically, a sound money regime in Japan with a hard yen might have been a beacon of freedom—both political and economic in Asia analogous to the hard DM in Europe through the 1970s and 80s. But that was not to be.

In sum, soft money policies in the US snuffed out the possibility of hard money regimes elsewhere and sustained ugly repressive governments around the world. Negative interest rates in Europe and Japan were symptomatic of money there having become a tool of Big Government and the enfeeblement of free market liberalism. Yes, in principle either Europe or Japan could have defied the soft money lead of the US hegemon—as Germany defied the lead of the inflationary Fed in the late 1960s, 1970s, and mid/late 1980s. But such defiance depends on a domestic political climate where sound money can win elections and the big exporter fear/distaste of large currency appreciation holds no or little sway in the political arena. Winning elections depends on sound money allying with other causes which are popular at the time. That general constellation was not present in the years running up to the Great Pandemic Inflation of the early 2020s.

References

Brown, Brendan (2014) Euro Crash Palgrave 2014

Brown, Brendan (2023) "The Qualities of the Monetary Base Essential to Sound Money: Fiat and Gold" Quarterly Journal of Austrian Economics, Vol. 26, No. 4, Winter 2023

Brown, Brendan and Pringle, Robert "A Guide to Good Money" Palgrave 2022

Fogel, Robert (1970) “Railroads and the American Economy: Essays in Econometric History” John Hopkins University Press
Kahneman, Daniel (2011) “Thinking Fast and Slow” Penguin Books
Rothbard, Murray (2002) “A History of Money and Banking in the United States” von Mises Institute

PART II

Inflationary Combustion

CHAPTER 4

Famine, Fiscal Explosion, and War

Milton Friedman famously wrote that "inflation is always and everywhere a monetary phenomenon" (Friedman 1963). His meaning: any sustained period of rising prices has associated with it (in a causative sense), money supply rising persistently and veering substantially in excess of money demand–supply, and demand for money being continuously rebrought into balance by a rise in prices.

This statement is problematic especially in the context of the actual money regime, where the monetary base has become dysfunctional as already explained in this volume. Dysfunctionality relates here primarily to the dilution of base money's special qualities whether as medium of exchange or store of value. Dilution agents have included such factors as "too big to fail" support for banks, deposit insurance, and generous lender of last resort assistance. Dilution means that the monetary services renderedto individuals by components of the monetary base whether directly or indirectly as backing for bank deposits become less intense. Another example of dilution agent is the regulatory plus oligopolistic restrictions, which penalize the use of cash (rather than cards) in the purchase of goods and services (see Brown 2023).

Friedman's implicit definition of inflation was a sustained rise in consumer prices. But as we have explained here, the symptoms of monetary inflation, whether in goods/services markets or asset markets are not always easy to detect, all the more so in early stages. Symptoms in goods

B. Brown and P. Simonnot, *Bad Money*,
https://doi.org/10.1007/978-3-031-95425-2_4

and services markets can be camouflaged by a rhythm downwards of prices driven by non-monetary factors, which would have full expression under the soundest of monetary regimes (see Bagus 2016). The diagnosis of inflation then depends on comparing possibly stable consumer prices with a hypothetical fall which should have occurred if money was under control. Examples of these downward rhythms include the sustained fall in prices during periods of positive supply shock (emerging abundance of scarce resources, for example, after a period of famine), business cycle downturn, or spurt in productivity growth. Friedman never went along with the concept, in any case, of asset inflation, seeing this as difficult to reconcile with "positive economics", where hypotheses must be econometrically testable.

So how to rephrase the idea that inflation is every time and everywhere a monetary phenomenon?

We could start with the counterfactual. In a good money system sustained but overall limited rises or falls in average consumer prices are possible without any monetary malaise having set in.Most likely these would reflect a powerful combination of non-monetary forces.For example, a lull in productivity growth perhapse related to a slowdown in technological change could go along with a modest rise in prices.More generally supply shock could bring about a period of price rises, albeit constrained by the tight limit on the growth of money supply.Note that a good money system can provide for a long drawn out program of modest monetary injections (in fact monetary inflation) so that money's purchasing power falls back to a norm having risen during an episode when non-monetary disinflationary forces were strong. Those corrective injections come to a stop if meanwhile there is a gathering of non-monetary inflationary forces-such as an emerging supply shock or a bout of sub-normal productivity growth. As we shall see in chapter 10, the gold standard contains such a mechanism, where sustained falls in prices to a lower level prompt increases in the output of newly mined gold.

Just as good money does not mean the value of money is continuously constant, bad money need not be in a perpetual state of high inflation. Bouts or episodes of high inflation often come about where catalytic events combine with the bad money system which lacks any solid anchor to produce combustion. (For the sake of precision here, bad money systems can also sometimes produce high inflation without there having been a catalytic event as described; rather money just gets out of control without one big event to point to; the inflation in the US—and indeed internationally-from the mid-1950s to the mid-1960s might be such an example—see chapter 3). A good money system by contrast has defences (most of all the solid anchoring system already described) which prevent combustion from occurring.

Take various key examples of such combustion processes.

Sometimes the combustion starts with a fiscal explosion. We can describe this as a sudden perception of serious deterioration in the fiscal balance, meaning a big increase in the amount of red ink there. Sometimes of course such a fiscal explosion is linked to (contemporaneously or lagging) another simultaneous shock, for example war shock, or famine/pandemic shock. Those types of non-fiscal shock in themselves might have had the potential to produce an inflation combustion. The two together (fiscal and non-fiscal shock) can produce an even more fearful combustion in the context of the bad money system with no solid anchoring mechanism.

On its own, the combination of a fiscal explosion with a good money system could see prices fall eventually rather than rise. Moreover, the good money system could potentially emit forces in the political arena, which would restrict the extent of the explosion. One such force could be fear of default in the marketplace leading to a slump in government bond prices, which would be highly unpopular. But the anchoring mechanism can come under stress in the process, including calls for suspension of key components-whether constitutional limits on base money growth or gold convertibility or anything else.

Suppose the fiscal explosion takes the form (as usual) of some combination of tax cuts and increase in public spending. Across goods and services markets, this is likely to be reflected in upward pressure on prices in the first instance in line with raised demand. At the same time many households and businesses might perceive their real incomes to have increased-even when assessed over many years as in accordance with the concept of permanent income-because of the fiscal explosion (this assumes no pervasive so-called Ricardo effect where individuals feel worse off taking account of future likely tax increases).

So, if we were in a good money regime where (by definition) the supply of base money grows at a very slow pace and the demand for base money assets, all paying no interest, is broad strong and stable, then fiscal explosion would on impact most likely cause excess demand for money—reflecting an increase in incomes (unless individuals were to wholly discount future increases in taxation as under the so-called Ricardo effect—see Hayek 1942)). This would have two consequences—first, money market rates would rise (reflecting the shortage of base money—which pays no interest—relative to demand) and second, a wide range of individuals/businesses would intend to pull back their spending (on non-monetary goods and services) so as to re-build their consumption of monetary services (see Brown 2023) which has suffered in consequence of erosion of real value of their money balances by higher prices. (see Brown 2023). These shifts in spending could push prices down below where they were on the eve of the fiscal explosion, albeit having been higher following the initial impact.

That reversal of price rises which had occurred early on following fiscal explosion is challenging for the good money regime to deal with—quite different from the suppleness with which it responds to natural rhythm of prices as driven by factors already mentioned in this volume. These factors (non-monetary forces) have included episodes of sustained rapid productivity growth, sudden intensification of resource shortages (as in famine or energy supply cut-off), or business cycle downturn. In these latter examples, businesses adjust their prices in view of their sales environment in the same direction as required for re-balancing between supply and demand for money. Nonetheless, in the good money regime, the money guardrails do hold. And indeed, the expectation that they will hold mean that the possibility of default (actual default in nominal servicing obligations, we do not include here default by inflation) in the government bond markets exercises restraint on fiscal policy.

How would fiscal explosion joined with war, famine, or pandemic hit the monetary constraint under a good money regime, avoiding thereby an inflationary outcome? Here we have a combination of shock to monetary equilibrium—from fiscal explosion coupled with a supply shock. In principle, a slow-growing monetary base coupled with upward shift of prices responding to an increase in government spending and from the reductions in supply of goods/services would mean a shortage of base money. And so, the higher prices might come under some reverse pressure (back down) as individuals reduced their spending to rebuild money holdings in real terms, and higher money market rates had some dampening influence. But this reverse pressure could fade as individuals take account of declines in their real incomes as due to the supply shock and lower their demand in consequence for the intense services rendered by base money. That is different from the case of fiscal explosion on its own, where there is no real income decline-indeed possibly an increase, and so the decline in prices from the initial jump on impact would have further to go.

Historically, there have been examples of fiscal explosion twinned with war shocks conducted under gold money regimes. These include France in the Napoleonic Wars (see Bordo and White 1999), France during the Franco-Prussian War (see Wiegand, 2019), Russia and Japan during the Russia-Japan War 1904–5 and subsequent revolution (Siegel 2014). The resource shortages (including labour) which accompany these fiscal explosions contribute to the rise of prices during them and are fully consistent with monetary base growing at a still very slow pace. When the combined war shocks (fiscal explosion and supply shortages) come to an end, then prices most probably under the good money system fall back to a level near that on the eve of those happenings. This is all quite different from the experience of war and fiscal explosion under bad money regimes.

Bottom line: under a good money regime, war—equivalent in economic terms to a supply shock (resource shortages/fall in productivity plus fiscal explosion—would produce some considerable rise in prices (as driven by the supply shock and government expenditure). But an incipient shortage of money meaning high money market rates and individuals striving to cut back spending to restore their consumption of intense services from base money would restrict the overall rise in prices. In the ensuing peace, we would see the reverse of this. The positive supply shock, rise in productivity and fall in government spending should mean a fall in prices.

Under a bad money regime, by contrast, the government and its central bank are likely to resist the rise in interest rates which accompany the eruption of war and fiscal explosion. A key objective of monetary policy makers is cheap funding for the government; there may also be concerns to avoid severe continuing episodes of financial stress. The central bank and those to whom it answers may have a plan (perhaps secret!) to raise monetary taxation—easier to do so than raising explicit taxation on incomes and capital.

References

Bagus, Philipp "In defense of deflation", the Austrian, April 28, 2016
Bordo, Michael D and White, Eugene "A Tale of Two Currencies: British and French finances during the Napoleonic Wars" Cambridge University Press

online October 19, 2009, also in "The Gold Standard and Related Regimes; collected essays" Part 4, Chapter 10, pp. 367–81, 1999

Brown, Brendan (2023) "The Qualities of Monetary Base Essential to Sound Money: gold and fiat" Quarterly Journal of Austrian Economics Vol. 26, Issue 4

Friedman M (1963) "Inflation Causes and Consequences" Asian Publishing House

Hayek, F.A. v (1942) "The Ricardo Effect" Economica Vol. 9 No. 34 May pp. 127–162

Siegel, Jennifer "The International Financial Challenges of War and Revoloution 1904–1906£ Chapter 2 in "Peace and Money:French and British Finance in the Service of the Tsars and Commisars" pp. 50–85 2014 Oxford Academic

Wiegand, Johannes (2019) "Destabilising the Global Monetary System: Germany's adoption of the gold stand in the early 1870s" WP/19/32 IMF Working Paper, February 2019

CHAPTER 5

Pandemic Spasm to Great Inflation

Alex Pollock in his brilliant short tome "Finance and Philosophy" (Pollock 2018) writes:

So the future is unknowable, we're confused by the present, and we misinterpret the past—at least in finance and economics if not real science.

Well within a year of its publication date (2019), great surprise hit again, with the emergence of the COVID-19 pandemic. Surprise does not mean a black swan—or otherwise put, a total bolt from the unknown. Thinking and skilfully imaginative individuals may well have thought there was some finite possibility of a great pandemic occurring, albeit sketched in very hazy terms. The evolution of that possible future state of the world into reality is bound to have some unknown elements. There could be a trade-off between hard effort to reduce the amount of the unknown by careful mapping of future possible realities and nurturing a deeper intuition, which could flash forebodings and forewarnings.

So it was with COVID-19. Anyone who thought carefully about the economic consequences of pandemic might well have imagined that a fiscal explosion could accompany this. And given the rottenness of the current monetary regime, fiscal explosion was likely to lead on to monetary inflation. Flawed Keynesian prescriptions could play a role beyond fiscal explosion in driving monetary inflation. According to these, the economic downturn accompanying pandemic should be countered by

B. Brown and P. Simonnot, *Bad Money*,
https://doi.org/10.1007/978-3-031-95425-2_5

stimulus, including the use of new non-conventional monetary tools—no matter that the downturn reflected to a considerable degree supply shortages.

But who was writing about all these possibilities even a year before the pandemic emerged? Perhaps we could find some mention in the stress-testing undertaken by individual businesses concerned to protect themselves in some degree against all known possible untoward circumstances. General demand in the marketplace for such analyses was not evident—perhaps because so many sophisticate practitioners are understandably cynical about any gains to be made from studying reams of such material. And there is the issue of deliberate official secrecy. Wuhan, the virus experiments there, and the likely role of certain US government health officials in their initial promotion, were just not public knowledge.

Philippe, in our early dialogue on the pandemic, saw far beyond its terrible immediate human toll. He was full of foreboding about its economic, social and political consequences—none of them good for economic and political freedom. He insisted that we add a chapter to our last book already going through the editing stage (Brown and Simonnot 2020); in the epilogue to our dialogue there, we discussed the inflationary consequences of the policy response in the US and Europe. The fiscal explosion and its monetization (ostensibly by the Federal Reserve pegging the policy rate at near zero and presiding over a vast expansion of its balance sheet including the purchase of Treasury bonds) promised ill. The policies of the Federal Reserve and the massive government deficits made possible by these were such a far cry from anything which would have happened under a solidly anchored monetary system.

The outlook for CPI inflation would be influenced not just by the extent of monetary inflation—inherently difficult to measure with any precision or timeliness in a dysfunctional monetary system —but also by non-monetary forces. The scarcity of certain goods and services under the influence of negative supply shock would mean direct upward pressure on the prices of these. Subsequently, the supply shock would go into reverse as scarcity (as due to multiple source dislocations) gave way again to abundance once the pandemic was over. If throughout the pandemic and its aftermath monetary inflation remained strong then the dollar (and almost many other monies) would lose cumulatively a large amount of domestic purchasing power (in fact near 20% from 2020 to 2024). Two early tell-tales of the monetary inflation were the sky-rocketing price of gold through 2020–1 and powerful asset inflation. As is often the case—but not always—in sequencing suspected symptoms of monetary inflation these emerged earlier in asset markets than in goods and services markets. US consumer price inflation started to accelerate sharply in 2021.

The pervasive policy discussion amongst macro-economic policy-makers—including monetary officials—amidst the pandemic shock and accompanying economic downturn took its cue from the great recession of 2008–9. There was the superficial similarity of a financial crash at the start, (lasting much less time in the case of the pandemic—see Pollock and Adler 2022). The now familiar unconventional monetary tools were pulled out of the box together with fiscal stimulus. The lesson preached by those in the US corridors of power and by their accolades outside was that this time the fiscal stimulus should be bold unlike the so-called tame US fiscal stimulus of 2008–10.

All of this made very little sense. Yet such themes became the pervasive rationale of government and central bank action in the US and abroad (with some exceptions as related later in chapter 11). The plan was to intervene massively to prevent financial market distress feeding on itself in any way whilst boldly stimulating demand (consumption and business spending). It seemed that Chief Powell and Treasury Secretary Mnuchin were determined to prove that they would be bolder than Chief Bernanke and the White House Economic Team back in the early days of the Obama Administration.

Yet the traditional neo-Keynesian (and Bernanke-ite) ideas on which these policies were based had even more than usual dubious relevance to the actual situation of economic spasm—not a phenomenon which fits into normal cyclical analysis. Rather, the emergence of pandemic had closer parallel to famine—a sudden impairment of the supply side of the economy. And this impairment also included a change in characteristic of many goods and services (especially the latter); these could now be delivered only in a form where a risk of serious infection (by COVID-19) would be present. The same was true regarding the provision of labour services in now many potentially infected workplaces.

Who, except the most foolish, arrogant, crony-like or corrupt, would pretend that they could in any way assess whether under such circumstances aggregate supply exceeded aggregate demand (justifying demand stimulus according to "Keynesian logic"). Such aggregates were surely even more nonsense than in usual times!

What we could say with some confidence is that underlying real incomes or real economic well-being in aggregate-amidst some heterogeneity-had surely decreased under conditions of pandemic. In turn if base money were on some sort of very slow rising profile over the long run there could possibly be some excess supply of base money over real demand for it—demand falling under the influence of shrunken real incomes. Less demand for base money in real terms would mean that its purchasing power could decline to some extent during the pandemic even under sound money conditions. That decline in demand for base money was not for sure, as so much uncertainty at first along with raised bankruptcy risks could provide some backstop. And the fall in individual assessments of permanent income (to which demand for money might be more sensitive than actual income) could be moderated by expectations that the duration of the pandemic would be short. Alongside, there would be big changes in relative prices consistently, with items now in very short supply relative to demand recording large price gains—whilst other items facing sharp fall in demand recording price cuts. All of that would go into reverse once the pandemic receded.

One of the strangest aspects of the pandemic from Spring 2020 onwards (after the immediate panic during the initial spasm) was the widespread sense of economic well-being, at odds with the above supposition that surely there would be a pervasive sense of being worse off. And to match virulent asset price inflation was taking place adding to the sense of well-being for many. (We are talking about primarily US here—at the other end of the spectrum we have a variety of opposite experience including China as will be described in Chapter 11). Evidently, something was wrong here—how could there be such a sense of economic well-being amongst the setbacks of COVID 19 made worse in many cases by lockdowns enforced by Big Government?

The something wrong though did not have a given time expiry date. Some firms—new and old—could make huge profits in the pandemic economy. One thinks here of the giant tech monopolies all of which made great profits under the circumstances of the pandemic economy. In general, their business gained from individuals' efforts to avoid disease constagion by substituting digital communications for physical contact whether in the work-place or at home. Some would say these monopoly positions became even more enhanced. The vicious circle from asset inflation to their degree of monopoly power became even more hideous.

The divergence between economic well-being aggregated across perceptions of individuals and production of goods/services for society was a phenomenon of monetary inflation. Somehow the machinery of money working together with vast fiscal transfers was behind the delusions of individual prosperity in a global economy whose total output capacity had suddenly shrunk. Would there be a subsequent disinflation crisis in which the micro-perceptions and macro-reality would close together?

That is all running ahead of the story. But let's reflect on how the pandemic spasm would have played out without monetary inflation. We could well imagine that the decline in economic well-being amidst famine-type supply shock would have gone along with a strong tendency for households and government to dissave. Both would try to sustain or even increase spending now by borrowing. That would have a corollary in intentions to spend less than otherwise in the future. This tendency would have most likely gone along with higher long-term rates—though that is not self-evident or certain given the possible shrinkage of present investment opportunity and related dip in capital spending, meaning that society would in fact "live off" a diminution of the capital stock. Credit-rating concerns would have been a constraint on the extent of possible borrowing—whether by many individuals, businesses, or government itself.

At the individual and business level, there would be partial workarounds regarding credit market constraints. Public authorities could provide limited guarantees to "social credit programs". Governments could prevent their own debts suffering downgrades in credit quality by legislating broad-based solidarity taxes albeit starting at some fixed date in the future. In the corporate sector, businesses suffering huge income shortfalls and thereby entering bankruptcy territory could complete debt-equity swaps. In these present creditors would receive equity rather than pursuing the course of a full-blown bankruptcy. And finally, the prospect that prices would fall once the supply shock started to reverse (as the pandemic came to an end) would provide a natural incentive for households and businesses to delay consumption (or put up with shortfalls of present consumption). This would derive from the view that there would be better value in the future.

This possible sound money counterfactual was very different from reality as we shall find out in subsequent chapters.

And to add insult to injury, the Federal Reserve pursued two further back-to-back monetary accommodations of vast government deficits following the end of the pandemic—first with respect to the Biden Administration's fiscal explosion of 2022–3, and then to its public spending bonanza continuing in 2024 ahead of the elections in November that year. The tendency of prices to fall as pandemic shortages came to an end meant that the monetary accommodations of 22–4 were accompanied by a moderation of reported CPI inflation. Without that further dose of monetary inflation— an addition to the monetary inflation forces which had built up from 2020 to 2021—prices on average could have fallen far towards the eve of pandemic level. Yes, that could have meant short-term interest rates at much higher levels than actually occurred.

References

Brown, Brendan and Simonnot, Philippe "Europe's Century of Crises under Dollar Hegemony" Palgrave 2020

Pollock, Alex J "Finance and Philosophy; Why we are always surprised" Paul Dry Books 2018

Pollock, Alex J and Adler, Howard "Surprised Again – the Covid Crisis and the New Market Bubble" Paul Dry books (2022)

CHAPTER 6

Four Shots of Fed Inflation 2019–25

The most asked question in the financial media through late 2023 was why the US recession, so widely foretold at the start of that year in consequence of the previous year's big increases in the Fed's policy rate—from 0 to 4% by end-2022 and then to 5% by Spring 2023—failed to arrive. Instead, a solid growth outcome materialized, including a continuously strong labour market. US stock markets had delivered stellar performances—S&P 500 up almost 25% to end-2023, a result which was to be repeated the following year (to end-2024). Had the economists and financial experts mostly got it wrong due to some basic flaw in their analysis? Had they been too pessimistic, underestimating the skill of the Powell Fed to engineer a "soft landing" in which inflation would fall back towards target without the emergence of recession?

Readers of this volume so far can already decipher part of the answer. Fed policy had not become disinflationary despite the headline-grabbing rate rise through summer and autumn 2022. The massive positive supply shock, as pandemic dislocations faded away, under a sound money regime would have been accompanied by sharply falling goods and services prices across the board. Instead, the Fed took the opportunity of the positive supply shock to relieve itself of any tentative intention (formed perhaps during summer 2022?) of pursuing "severe" monetary disinflation. The word "severe" was never used in public communication and in any case would have had to include a strategy for neutering unspent inflation

B. Brown and P. Simonnot, *Bad Money*,
https://doi.org/10.1007/978-3-031-95425-2_6

forces—including still present asset inflation—with their origins in the vast monetary inflation of 2020–1. Unsurprisingly, no strategy ever emerged, even in embryo form. In fact, the continuation of strong monetary inflation was surely evident from the fact that reported CPI inflation at end-2023 was still more than 3%, albeit that the Fed claimed success in its "struggle" to bring inflation back down to target (2%) from 6.5% at end-2022 despite a further fiscal explosion. Fed success on its inflation target was still in question at end-2024 with CPI inflation at 3% year-on-year.

The "soft landing" boast, in any case, jarred with evolving reality in important respects. For example, there was the uncomfortable fact for some observers of a new build-up of asset inflation in late 2022 and through 2023, surely a tell-tell sign of monetary malaise. Illustrations included a decline in credit spreads from a substantially higher level reached briefly in early Autumn 2022 when much of the talk in the market-place had been about Fed disinflation; tremendous growth of private credit (outside the conventional banking or public debt markets) in which private equity groups (whose previous heady growth had been one big feature of asset inflation since at least the start of the twenty-first century) were strikingly active; a related boom in demand for financial engineers; and still scorchingly high speculative temperatures (irrational exuberance). Virulent asset inflation remained evident through 2024 and into summer 2025 (the time of writing), including further dizzy performance spurred by tremendously optimistic narratives about artificial intelligence and related scope for monopolistic profits far into the future.

True, by late 2023, consumer price inflation could be portrayed on certain measures as on the last lap of the approach road to the central bank target range. And in 2024, some asset markets which had been hot for so long, even approaching manic conditions, were cooling at least in some respects. For example, private equity groups were attempting to shore up growth despite sluggishness in their core business (highly leveraged takeovers taking advantage of low credit spreads and a rising equity market) by engaging in obviously problematic strategies. These included big participations in private credit (reciprocal arrangements here with other private equity groups), leveraging the structure of the private equity group itself (where previously unleveraged), and buying up insurance companies who in turn were increasing their participation in private equity (see Smith et al. 2024). None of this provided strong evidence of overall "slowing" of monetary inflation, especially given historical evidence from previous asset inflations where some markets might cool in a mid-stage of the disease whilst simultaneously others become scorchingly hot at the same time (see Brown and Pringle 2022). In any case, the Fed and its apologists (see, for example, Blanchard and Bernanke 2023; Guerrieri et al. 2021) did not claim that serious disinflation should be on its way to compensate individuals for the weighty cumulative loss of purchasing power of money since 2020.

The hypothesis here is that the great monetary inflation which reached a crescendo during the pandemic in the US (also in the euro-zone and the UK) continued well beyond it. Importantly, the big cumulative fall in the value of money (dollar loses near 20% of its internal purchasing power 2020–4) substantially reduced for many borrowers the over-leverage which had built up during years of asset inflation starting in the previous decade and especially during the pandemic. This reduction occurred for borrowers whose assets and income flows in nominal value rose cumulatively in line with or by more than prices of goods and services on average. The US government and many foreign governments were one category of such a borrower (in this case income flows came from tax revenues); but there was also a wide span of non-financial private sector borrowers in other categories.

That de-leveraging by fall in the value of the money was not a new phenomenon. Something similar had been seen in the 1960s and early 1970s when big inflation surprises had reduced indebtedness in real terms. Notably, in the US, a financial crisis did not emerge alongside the severe economic downturn of 1973–5. Indeed, it was only in the Mexico/Latin American debt crises of 1981–2, when real interest rose into the stratosphere for a multi-year period, that financial system failure almost became fact.

De-leverage by surprisingly high inflation is not uniform across all sectors. It is strongly evident in the case of fixed-rate indebtedness of the government—staving off any type of default crisis there. It is also evident in areas for example of the private equity sector where firms are selling goods and services whose prices rise as the value of money falls. That would be the case for example for private equity-controlled firms running hospitals or prisons—or a whole range of activity related to infrastructure projects.

The de-leveraging by monetary debasement had a corollary in huge losses somewhere else (candidates included the pension funds holding huge amounts of government bonds and credit paper; also we should consider here a wide range of individual and institutional wealth holders, even if for now the huge gains related to asset inflation elsewhere in their portfolios more than made up), but much of this remained hidden from view and would not necessarily trigger financial crisis any time soon. That could change if insurance policyholders had scope in time to demand repayment (albeit with long notice periods to the institution involved).

In sum, our hypothesis in this volume is that monetary policy under the Powell Fed from 2018 to 25 should be in effect described as seriously inflationary, albeit at a variable tempo. There were in effect four shots (injections) of monetary inflation. A fifth shot i may well be under way at the time of writing (Summer 2025) in the midst of the "tariff offensive" launched by the Trump Administration.

The first shot (injection of monetary inflation) had started in Winter 2018/19, well into the aftermath of the Republican/President Trump unfunded tax-cuts of Spring 2018. The Fed had accompanied these with around 100 bp of cumulative rise in the policy rate from around 1.25–1.5% in Spring 2018 to 2.4% in December that year. i Shifts in the policy rate are a notoriously troubled indicator of whether monetary conditions have ceased being inflationary or even turned to disinflationary. Such trouble is evident in 2018/19. A 100bp cumulative rise in the Fed funds rate from an extremely low level coinciding with virulent asset inflation could be a triviality in the bigger picture. Yet Chief Powell, despite no evidence that his modest rate rises to still a very low level had exerted any disinflationary influence, bowed to pressure from the White House to start undoing these in Spring 2019. The Powell Fed had been strongly criticized for having "tightened policy" in the first place by the White House. Various conservative economists joined President Trump in that criticism, some but not all tainted by a simultaneous scramble for top jobs in the Fed and elsewhere, which depended on Presidential nomination. These conservatives argued that inflation was drifting again below target (of 2 per cent) and so evidently estimates of the Phillips curve (which plots a supposed trade-off between falling unemployment and rising inflation) were yet again unreliable; unemployment now below 4% was not accompanied by any inflation upturn. The global and US economies seemed (according to contemporary data) to be slowing from Spring 2018 onwards. So surely now was not the time to thwart the supply-side radical reforms of the Administration and the Republican Majority in Congress (facing mid-term elections in November 2018) by cooling aggregate demand.

The fellow-travellers who supported the White House's drive for easier money through Autumn 2018 and into the subsequent Winter 2018/19 ignored the general point in this volume that there is a natural rhythm of prices as driven by non-monetary forces. Given the global growth cycle downturn and the fall in commodity prices reflecting the China slowdown (alongside the US-China tariff war), there should have been then an episode of falling prices; all the more so if the US tax cuts were potentially stimulating an acceleration of productivity growth. To sustain a 2% inflation rate under such circumstances meant shoring up monetary inflation. The Fed failed to neuter an overhang of unspent inflationary forces already emitted by monetary inflation in the recent past. A new strong pick up in the price of gold in 2019 and other symptoms of stronger asset inflation (such as falling credit spreads and booming financial activity amidst much irrational exuberance especially in private equity markets) all suggested that the Powell Fed in 2019 was on an inflationary path. That was the first monetary inflation "shot".

The second shot, this time huge and powerful, was the radical monetary stimulus through the pandemic in 2020–21 using extensively and in new ways the unconventional toolbox. This had gone along with a monetization of the vast fiscal explosion in that same period. The Fed had lowered the policy rate to zero and embarked on boundless quantitative easing, which concentrated on the purchase of Treasury bonds. But there was much more than that: the effective pre-emptive bailing out of financial and non-financial firms via a massive Fed-organized asset purchase program all financed by expansion of the Fed's balance sheet (see Cochrane 2024).

Then the third shot; just as the most powerful positive supply shock of peacetime since arguably the end of the Korean War began to unfold through 2022 (albeit blurred by the eruption of war in Europe starting in February that year which caused natural gas prices there to reach for the sky—transitorily) as the pandemic receded, the Fed again monetized the next fiscal explosion of Bidenomics. This explosion stemmed from vast environmental and infrastructure package (the so-called IRA—the inflation reduction act). We should interpret "monetization" at this time as holding back short and long-term rates from rising to anywhere near the level which would have been consistent with a pivot to sound money. Instead, the unspoken objective was to contain the cost of vast new government borrowing. The Fed backed down from its hiking rate program (in 75 bp moves) when the bond and equity markets together seemed to enter a free fall (as in late summer 2022) on speculation that the Fed was indeed pivoting to a Volcker 1980/2-type disinflation.

And then, fourth shot, came the monetization of the campaign to re-elect a Democrat as President in 2024. As it seemed to many that the US economy was losing steam into Winter 2023/4, with evidence of some cooling in the long hot labour markets and even the private consumption boom/bubble faltering, the Powell Fed suddenly broadcast a revised view. This included projections of substantial policy rate cuts in the year ahead. Of course, there is no way of proving "beyond reasonable doubt" that this Fed change in policy was a politically-driven decision. But why the suddenness of the change?

In any case there was no way of predicting reliably in advance just how forceful or successful the monetization in the Biden re-election campaign would be. In the US laboratory of monetary history, there is much evidence of monetary policy tuned to electioneering (see chapter 13)—all subject to the proviso that proof to the standard of no reasonable doubt is missing, at least in the sense of demonstrating intent of those administering/deciding policy. And in the context of a dysfunctional monetary system with no remnant of solid anchoring there could be huge gaps between intent and outcomes. How in real time could anyone assess the inflationary or deflationary force of monetary conditions—leaving to one side the huge focus on policy rates which in fact for most of the time give us little or no clue.

So fast forward to the Powell Fed decision to announce at end 2023 an intended pivot over the year ahead to a policy of cutting interest rates and by significantly more than broadcast up until that point. Prosecutors advancing the charge of politicization of monetary policy had some strong cards to present. There was much evidence from the past of Powell's "high political sensitivity"—including the three previous monetizations as discussed plus his record for assiduously cultivating congressional contacts. Then there was the "bad blood" between President Trump and Chair Powell (though not at the start when Trump had approved Treasury Secretary Mnuchin's choice of Powell as Fed Chair in late 2017). But no, the charge could not likely be proved beyond reasonable doubt. Who knew for sure anything about intent—even though as in the past the chair's close links to private equity could add to the story here. Perhaps the chair really believed that getting the US back to the 2% inflation standard constituted a real triumph and additionally that he could perceive in the stars some insightful message about r star. (the neutral level of interest rates).

Beyond these political or otherwise calculations of Chief Powell and his confreres inside or our outside of government was a lacklustre reality which we could sum up under the title "payback". The persistent and through long stretches virulent monetary inflation, especially in the dimension of asset inflation, had accumulating ill consequences. Would those come to a head at some stage in an almighty financial crisis? That was not certain though a significant possibility. We should acknowledge soothing factors such as the real write-off of debts by inflation as described and the camouflaging of losses in areas of the financial system where there was no immediate or early day of reckoning. And even where reckoning was early there was the full extent of potential government bailouts as evident in the Spring 2023 regional banking crisis and earlier in the February/March 2020 pandemic market crisis. A tentative lesson from the laboratory of history is that great panics and crashes-not including the giant spasms in response to shock of imminent great war (as in July 1914) or of Great Pandemic (February 2020) = occur always in the context of a visible monetary disinflation already under way. So there was comfort here from the improbability of the Powell Fed deliberately pursuing serious monetary disinflation.

On the other hand, the longevity of the prolonged asset inflation from this point (winter 2023/4) was an open question, given the possibility of an endogenous cooling (meaning a cooling from within rather than administered by Fed tightening). Relevant here was accumulating malinvestment (for example, the non-optimal way in which new technology was exploited, the related strengthening of monopoly capitalism, and ultimately a sombre rate of progress if any in overall living standards). There was a big question mark over the sustainability of US consumer spending at levels far above normal as catapulted there by the mega fiscal and monetary stimulus of 2020–4. The private equity bubble could implode under the weight of past fantastic excesses. And who could be fully confident in the extraordinary wave of physical investment driven by the innovation of artificial intelligence continuing with a subsequent consolidation?

Even without the trade policies of the 2nd Trump Administration, the globalization "bubble" of the past two or more decades might well be deflating now. A principal form of malinvestment driven by asset inflation during the previous quarter century or more had been the capital spending boom in globally integrated supply chains. The speculative narrative of that boom had been the big cost savings possible from spreading the production process globally taking advantage of new control systems for managing intricate supply chains made possible by digitalization. Rational scepticism concerning the possible downsides of globalizing production—including possible dislocations and mal-control issues—might not have got due weight in equity market pricing under the influence of asset market inflation including the "hunt for yield" (see chapter 15).

At the time of writing (Summer 2025), a key question in the US and global economic outlook is whether the Powell Fed has started to prepare and even administer a fifth shot of monetary inflation. We return to this question in Chapter 12 under the topic of bad money in economic war. Here is a preview.

In preparing the monetary shot (injection), the Fed would be responding to concerns that the roll-out of the Trump Administration's new trade policy means a high risk of business cycle downturn in the near-term. The case against the shot turns on the inappropriateness of stimulus in response to what is fundamentally from the perspective of the US economy a supply shock. The epicentre is trade with China, but also extending well beyond—for example, potentially high reciprocal tariffs and product-specific high tariffs including automobiles, pharmaceuticals, microchips and steel.

The essence of the present trade policy supply shock is that a whole range of goods from foreign suppliers to the US now face a hurdle in the shape of a tariff. Restricted supply means upward pressure on prices of the goods in question plus on prices of other goods which are close substitutes for these. Whether this translates into a sustained fall in the value of money depends on the monetary regime. A good money system would emit forces which contain the given price pressure and bring declines in prices outside the area of supply shock. It will take time, effort, and skill for various types of substitution by consumers and producers to reduce the effective hurdle. Strategies include replacing goods now subject to high tariff with goods subject to lower tariffs or no tariff at all. Such replacement occurs both by varying the type of good and its country of production.

Unlike the supply shock of the pandemic, the supply shock emitted by US trade policy is US-specific. The rest of the world faces a demand shock—heterogeneous in that the US tariffs are to a degree product and country-specific. The roll-out of the supply shock is largely determined by policy announcements from the White House. There has been much speculation about one part of the trade shock transcending China—the so-called "reciprocal tariffs". According to information at the time of writing (May 2025), these are to be levied after a 90-day pause announced in April (meaning a threatened imposition in July) and will apply to those countries which do not reach deals by then with Washington.

The supply shock implicit in the Trump Administration's trade policy stems from its high and variable rate across different imported goods and countries of origin. If by contrast the Administration were to levy a general and uniform consumption tax on all goods of whatever type and wherever produced (at home or abroad), there would be no supply shock. The essence of the supply shock is disruption to present patterns of production and consumption as between goods and countries. The levying of tariffs or of a general consumption tax under a sound money regime would not bring about a similar sustained long-run fall in the value of money (indirect taxes included in prices of goods and services). Quite likely there would be no fall of consequence-the details depending on the supply and demand conditions for money.

Back from the hypothetical consumption tax to the actual trade supply shock. This induced aggregate business and consumer responses on a massive scale so as "to beat the clock" ahead of Implementation Day. Hence, even the most gifted forecasters would have an almost impossible task in assessing the present and near-term situation of the US and global economy. A monetary shot program under such circumstances taking account of an inevitable recoil in global trade after Implementation Day is evidently a gamble at best,

Specifically, US individuals and businesses aware that new tariffs and higher tariffs are likely on their way soon (China trade already shut down) step up their spending on imports now so as to get ahead of their implementation. Some of that spending may have a corollary in the delaying of purchases of goods home-produced in the US.

Merchants help individuals and businesses in their various strategies to avoid tariffs or higher tariffs. They do this by accumulating much larger than normal inventories of the given imports. Hence, even after the new tariff regime comes into effect, the merchants can continue selling at the pre-tariff set of prices. That build-up of import inventories might be matched by the same merchants spending less for example on physical investment projects given the constraints of cash flow management.

All of this has a counterpart in raised production and export sales to the USA from the rest of the world. In foreign countries outside China the export boom to the US could give way to a collapse in production beyond the deadline for the next big round of tariffs. US demand for domestically produced US goods could simultaneously increase.

Suppose the Powell Fed amongst all this trade turbulence has proceeded with its fifth monetary shot. The actual and prospective size of monetary injection program is hard to estimate in real time. Symptoms of asset inflation-including record low credit spreads, fantastic speculation in the AI space-are evidence supporting the hypothesis of fifth shot under way but not conclusive given the notorious lags between monetary impulses and their assessable results. Present moderation in reported consumer price inflation through Spring and Summer 2025 is not strong evidence to counter the fifth shot hypothesis. And there could also be already actual countervailing good supply shocks-meaning new abundance of resources. These could include a spurt in producitivity growth due to AI innovations. Or there could be simultaneous new abundance of energy supplies, promoted in part perhaps by a peace in Europe. Such positive supply shocks would mean that a new program of monetary injections would not emit clearly visible symptoms at first in goods and services markets. Under a good money regime such positive supply shocks should translate into a welcome periodic fall in overall consumer prices and there would be no scourge of asset inflation.

How to measure the effectiveness of the hypothetical fifth shot? The actual path of consumer price inflation is a treacherous indicator at best of monetary inflation. Under a sound money regime, in conditions where income loss from trade supply shock is being matched to some extent by income and capital tax cuts or public spending increases, prices of consumer goods and services on average would follow a likely winding path along which there could be sustained moves in one direction or another. These moves, however, would be cumulatively limited and likely reversed over the long run. The actual outcome would depend on how the disturbances alter the demand for base money in real terms.

Under the status quo of the present bad money system, the Fed adjusts its policy rate ostensibly so as to fulfil its dual mandate of low unemployment and low inflation. Accordingly, as we have discussed already in this volume (see chapter 4) supply shocks such as the change in US trade policy, are at high risk of triggering inflation combustion, meaning an intensification of monetary inflation.

References

Blanchard, Olivier and Bernanke, Ben "What caused the pandemic era inflation" NBER Working Paper, June 2023

Brown, Brendan and Pringle, Robert "A Guide to Good Money: Beyond the illusions of asset inflation" Palgrave 2022

Cochrane, John "Fiscal Narratives for US inflation" Stanford University Working Paper, January 29, 2024

Guerrieri, Veronica et al. "Monetary Policy in Time of Structural Reallocation" Jackson Hole Federal Reserve Conference Paper, August 2021

Smith, Ian; Lough Will; Agini Samuel "Is Private Equity's Bet on Life Insurance turning Sour?" Financial Times, March 24, 2024

PART III

The Inflation Mongers

CHAPTER 7

The Inflation-Mongers Say "Transitory"

Those directing US economic policy during the pandemic were careless about the inflationary consequences of their chosen path. This does not mean that they aimed for severe inflation. But they decided on a policy which inevitably increased the danger of high inflation occurring even if that was not their central expectation. The policy makers whether in the Federal Reserve or the White House were cavalier about their ability to steer the US through and beyond a period of high inflation should this materialize. In any case inflation from their viewpoint was not a monetary disease to be eradicated. A modest amount with regrettable spikes as could be explained by supply shocks was wholly acceptable to them. The status quo monetary regime which they endorsed had as its aim perpetual inflation albeit at a so called modest pace. The regime had a long history of repressing and resisting wholly benign build-ups of non-monetary disinflationary forces. Hence, the epithet of inflation-monger.

There is a parallel here to the warmonger who conducts international relations in an aggressive fashion but who does not expect to take his or her country into a war; but that may happen because threats and counter-threats get out of control, fuelling ambiguity and stimulating anxiety. Philologists tell us that the origin of the word "warmonger" has to do with monger in its Old English senses of "dealer" or "trader". The warmonger may even be of the persuasion that war if it comes will be quick and not bloody. The warmonger may well have heard or even

B. Brown and P. Simonnot, *Bad Money*,
https://doi.org/10.1007/978-3-031-95425-2_7

considered the warnings from pessimists that it could end up being a catastrophic stalemate or worse. Although the warmonger may not be aiming for war, he or she is not at this stage amongst those who are the most anguished by the suffering which would occur if this were to erupt. This apparent low level of human sentiment may also be related to profits that he/she would make out of war, whether directly or via business relationships.

What are the parallels with the inflation-mongers in the regime of the 2% inflation standard and especially during the episode of the COVID-19 pandemic? They are bellicose about getting inflation up if it is too low (below 2%). They turn swiftly and severely to a policy of stepped-up monetary inflation in response to any likely shortfall in inflation (below 2%) and interpret this situation to include perceived danger or actuality of recession. They are ready to apply powerful instruments from their non-conventional toolbox for these purposes. Their intention is not to get inflation thereby much above 2% but if that happens, they are not greatly concerned due to their boast of being able to rein this mistake back well before high inflation becomes sustained. And they may not be the most anguished by the emergence of high inflation were this to occur given that he or she personally, or the cronies or Congress people or White House people who hold sway over him or her, are positioned so that their business profits and wealth would increase with inflation whilst potentially suffering terribly from deflationary crisis. The Congress and White House people may not just be thinking about their own personal positions but also thinking (to themselves) that the inflation tax which the emergence of high inflation would bring in could be useful (so long as they can somehow keep it camouflaged—perhaps by continuing asset inflation which showers gains on many voters). Was this the state of mind of leading monetary officials in the US when the pandemic emerged and of those to whom they answered (whether in Congress or in the re-nomination committees of the White House)? The same charge could be laid against policymakers in Europe and Japan.

Philippe and I jointly wrote our first piece on the potential inflationary outcome of pandemic monetary policies in our epilogue to our dialogue published in late 2020. Our hypothesis was that the pandemic would bring a substantial deterioration in the quality of fiat money as led by the dollar hegemon. Neither of us yet had coined the term inflation-monger but the constituents of that concept were very much in our discussion. And in retrospect, the extraordinary "inflation is transitory" claims of the dominant monetary policy makers, most of all at the Federal Reserve but also in Europe, were a central aspect of the inflation-mongering.

The central banks which proclaimed they were fighting depression or severe recession that the pandemic might cause did not concern themselves with the high inflation scenarios mentioned by the critics. In any case, some override of inflation above 2% could even be welcome towards achieving an average 2% inflation over time given under-shooting of the target in some recent years. And they believed that they had the means to curb high inflation if this began to emerge threatened to emerge and they could prevent there being any damage during the crackdown on inflation which had got too high.

The "inflation is transitory hypothesis" waned through l2021 as actually reported CPI inflation entered an alarming uptrend. By winter 2021/2, the high recorded CPI inflation and the approach of the mid-terms (November 2022) amidst political evidence of voter concern about high prices had persuaded the Fed to back away from pronouncing that high inflation was "just transitory". Again, however, by Summer 2022 when markets were swooning under the influence of big Fed rate rises, and inflation had visibly peaked on the CPI and other official measures, "team transitory" again became vocal (see, for example, Dolan 2022).

The proponents of "inflation is transitory" in the depths of the pandemic seemed to be saying that they expected the reported sharp rise in CPI inflation to be "reasonably short-lived". They explained the hypothesized short life by attributing the present severe rise in prices to the actual acute negative supply shock (in this case the dislocation and reduction of supplies by the pandemic). In general, they had no notion of prices in general falling back to the eve-of-pandemic level as the supply shock was reversed once the pandemic faded away. Rather the rise in prices which occurred during the pandemic – whatever that turned out to be cumulatively—would be "locked in"; beyond, the rate of rise of prices would fall back to the target, in this case 2% per annum.

We can think of this in terms of a price hill. Sound money advocates would interpret "inflation is transitory" under their regime as meaning that a likely moderate rise in prices to a near-term peak would be followed by a decline from the peak back to near initial levels. By contrast for the inflation is transitory team including the Fed and its enablers in Congress and the White House—the inflation mongers—the meaning (whether intuitive or explicitly considered) was that there would be a sharp rise of prices during the period of negative supply shock; there would follow another up-hill stretch as prices continued to rise at a faster pace than the original target even once the pandemic had faded. This further period of above-target price rises should be short and not cumulatively severe (just various lags in price and wage adjustment, especially in areas where there had been quasi-rationing and price controls), but the positive supply shock would bring this further above-target CPI inflation to an early end. Then, with the pandemic supply shock reversed in its entirety, CPI inflation would return to its original target.

This notion of "transitory inflation" was fuzzy at best and malevolent at worst. Why should there be a period of continued above-target rise in prices once the original supply shock was moving into reverse: and how long and severe could this period be consistent with the definition of transitory. And how large could the cumulative rise in prices be during the period of above-target inflation and subsequently locked in before target inflation resumed for all this to meet the definition of transitory?

One critique of transitory was that the pandemic would ignite an inflation combustion process. Accordingly, these critics warned of a cumulative rise in prices far beyond what could be described as some modest locking in of increases during the period of supply shortage. There would be a continuing high inflation trajectory beyond. Some of the opposition to the "inflation is transitory team" cited the example of the oil price shocks in the 1970s, especially the great shock of 1973, and how this "ushered in" high inflation through the rest of that decade (see Carstens 2022). Implicit in this critique was a malfunctioning of the monetary regime—what we describe as "Bad Money". "Team Transitory" quoted the example of the Korean War, the short albeit sharp inflation of 1951–2, followed by years of near price stability (see Gagnon and Rose, 2001). In fact, the devil was in the details of each historical episode. By the time of the oil price shock in Autumn 1973, CPI inflation in the US was already running in double digits reflecting years of inflationary Fed monetary policy; monetary policy had been tightened sharply in the months before the oil shock. The subsequent prolonged high inflation through the rest of the 1970s (after the Great Recession of 73–5) occurred in the context of further monetary inflation impulses and a second oil supply shock emitted by the Iranian Revolution in 1978.

In effect Team Transitory which included the Federal Reserve through 2020–1 considered actual monetary conditions to be appropriate (as taken in combination with the extraordinary fiscal policy). Their central scenario was that the plotted path of policy rates (according to which there would be only a modest rise ahead from present near-zero level starting some considerable time into the future) would mean a "tolerable" cumulative overshoot of the targeted inflation path and an acceptably short period of time before the inflation rate fell back to its annual target. As such we can say that by late 2021 and early 2022 the doubts were increasing markedly both inside and outside the Fed about whether that was a reasonable central scenario or whether there would have to be a substantial course correction. And related to all that is the question about the seriousness of Fed intent and the competence of that institution to translate serious intent into appropriate action.

In particular, did the Fed stick with a central scenario and ignore the alternative scenarios of increasing likelihood because the latter could actually suit the purposes of those it was in close relationship with (whether Big Government including Congress or the cronies in the financial industry). Even when the Fed decided to "pivot" or make a "hawkish turn", did some members of Team Transitory outside that institution overestimate the Fed's seriousness, honesty (as to purpose), and competence? Yes. Did they get their history wrong? Yes.

To suggest, as some of Team Transitory did (see also Krugman 2022), that the Korean War aftermath was going to repeat itself ignored the very different situation of the mid and late 1950s from the early 2020s. In the former case we had a shift in monetary regime (in the US the Treasury-Fed Accord 1951 (Hetzel and Leach 2001) and the gradual journey—as Germany led the way in removing exchange restrictions—towards non-US investors in general (outside official monetary institutions who already had that privilege) being able to convert dollars into gold at the fixed price of $35 per ounce). And the 1950s were an age of economic miracle—in Germany, Japan, and indeed the US—with rapid productivity growth putting downward pressure on prices. The early and mid-2020s do not seem to be a repeat in this regard, albeit that some rosy scenarios about the pace and success of digitalization might rank alongside.

So, let's sum up who was on the opposite side to Team Transitory?

First, there were the sound money theorists. They bemoaned the deep flaws in the 2% inflation standard (see Brown and Pringle 2022; White 2021). Furthermore, any claimed triumph about a restoration of the 2% inflation standard—if indeed there were a spell of a gentle rising price level after the Great Pandemic Inflation—would be shallow. New huge uncertainty about the value of money would take its toll on economic welfare. And there was a more general point. Sound money has a solid anchor which prevents supply shocks becoming the catalyst-as combustion agent-to episodes of monetary inflation now and in the future. These episodes, characterized by severe goods and asset inflation, taken together are inconsistent with money sustaining its value in the long run. Under a sound money regime there is no pandering to the inflation mongers who claim that current severe symptoms of inflation are just transitory and not indicative of economic damage or broader hazard.

Second, we should consider those who were not intrinsically against the present regime but who were nonetheless pessimistic about any early and large decline in inflation (see Eggerton and Kohn 2023). They tended to emphasize the problem of inflation expectations and related to this the formation of wage-price spirals. We could describe them as exhorting monetary official of the present regime to do better without positioning themselves against the regime on basic considerations. Some of these worried that the central banks would lack the determination or backing in the political arena to implement sufficiently severe monetary disinflation to confront the issue of inflation expectations ratcheting upwards.

In practice, this anti-transitory team missed focusing on an important issue. There would be a big positive supply shock at some point when the dislocations of the pandemic faded. The recorded rate of CPI inflation down should come down sharply at that point. Reining in monetary inflation then could well require that monetary conditions become ostensibly tight (with interest rates likely climbing far) simultaneously with the positive supply shock—just at a time when reported CPI inflation was falling. Would regime officials reach that conclusion and even if they did would they "have the spine" to fight strong opposition to monetary tightening under such circumstances in the political arena?

Third, another team of inflation prognosticators focused most directly on the politics of monetary policy. The 2024 election loomed. Maybe indeed reported CPI inflation would be falling through 2023 and early 2024 plausibly related to the big positive supply shock (of resumed global supply chains for example) and some dampening effect of the higher nominal interest rates. The Fed would interpret the fall in CPI inflation and any pull-back in economic growth (together with cooling of labour market) as grounds to start cutting the policy rate even though symptoms of monetary inflation especially in asset markets remained troubling.

When the score card came in—a cumulative near 20% fall in the internal purchasing power of the US dollar from 2020–4—a period of time which included both the pandemic and two years of its aftermath—the sound money group of critics say that much more was at stake than an error in Fed policy judgement. The 2% inflation standard was the ensconced monetary regime when the pandemic struck had revealed its fatal flaws. A new lease of life for the regime based on the hope that supply disruptions and fiscal explosion would not recur was a foolish way forward. Yet at the time of writing that seems to be what lies ahead.

References

Brown, Brendan and Pringle, Robert "A Guide to Good Money" Palgrave 2022

Carstens, Augustin "The Return of Inflation" SUERF Policy Note Issue No. 273 April 2022

Dolan, Mike "Inflation beaten? Team transitory re-emerges" Reuters, August 3, 2022

Gagnon, Joseph £ and Rose, Asher "Why did Inflation Rise and Fall so rapidly? Lessons from the Korean War" Peterson Institute for International Economics, Richmond Federal Reserve Economic Quarterly, Vol. 87, No. 1 Winter 2001, pp. 33–56

Gauti B Eggerton and Donald Kohn "The Inflation Surge of the 2020s: the role of monetary policy" Hutchins Center Working Paper No. 87 August 2023

Krugman, Paul "I was wrong about Inflation" Opinion, New York Times, July 21, 2022

Robert L. Hetzel and Ralph F Leach (2001) "The Treasury-Fed Accord: a new narrative account" Economic Quarterly, Federal Reserve Bank of Richmond, pp 33–55

White, William "It's worse than "reverse": The full case against ultra low and negative interest rates" Working Paper No. 151, March 2021

CHAPTER 8

Delays in Monetary Diagnosis Abet the Inflation Mongers

A big conundrum in the "inflationary is transitory" discussion was the role of money. Monetarist commentators made much of the monetary aggregates—the explosive growth of M2 in the US, for example, from 2020Q1 to 2022Q1 and the high inflation in the wake of this (see Sargen 2024). The problem here was that money had become a mere shadow of its former self. In principle, "money out of control" could still unleash powerful forces that would be the proverbial "monkey-wrench in all the other machinery in the economy" (see Friedman 2006); but there was now no or little way by studying the supply of money to assess at all precisely or reliably or in timely fashion how far money was "out of control".

By the point that any provisional diagnosis of monetary inflation can be made with a significant degree of confidence, it is likely to have been around for some considerable time. That long potential lag is useful to inflation mongers who sooth worried citizens by producing central case forecasts which seem to be consistent with the official inflation target. The inflation—mongers can seek to hedge their reputations by mentioning way-out scenarios—showing these in fan diagrams—where inflation turns out to be higher or lower. So, if high inflation comes, they can claim to have foreseen the danger. But the monger implements no action in the present against that danger. And clandestine allies in big government or big business or Congress or elsewhere who may "in their

B. Brown and P. Simonnot, *Bad Money*,
https://doi.org/10.1007/978-3-031-95425-2_8

most secret thoughts" feel that some inflation overshoot would be good for their plans do not express open criticism of failing to take pre-emptive action, which would contain the danger.

Back to the difficulty of diagnosing monetary inflation early: Base money had become so diluted, and its functions so curtailed by government and other interventions (whether too big to fail lending, deposit insurance, generous lender of last resort or disadvantages which mean less intense services from holding reserve deposits, or regulatory and oligopolistic restrictions which disadvantage the use of banknotes in payment for goods and services), that at the margin of holdings its special qualities rendered no benefit. Hence, changes in its supply did not prompt intended shifts in expenditure such as occur in well-anchored monetary systems (see chapter 4, also Brown 2023; Brown and Pringle 2022). Rather assessments about monetary conditions would depend on highly treacherous conjectures about the significance of policy interest rates as measured relative to assessed "neutral levels" or data for "broad money aggregates" (for example, M2 or M3). Constituents of these broad money totals excluding monetary base had become near perfect substitutes at the margin for a whole range of alternative short-term high quality and liquid debt paper. Hence, experts seeking to make a diagnosis of monetary inflation have to focus on the symptoms of monetary disease appearing (whether in terms of goods/services inflation or asset inflation). The symptoms might emerge only with considerable lags behind the start of monetary inflation. And in turn, the symptoms might continue for some time after monetary inflation has indeed faded.

In a classical well-anchored monetary system (as outlined already in the Preface to this volume and also in Brown 2023), the power of money derives largely from the response of individuals to windfall changes in their holdings of the consumer good described as base money (banknotes and reserve deposits in a fiat regime; gold coin and bars in a gold regime). We should think of this good (measured in units of purchasing power) as rendering intense monetary services (whether as medium of exchange or store of value).

For example, damage and corrosion (for example, by inflation which reduces the real amount held) to the stock of money (considered as a consumer good) has a direct effect on individuals' planned spending on non-monetary goods as services as they attempt to rebuild their holdings. This direct effect of money on spending depends on base money at the margin of holdings rendering intense monetary services which are highly valued by individuals, explaining why they hold substantial amounts even though there is no interest to be earned on them. (In the immediate, they may be induced to put up with less by a rise in money market rates). The anchoring of the monetary system-its capacity to stay on non-inflationary course rather than being rocked by economic storms—is rooted in this individual spending reaction, though supplemented possibly by an interest rate effect as described. In a well-anchored system, an upward lurch of consumer prices as triggered by supply shock is likely to set off forces that pull them back (so long as the shock does not trigger a big fall in demand in real terms for monetary base as possibly could be the case if individuals feel much poorer in consequence of the shock).

A well-anchored money (an essential condition is a large money base with super-money qualities at the margin) does not suffer permanent loss of purchasing power due to supply shocks (such as pandemic or war). Rather, as individuals find that their holdings of the money consumer good has fallen (in real terms), they plan to cut back their consumption of non-money goods. In aggregate, this puts downward pressure on a wide array of prices all outside the area of famine where prices remain higher than pre-famine.

By contrast, in the case of a non-anchored money, supply shocks tend to send prices to a permanently higher level. Yes, the monetary authority may seek to mimic in part the rise in nominal interest rates which would occur for a solidly anchored money, but there is no direct effect on spending from a fall in the real value of money outstanding. Shocks, whether supply shock or fiscal explosion, will likely leave prices permanently higher than otherwise. Hence, under a bad money regime, war and pandemic—both shocks which restrict supply—inflict a permanent loss on the value of money, unlike what would occur under a good solidly anchored money. Fancifully, or perhaps not so fancifully, a hostile large energy producing nation, by inflicting a global supply shock, can set off a chain of likely monetary sequences which will result in a loss of the dollar's purchasing power.

That was the case with the bad money regime in place at the start of the pandemic. One feature of the monetary system's ailing condition on which we have already commented on is the payment of interest by the Fed at the policy rate with respect to reserve deposits which started in late 2008. That meant at the margin base money no longer rendered intense monetary services. And already before those layers of legislative and discretionary government protection for bank deposits had greatly reduced the scope of intense monetary services from base money—so demand for this, if it had remained non-interest bearing, would not have been broad. In itself the explosion of base money through 2020–1 (as part of the QE policy) would not have had a direct impact on overall spending (we are not considering at this point the fiscal explosion alongside); the fact though that the policy rate was compressed to zero and the Fed was telling everyone that it was not even thinking about when to start contemplating scenarios for raising this from zero), never mind the fiscal explosion, was inflationary. The scope and extent of that inflationary impulse, though, was hugely uncertain.

The nature of the monetary regime (the 2% inflation standard) and the policies it followed were essential conditions for the fiscal explosion in the pandemic to take place and for its knock-on effects to spending overall. Had there been a well-anchored monetary regime and if indeed accordingly the central bank could not pile up holdings of government debt, the fiscal explosion would have been curtailed in scope by the spectre of default risk. The central bank would not have been able to pin the policy rate at near zero throughout.

The spectre of actual default in nominal terms would have been for real (under the good money regime) if the government had persisted with huge deficits; the market for its debts would have borne pressure—first in the form of a rising default premium, eventually in the form of a total cut-off of new supplies of finance. Instead, the assumption that the government had the power via the central bank to perpetually stave off actual default in nominal terms by expanding its (the central bank's balance sheet) meant that default would be in the form of inflation write-off rather than abrogation of debt agreements.

This assumption (that government could stave off nominal default by money printing) was not guaranteed to be always valid, but likely to remain so. In principle, at some point in the future, a mood swing in the political arena against bad money could mean a new start which would include some downward revision of outstanding nominal debt contracts for government bonds. This write-down would take most likely the form of forced conversion (to longer maturity and lower interest rates) and perhaps an abrogation/curtailment of inflation-protection clauses in the indexed bond markets. It is such risk scenarios that the credit-rating agencies focus on when they consider the overall risk of government debt in nominal terms. In principle, they are not in the business of assessing risk as related to governments wiping out principal in real terms by inflation.

The bulge in issuance of bank deposits by the banks, which pile up reserve deposits (in turn matched to a large extent during the pandemic spending bulge by government debts purchased by the central bank), is explained by the enhanced appeal of these to savers at such a time. Individuals can, in large part, see that the long-term bond market is manipulated by the QE policies of the central bank. Hence, there was no direct stimulus to spending from the rapid accumulation of bank deposits; the stimulus came from policy interest rates pinned down to zero and the government's pay-outs to individuals and businesses as funded by government debt issuance. In principle, future tax payments to fund these government debts could have weighed on present private sector propensities to spend (the so-called "Ricardo effect"). Offsetting this, however, could have been a widespread sense or intuition (illusory in part) that the government debts would somehow be repaid by "inflation tax" which would fall on other people's shoulders than one's own, especially if the individuals concerned were doing well out of current asset inflation.

By the same token, the contraction of broad money supply aggregates which occurred through late of 2022 and most of 2023 in the US (reversing only a small part of the previous bulge) and some foreign countries should not have been seen as in itself empowering recessionary forces or a return of prices (of goods and services) on average back down in the direction of the pre-pandemic level. QE (quantitative easing) had gone into reverse in June 2022 with the start of QT (quantitative tightening) (see Sablik, 2022; Engemann 2019). So what? Monetary base had lost (due to dilution of its qualities as described) any significant power to drive expenditures one way or another.

Interest rate levels, with Fed funds rate reaching a high plateau of 5.25% in Spring 2023, remained a very treacherous guide to the tightness or not of monetary conditions. Overall, strong symptoms of asset inflation through 2023 and 2024 and the fact that year-on-year CPI inflation was still running at over 3% at end-2023 and end-2024 despite a massively positive supply shock (increased supplies after the disruption of the pandemic) suggested that monetary inflation was still very much alive.

References

Brown, Brendan "The Qualities of Monetary Base essential to Sound Money: Gold and Fiat" Quarterly Journal of Austrian Economics, Vol. 26 (4) 2023

Brown, Brendan and Pringle, Robert "A Guide to Good Money" Palgrave 2022

Engemann, Kristie M "What is Quantitative Tightening" Federal Reserve Bank of St. Louis, July 17, 2019

Friedman, M "The Optimum Quantity of Money" Aldine Transaction, London 2006

Sablik, Tim "The Fed is shrinking its balance sheet: what does that mean?" Federal Reserve Bank of Richmond, Economic Focus, Q3 2022

Sargen, Nick "A Monetarist View of Where the Fed went wrong on Inflation" Forbes, October 6, 2024

PART IV

Culprits and Scapegoats

CHAPTER 9

Rival Explanations for the Great Pandemic Inflation

In the previous part of this volume, we discussed much about how the Great Pandemic Inflation emerged, drawing on the concept of bad money (otherwise described as anchorless money) as set out earlier. In this chapter, we review alternative themes out there about what and who was responsible.

We start with Bernanke and Blanchard (see Bernanke B and Blanchard O 2023). These authors point out that between mid-2020 and mid-2021, the Fed stuck with an official forecast that CPI inflation would rise to only a little above target during 2022 and by 2023Q4 would be back to within target. On the basis of that forecast, policy was consistent with the "average inflation target" which the Fed had introduced into its new operating procedure in 2020. According to this, some overshoot of the inflation target in the present could be justified as an offset to undershoots in the recent past. Also, as part of the change in the procedure the Fed was to be on its guard against continuing to respect estimates of NAIRU (level of unemployment at which inflation is low and stable) being too high in view of evidence from the second decade of the twenty-first century (when inflation did not even get up to target with unemployment lower than estimates of NAIRU). The NAIRU concept is of course firmly embedded in the neo-Keynesian analysis of inflation based on the continuously updated versions of the Phillips curve (which relates unemployment to inflation) (see Ball and Mankiw 2002).

B. Brown and P. Simonnot, *Bad Money*,
https://doi.org/10.1007/978-3-031-95425-2_9

Bernanke and Blanchard do not criticize the adoption of the new framework. No talk about fighting the last war and the bizarre nature of the Powell Fed's continued preoccupation through 2020 with the theme of inflation too low as had been the case in the years running up to the eve of the pandemic. But that should all have seemed like ancient history at this point (2021). Surely the Fed should have aborted its work on the policy document and focused on the task at hand—to prevent money getting out of control during the pandemic?

Instead, according to the rewrite of the framework, the Fed should be as concerned now about the risk that its estimate of the NAIRU (level of unemployment at which inflation is stable and low) was too high as too low. Almost tamely, Bernanke and Blanchard turn to the notorious Phillips curve in the context of the new 2020 framework for insights into the pandemic inflation. In our dialogue (the precursor to this book) Philippe Simonnot and myself made much of Bernanke's failure to re-examine the Fed and its applied doctrines in modern times (see Brown 2022), even though that could have meant admitting mistakes when he was in charge. Public remorse is rare amongst once high-level officials and this ex-Fed Chair provides no exception to that rule.

These authors (Bernanke and Blanchard) find that labour market tightness was not to blame for inflation during the pandemic (hardly extraordinary given the high unemployment in the pandemic struck labour market, albeit that it was possible in principle that labour supply had shrunk by more than labour demand—but who could possibly estimate any of this?); rather the chief culprit was the spike of many producer prices under the impetus of resource shortage and the big sustained jump in private consumption. The essence of this spending spree according to the authors was an abnormal concentration (of consumers) on goods purchases matched by some decrease in spending on services whose consumption and production was subject to infection risk—a thesis to which we return below. They do not consider at all the hypothesis that the consumer spending spree was driven by monetary inflation, a concept which they do not endorse. The authors warn (at their time of writing, early 2024) that continuing labour market tightness could become a source of continued high inflation going forward. All of this is on another planet from the concern of sound money theorists that there should be a solid anchor, which would mean monetary inflation cannot take off at all and that the value of money after the pandemic should tend to return to its level on its eve.

Kohn and Eggertson (2023) definitely do not agree with the previous viewpoint that a supply shock induced rise in key prices was responsible for the pandemic inflation. They criticize directly the conduct of monetary policy and the inappropriateness of the Federal Reserve at a time of considerable inflation danger in the first year of the pandemic going ahead with a revision to its framework driven by official angst to make up for inflation having been too low in recent years (see Bokun & Kliesen 2020).

The authors (Kohn et al.) do not call a spade a spade—the policymakers who approved and implemented that framework were inflation-mongers. Yes, those same policy makers may have shared the view that the tightening of monetary policy through 2018 was a mistake in the sense that the Fed proved to be over-concerned about the tightness of labour markets and so raised rates too high with the result that inflation in 2019 slightly under-shot target. But was 2020, the first year of pandemic when risks of stimulating monetary inflation were abnormally high (not least with all the red ink in the Federal deficit), the time to be introducing reform of the framework which would condone the Fed driving inflation higher?

The kindest interpretation is that reform of the framework had been a job at the Fed under way for some time. The job including its conclusions were already near complete on the eve of the pandemic just took several months more to be translated into elegant prose pieces whose publication would be paired with a public relations blitz lauding Fed transparency. Lees kind interpretations would include elements in the inflation-mongering descriptions in the previous two chapters of this book. And where were the critics in Congress who at least could have questioned whether this was a case of maddening flaws in a powerful bureaucracy (the Federal Reserve)?

Back to Bernanke and Blanchard: how do they explain the policy-rate (Fed funds rate) piloting by the Fed going so badly wrong during the pandemic (2020–21) and its aftermath? As mentioned, they focus on the extreme swings in the pattern of consumption; through the acute live phase of the pandemic (2020 and early 2021) in the US, there was a stampede into the buying of goods and a move away from services (whose delivery became subject to serious infection risk) and within goods there were hot favourites. The prices of the goods in new stark excess demand shot up. But the prices of other goods and services did not fall. Hence, there was a jump in CPI inflation and this in turn got built into expectations. The labour market at this stage was not the source of inflation according to these authors—with wage rate increases trailing by large margin CPI inflation.

The "fall-guy" according to these authors is the sharp relative price changes which should occur in response to the shift of demand from services to goods. At the Fed's Jackson Hole Conference in August 2021, an invited paper was presented (Guerrieri et al. 2021) which purportedly justified monetary inflation so as to produce consumer price inflation above target which would facilitate a speedier than otherwise relative price change in the situation of large structural change in demand (as during the pandemic).

How should sound money advocates respond to this hypothesis? They would maintain that under a good money regime with its essential characteristic of a solid anchor (see pp. 21–22 in this volume), the sharp rise in some prices due to the shift in composition of overall demand would have set off forces downwards on other prices. Individuals would have found themselves short of a key consumer good—base money—as measured in units of constant purchasing power and have reined back their intended spending on non-monetary consumer goods and services. In the immediate—technically so as to preserve stock equilibrium between demand and supply for reserve deposits in the overnight markets—the money interest rate would have risen, perhaps sharply. In consequence, some individuals (and businesses) would make do with considerable shrunken holdings of the money consumer good in the immediate. The actual fiat money regime under the banner of the 2% inflation standard totally failed to mimic in any way the forces just described which would be unleashed under a solidly anchored good money.

Bernanke et al. have much to say about how inflation expectations became "inflamed" by the sharp rise in individual prices of goods as described above; but there would have been no such inflammation if everyone and their dog had known and assumed that a solid anchor to the monetary system was at work. This solid anchoring would have included an only slow long-run growth in monetary base which itself rendered "super money" qualities at the margin for which there were broad and strong demand. Hence, a rise in prices of goods in sudden excess demand (relative to constricted supply) would have been a direct negative effect on intended spending with respect to non-monetary goods and services in general. This would have brought downward pressure on a whole range of prices and prevented the price rigidities (especially for services subject to infection risk) of which the authors complain. It was a failure of the monetary regime in place that it provided no solid anchor which would have prevented the monetary system going haywire—emitting giant inflationary forces—in an economic storm—in this case great pandemic.

The authors' (Bernanke and Blanchard) concern about how inflation might stay high beyond their time of writing (early 2023)—a failure to detect tightening of labour market (unemployment falling below the true level of NAIRU due to faulty estimates of this)—justified from their viewpoint some potential tightening of monetary policy. The problem here is to make the analysis (and faults in the analysis) of the labour market so central to what went wrong. But why home in on one market like this (the labour market) rather than the overall monetary conditions—and specifically the holding of interest rates down at close to zero for such a long time despite clear evidence of fiscal explosion and strong symptoms of asset inflation which in general tend to proceed the symptoms of goods and services inflation. Massive fiscal explosion coupled with so much evidence of asset inflation surely should have caused the monetary inflation alarms to ring?

There is another strand to this focus on the labour market as one source of the inflationary outcome. Goodhart (2020) (also see Goodhart and Pradhan 2020) maintained that the end of abundant labour supplies coincided with the onset of the great pandemic inflation and is set to continue as a source of inflation pressure. During the quarter century following the collapse of the Berlin Wall, huge new supplies of labour to markets in Europe and the US meant that unions lost their power and wage pressures could no longer form and drive an inflation process. By the early 2020s, this wave of immigration had dissipated.

As a first point, it is far from clear now half-way through the 2020s that immigration pressures into the US and many foreign countries including in Western Europe have dissipated. In many countries, including the US and UK, there was a post-pandemic wave of immigration. As of 2025 that wave has apparently come to an end partly under toughened up controls on population inflows but long-run forecasts on immigration are full of uncertainty. As a second and more important point it is dubious that fundamental supply factors in the labour market are a source of monetary inflation. We can paraphrase Friedman to say that inflation is always and everywhere a monetary phenomenon (see our discussion of this point already in this volume, chapter 4). Yes, sustained periods during which there is a spurt of productivity can mean a downward rhythm of prices fully consistent with no monetary inflation or deflation. In reverse, a sustained fall in productivity growth can mean prices in general rising as consistent with sound money. But this is not the case that </Primary></IndexTerm> et al. is making; they are not arguing that a slowdown in immigration would mean an extended period of much slower productivity growth.

We come next to the fiscal view of inflation, largely associated with Cochrane (see 2023 and 2024). The contention here is that the massive fiscal explosion which occurred during the pandemic would rationally fuel expectations of a much higher price level further ahead. Many rational individuals would doubt that government could raise conventional taxation so as to service the debts so it would instead resort to inflation taxation and other forms of monetary taxation. By fostering an extended period of inflation unmatched by nominal rate increases (which would remain strictly under the control of the fiat central bank), the government would collect this windfall taxation. Knowing this is what most likely lies ahead there would be anticipatory spending—with individuals buying goods now in anticipation of these being higher priced in the future; this could be most obvious in real estate, but also more generally (though in principle most of all in consumer durables).

Collectively, however, such anticipatory buying does not mean that inflation tax is avoided in aggregate—only distributed away from the alert early birds to those who do not realize the situation. If all are early birds, such redistribution is not possible. And there is still an issue around the so-called Ricardo effect. Citizens knowing that inflation tax looms and with no reason to think they are smarter at avoiding inflation tax than anyone else may increase their current saving.

In broad terms, a key issue not raised by Cochrane up front is how, in a dysfunctional monetary system (no anchoring, monetary base so diluted that at the margin there is no value to its super-money services), individuals estimate when and by what means the government will levy its inflation tax? Yes, there may be a vague or widespread intuitive sense that much higher prices are to come at some point in the future—but does that justify replacing ageing consumer durables early (when much change is underway) and or stocking up on a greater amount of consumer durables? The upward pressure on prices during the pandemic occurred at a very uneven rate, most aggressive through 2021 and the first half of

2022. It is not clear that many individuals got their timing right and were able to stock up in advance of the sudden price spurt for selected goods. In fact, shortages may have meant that the goods were just not available for such stocking up. And if there were a substantial amount of "buying in advance" of goods to beat a looming inflation tax, the monetary authority could resist this by pursuing a tighter than otherwise monetary policy in the immediate, never mind the fiscal arithmetic.

In sum, the fiscal balance is not the determinant of present inflation—rather it is monetary conditions. Yes, a large fiscal deficit and weak public finances can make the efforts of a monetary authority in a fundamentally flawed system even more challenging to salvage any sort of "monetary order" in terms of long-run price stability. But the efforts can bear some fruit; and we should not dismiss the possibility of political forces strengthening, which would bring a change in monetary regime in the direction of soundness well before the path to fiscal ruin has reached its destination. Individuals rationally would reckon with that possibility.

As a postscript, we should say that the assumption of government never defaulting in nominal terms and so inflation tax becomes potentially high and variable in the future depends on a continuation of the political status quo. The political arena, though, could change in ways which make default in nominal terms a significant possible reality. Then the inflationary printing of money to service the debt could be replaced by actual default. In consequence default by inflation might occur to a substantially lesser extent than in other alarming scenarios.

References

Ben S Bernanke & Olivier J. Blanchard (2023) "What Caused the US Pandemic-Era Inflation" NBER Working Paper 31417 June 2023

Brown, Brendan Book Review on "21st century monetary policy: the Federal Reserve from the Great Inflation to Covid 19" in Quarterly Journal of Austrian Economics Vol. 25, Issue 2, 2022

Cochrane, John H "Fiscal narratives for US inflation" January 29, 2024. Comments on "Origins of US inflation since 1950 by Christopher Sims at the 2024 AER P and P session on "understanding the return of inflation

Cochrane John H "The fiscal theory of the price level" Princeton University Press 2023

Dan Kohn & Gauti Eggertson "The Inflation Surge of the 1920s: the role of monetary policy" Hutchins Center on Fiscal and Mondetary Policy August 2023

Goodhart, Charles (2020) Inflation After the Pandemic: Theory and Practice VOX CEPR Policy Portal November 24 2020
Goodhart, Charles and Pradhan M "The Great Demographic Reversal: Ageing Societies, Waning Inequality, and an Inflation revival" Palgrave 2020
Guerrieri, Veronica, Lorenzone, Guido et al. « Monetary Policy in Times of Structural Reallocation" prepared for 2021 Federal Reserve Jackson Hole Policy Symposium (August)
Kathryn Bokun & Kevin Kliesen "Key Elements of the Fed's New Policy Strategy" Federal Reserve Bank of St. Louis, Working paper 88952 2020
Laurence Ball & N. Gregory Mankiw "The NAIRU in Theory and Practice" Journal of Economic Perspectives Vol. 16, No. 4 Fall 2002 pp 115–136

CHAPTER 10

Counterfactual Pandemic under Gold Standard

It is useful to challenge oneself and ask a key counterfactual question towards understanding the full extraordinary symptoms of malaise, some bizarre, experienced under the contemporary dominant monetary regime. In our dialogue, we (the authors) tried to harness the power of counterfactual analysis even if it has practical limits. We searched for a counterfactual question which could highlight what was wrong with pandemic era monetary policy in the US (and in Europe/Japan). The general question we raised: how would it have been if the shocks under consideration (war, pandemic, great recession, economic war, for example) had occurred under the gold standard? We can then compare what has happened under the 2% inflation standard or any other bad money regime with the outcome under a sound money regime. Already this book has gone down that track in the chapters on inflationary combustion (see chapters 4 and 5).

As illustration, let's start with the COVID-19 pandemic. Suppose most countries including the US had been on a full gold standard (gold coins circulating as a medium of exchange, banknotes 100% backed by gold, similarly the safest category of bank deposits used also in settlements for payments also backed by gold—see Brown 2023) when the pandemic erupted. The onset of the pandemic (when recognized as such) may well have gone along with some increase in demand for monetary base (which under the gold regime takes the form of circulating gold coins and gold

B. Brown and P. Simonnot, *Bad Money*,
https://doi.org/10.1007/978-3-031-95425-2_10

bullion), reflecting the increase in uncertainty. One type of uncertainty might have been the survival of the gold standard, meaning gold had a special haven role at such a time (on the assumption that individuals would not find their gold confiscated or forcibly converted into fiat were the gold standard to come to an end). Another consideration fuelling demand for base money would be the increase in bankruptcy risk in general as a result of the pandemic. Alongside money market rates would come under upward pressure, and there could be some negative knock-on effects to spending as individuals seek to build up their holdings of monetary base (gold).

This initial base money shortage could be relieved in some degree and even reversed if a subsequent decrease in incomes became apparent, meaning that many individuals and businesses would decide to economize somewhat on their recently built-up holdings of the consumer good called money at the same time as they cut back on other expenditures. The concept of income relevant here though—in determining demand for base money—may well be permanent income (taking account of income getting back to normal after the pandemic) rather than strictly current income. Capital market rates are not pre-determined in direction—that depends on how a multitude of individuals see investment opportunity and how their time preferences between present and future consumption change in response to the pandemic. For example, if current actual incomes fall, and households try to sustain consumption spending to some degree (via dissaving, for example), and of course government deficits increase, then capital market rates might rise. This tendency could be offset though by any new reticence overall regarding business investment.

Credit default premiums on government debt would likely widen in the pandemic unless increased state spending during the pandemic was convincingly matched by increased tax revenue over years to come in a credible fashion not just pie in the sky wishful budgeting). Governments whose servicing record was poor, or which were otherwise in disrepute as a borrower, would find their credit spreads (as measured by the difference between yields on top quality debt and those on the risky debt in question) widening most. Currencies with generally low gold backing (whether for banknotes or bank deposits) could suffer some degree of capital flight, meaning money market rates would rise most on those.

The outbreak of pandemic in the context of a financial system where there are no bailouts, whether too big to fail, lender of last resort or anything else, could trigger a run out of riskier deposits into safe deposits (often within the same bank), where safe have higher gold backing. Yes, there would be bankruptcy amongst some bank loan customers—but the damage would be contained in part by debt-equity swaps (in these, the creditors agree to the debtor in difficulty issuing them equity in exchange for the debt paper they now own). Yes, there could be a run on some suspected weaker banks with a grouping of bad debts, perhaps due to previous bad management. But that is what safe deposits are all about. We have seen earlier in this book that attempts to smother all bank deposit risk mean a loss of any prospect of good money (as the super-money qualities of base money are thereby diluted, meaning that there is not a large, strong and stable demand for this aggregate, meaning that it can function well in anchoring the monetary system).

In the long run, there is no presumption that the value of gold money as described will fall from the eve of the pandemic until its aftermath. At the very start, the value of money could increase in line with the initial monetary squeeze and shortage of base money. Then there would likely be some period of higher prices on average across all goods and services when the demand for money has fallen (in line with real incomes), and prices of some items in short supply can rise towards the sky. At the same time as we have those sky-high prices, there could be quite broad-based falls in other prices due to the shortage of money reflecting those price spikes; that downward pressure would emanate from individuals seeking to rebuild their holdings of money in real terms (having been eroded by the price spikes). Then as real incomes recover as dislocations fade in the aftermath of the pandemic, micro-forces pushing prices down coincide with further monetary shortage, this time caused by demand for money increasing in line with income rebounds.

It is possible that the demand for money will remain higher than trend before the pandemic given new awareness of potential shock and related financial uncertainty. In that case the value of money might persist at a higher level than prior to the pandemic (correspondingly on average prices would be lower). In the very long run that higher value level could be undermined by a boost to gold production that comes from lower average costs of mining (in line with generally lower prices) relative to the fixed nominal price for gold. Gold money regimes do in principle provide for small doses of monetary inflation potentially over a long time span so as to stabilize the value of money from a very long-run perspective. Another example of the same phenomenon is the rise in the value of money which occurs during a sustained spurt in productivity growth. In the very long run, though, that rise is reversed by the stimulus to gold production which comes from the lower level of prices relative to the fixed nominal gold price. The same point could be made with respect to supply shocks if these prove to be permanent. The limited rise in prices which occurs early on could be reversed ultimately if higher costs mean less gold production.

We have been discussing so far here the case of most of the world on a full gold standard. If it were only one large country on gold—specifically the US—whilst other countries had fiat moneys which were either floating against the dollar or tied to the dollar then the outcomes could be substantially different from above. The chief risk consideration would be those non-dollar currencies devaluing against the dollar given that any anchoring system they had being inferior to the gold anchor in the US, and that would be particularly pertinent at a time of great supply shock (as in pandemic).

We have such an example from the laboratory of history of the US on gold whilst most of the rest of the world is on fiat during a period of inflation-combustion—1915–16/17, otherwise described as the period of US neutrality in First World War. The US stayed on the gold standard throughout this period of neutrality, with gold coins circulating in the US and the dollar fully convertible into gold. Gold imports and exports remained free of restriction, though subject to higher costs of shipping (across the Atlantic) due to sea warfare and the risk of attacks on neutral (or not so neutral) shipping.

The main story here was that the Entente Powers, which like the Central Powers had exited the gold standard at the outbreak of war were shipping the gold which had once been the base of their monetary systems to the US to pay for munitions and other imports. The gold monetary base now within the US exploded—meaning in effect rampant monetary inflation, which showed up both as a powerful rise in goods and services prices and asset inflation. In effect demand for monetary base (gold coin and gold bars) in the gold bloc countries, now essentially only the US as against as previously most of the world, shrunk sharply as the counterpart to European belligerents exiting the gold standard. Hence, the value of gold fell sharply (equivalently prices in dollar terms rose).

In principle, the US could have cut short this monetary inflation via gold inflows from Europe by suspending the coining of gold; individuals could no longer present gold bullion to the mint in the US and be entitled to 1.1 conversion into dollars at the stipulated rate. Instead, there would have been a freely floating gold price during the period of neutrality. Taking the then official rate at 20.67 dollars per ounce, the free-market rate might have fallen to say 14 dollars per ounce. In effect the dollar would have been selling at a large premium above its official gold value. The buyers of gold and sellers of dollars would have been speculating essentially on a return to normal once the war was over. But it was not self-evident that there would have been any return to normal, because normalization could mean a big catch-up monetary inflation (see Brown 2015).

Alternatives could include long-time dollar/gold float, or a gold revaluation (say to 15 dollars per ounce of gold), or gold sterilization (where the newly created Federal Reserve might take in gold but simultaneously revise up its gold backing for banknotes and deposits to say 100% from the legal set 60%,). This latter step though might well have zero political support—as how much better would individuals feel for having a 100% gold backed currency?

The monetary experience of World War One is understandably an extreme case. Suppose the world had entered the pandemic on the gold standard. It is implausible that this would have had as sequel anything like the monetary history of the Great War. Perhaps one or two small or weak countries (in terms of monetary position) would have been forced off gold. But most plausibly these exits would have been viewed as generally transitory. And implausibly, there would have been gold sequestration such as to make any early return to a full gold standard impossible in the exiting countries.

Alternatively, we could consider a hypothetical gold money regime in which the US is the only country on a full gold standard (as defined above) whilst all other countries have fiat monies. Hypothetically, some of these could be pegged to the US dollar, but the issuing authority would make no commitment itself about gold convertibility. Historically, this situation has existed for brief periods such as 1919–24 in the case of the US (see Brown 2012), and possibly for France (together with other remaining gold bloc countries) from 1934 to 1936 (see Brown and Pringle 2022) and White (2023). It is plausible in this unilateral US gold standard a shock such as the Great Pandemic would ignite a flight of global capital out of the fiat monies into the safety of the gold dollar—so long as the dollar's convertibility into gold does not itself become subject to significant uncertainty. The climb of the dollar would in itself provide an antidote to any rise in prices overall in the US early in the pandemic on the basis of sudden resource shortages.

Under any US dollar gold regime which is well grounded and not in doubt we should not at all observe the phenomenon of asset inflation—the other symptom of monetary inflation along with the symptom in goods and services markets—in response to pandemic. That is a big difference with what we observed actually—a virulent asset inflation taking off already in Spring 2020 just a few weeks into the pandemic, only a very short interval of time after the few weeks panic and crash during the first quarter of 2020. Features of that asset inflation included manias in "pandemic stocks"—businesses which faced huge new demand for established or new products suited to a world where there was deep scare of infection; but rational scepticism would have suggested valuations on the basis that this would all be transitory; and there were the hot markets in certain residential real estate in now popular locations away from the main metro centres and with extra living space in desirable surroundings.

The end of the pandemic brought a reversal in some of this, but not of the asset inflation (and monetary inflation, which spawned the asset inflation) overall; rather there was a rotation of asset classes into and out of the hottest speculative zones. Some stayed there (including members of the so-called "Glorious Seven". There are parallels for this type of asset inflation under the extreme conditions of war when financed under a bad money regime as we shall discover in a subsequent chapter.

References

Brown, Brendan "Monetary Chaos in Europe 1914–31" Routledge Revivals 2012

Brown, Brendan "The Curse of the Federal Reserve" Palgrave 2015

Brown, Brendan "The Qualities of the Monetary Base Essential to Sound Money" Quarterly Journal of Austrian Economics Vol. 26 (4) 2023

Brendan Brown and Robert Pringle "A Guide to Good Money" Palgrave 2022

White, Lawrence H "Better Money" Cambridge University Press 2023

CHAPTER 11

Lessons from Low Inflation Countries in Pandemic

When we talk about the Great Pandemic Inflation—defined to include the period of the pandemic 2020–21 and post-pandemic 2022–4 (the latter includes also an initial supply shock from the eruption of Russia-Ukraine War in February 2022)—this was not a truly global phenomenon. There were at least three notable exceptions and a fourth partial exception.

The inflationist countries: included the US, euro-zone and UK. There the domestic money lost cumulative purchasing power between end-2019 and end-2024 by 19%, 17%, and 20% respectively. By contrast for Japan, Switzerland, and China, the domestic money lost cumulative purchasing power over the same time period by 8.0%, 5.9%, and 3.5% respectively. In South Korea, the loss of purchasing power of the domestic money was 12,5%.

So how to explain these differences and can we learn anything thereby about the drivers of the great pandemic inflation in countries afflicted by this?

Let's start by looking at the exceptions—first Japan. The fiscal deficit bulged here from 3% of GDP in 2019 to 9.1% in 2020, 4,4% in 2022, 4,2% in 2023 and 6,1% in 2024 (almost 23% of GDP cumulatively)—a considerably smaller bulge than in the UK and US. In the US, the cumulative fiscal deficit from 2020 to 2024 was 44% of GDP and in the UK 36%. Japan money supply growth on the M2 measure was not exceptional—18% cumulatively through 2020–23 compared to 20% in the US

B. Brown and P. Simonnot, *Bad Money*,
https://doi.org/10.1007/978-3-031-95425-2_11

and 12% in the eurozone. We should note that in the years 2015–19, prior to the pandemic, the yen lost only 2.4% of internal purchasing power, so there was a 5.6 percentage point deterioration in performance on this measure in the pandemic years. That compares to a deterioration on the same measure in the US of almost 11 per centage points and similarly in the euro-zone and UK.

So, fiscal deficits and money supply expansion were both noticeably lower cumulatively over the pandemic period in Japan than in the US. We should recall, though, the difficulties of interpreting monetary data anyhow under our contemporary dysfunctional monetary system with its totally corrupted monetary base. An alternative and also flawed measure of monetary policy is interest rates . For the record these did not fall at all in Japan from the eve of the pandemic; they were stuck at just below zero, as against the large rate falls at the start in the high-inflation bloc of countries.

We should also note some particularities that favoured low Japanese inflation in the context of contemporary unanchored monetary systems. Cost pressures from the pandemic and Russia war were less acute than in many other countries. Japan had continued access to Sakhalin LNG supplies at fixed prices (justifying this lack of solidarity with NATO by pointing to its need for energy security and the argument that withdrawal would benefit China which would take its place) and the hydroelectric industry domestically produced at fixed prices. We could also talk about contemporary Japanese social psychology. Long years of stable prices may have been a factor in why nominal wages did not rise in line with actual prices and why inflation expectations failed to rise quickly.

We could also hypothesize about the Ricardo effect. Japan had by far the largest gross government debt to GDP ratio before the pandemic started . Two decades or more of handwringing about Japan's weak public finances in the context of notoriously bad demographics had likely made many Japanese fully discount future taxation and spending cuts to match and all of this reflected (downwards) on their current spending. On the other side of the ledger, we have the more than 25% depreciation of the yen against the dollar from the eve of the pandemic to 2024 and the lift this gave to some cost inflation.

Let's turn to the case of Switzerland. As for Japan, in the 4 years up to the eve of the pandemic (Say, December 2019), even more so, the cumulative loss of purchasing power of the national currency had been small, in this case 1.7% only. So, the almost 6% loss during the pandemic and its aftermath (2020–24) was a significantly worse performance—but by much less than the 10% odd worsening in the case of the US or UK. The small size of any budget deteriorations stands out in Switzerland—the general government deficit rose to 3% of GDP in 2020 from a 1.3% surplus the year before and has stabilized at slightly positive again since. There was no magic or toughness in Swiss National Bank (SNB) policy—the officials there followed the same inflation targeting procedures as in other countries, albeit they had not adopted the symmetry of the ECB and Fed in 2003 (when both institutions declared that undershoots of inflation below 2% were as serious as overshoots); in fact according to its publications aims for CPI inflation of simply less than 2% (meaning that say 1% does not trigger any correction towards ease).

The SNB unlike the Fed, ECB or BoJ had not adopted QE with its emphasis on buying government debts; instead huge expansion of the SNB's balance sheet had come about at times related to foreign exchange market intervention; the SNB had worked to contain the monetary base expansion under such circumstance by the issuance of its money market certificates, but it is dubious how far these were actually distinct from monetary base (see Jordan 2022). The reputation of Switzerland as a haven—not these days so much from confiscatory governments but underpinned to some extent by the availability of its banknotes in large (1000 franc) denomination—helped the Swiss franc strengthen—by around 10% against the dollar and more against the euro during the pandemic period (2021–2). As the pandemic continued, the Swiss National Bank embraced a stronger franc as good for containing inflation pressures never mind the loss of competitiveness (in contrast to its previous policy of intervening heavily to prevent franc appreciation).

There were two factors moderating cost-side pressures in Switzerland during the pandemic. These pressures are a menace in unanchored monetary systems (including Switzerland) they can trigger permanent loss of the money's purchasing power via monetary inflation. These two moderating factors were first the high proportion of Switzerland's electricity needs being sourced from domestic hydroelectric power, with prices held far below trends in the wider European or global economy. Then there was the rapid progress of online shopping—which in Switzerland's case provided new opportunity for retailers in neighbouring countries to arrange delivery at their goods and services at much lower prices to Swiss consumers, especially in urban areas just next to France or Germany (as for Basel, Zurich, Geneva, Ticino). In a sound money system this leap in technology allowing much greater competition for non-competitive/oligopolistic retailers in Switzerland, would have been accompanied by a fall in the general level of prices. So for Switzerland to chalk up a 5% loss of purchasing power for its money when this revolution in distribution was taking place was not so impressive. If we measure monetary policy by the level of interest rates (a very treacherous procedure!) then during the early pandemic there was no change in Switzerland, as for Japan, (significantly negative) in contrast to the rate cuts in the US. Over the whole period 2020 to 2024 M2 fell cumulatively by 7% (rising at first then falling as money market rates rose); but M2 is a notoriously poor indicator of anything in Switzerland.

China is the most extreme example of a country with ostensibly low CPI inflation during the pandemic and its aftermath. Certainly, the record is striking. The Chinese currency lost 10% of its internal purchasing power from 2016 to 2019, but less than 4% from 2020 to 2024. There were two obvious factors responsible here. First, collapse of the real estate sector, which occurred from the start of the 2020s; in effect, there was a giant bubble bursting at the heart of the Chinese economy—the corollary of two decades of vast asset inflation. (see Zongyuan 2024; Brown 2024).

And then there was the hit to investment spending outside the real estate sector from the unwinding of integration with the global economy as wrought in part by a reversal of US policies with respect to China. It is plausible also that the boom in globalization from which China had gained for at least two decades was partly an aspect of malinvestment driven by prolonged US-led monetary inflation, with the participants over-estimating gains and underestimating costs compared to the yardstick of rational scepticism which would have prevailed under sound money. Anyhow, the twenty plus years of accelerated integration in the wake of China's access to the WTO (under Clinton Administration) went into reverse as starting with the Trump Administration Washington began to promote some greater wariness ostensibly at first via a tariff war but subsequently through a raft of measures to protect US security interests and promoting US domestic manufacturing. Foreign investment into China took the brunt—previously a motor of demand in China.

And then we should mention the different path of the pandemic in China and related psychology. There was no spontaneous widespread propensity amongst households in China to go out and spend , making up for lost time and lost life, as the lockdowns came to an end (almost two years later in China than US). Instead there was caution—perhaps explained by simultaneous concern about the economy and society (banks unsafe, government debt risky in long-run, income in old-age problematic, and savings in US dollars in danger of Washington freezing actions) as reflected in huge buying of gold and crypto (even despite restrictions on access to public platforms or exchanges for the latter).

Finally, a note on the partial exception of South Korea to the high inflation of the pandemic in the US and most of Europe (see Bank of Korea 2022). Relatively, tight fiscal policy is one important candidate explanation. External demand was also weak especially on account of China's economic softening during the pandemic and post-real estate bubble. But there was no strengthening of the Korean currency to help create a virtuous circle of low inflation in South Korea as in Switzerland. Quite the converse; pessimism on exports, the plunge of the yen (the currency of one of Korea's principal trading competitors and the weakness of the yuan all pulled the won down against the dollar. The won's depreciation surely helps to explain why despite Korea ending up with lower inflation than the US and Europe, it failed to match the low inflation performance of China and Switzerland. Counterfactually, the Korean central bank could have followed a tighter monetary policy to brake the won's fall; but that did not happen, doubtless partly under the influence of the politically critical export giants. From December 2020 to September 2022, the Korean currency tumbled from 1091 to 1444 against the dollar—unleashing forces of inflation in such an open economy (much more open than Japan).

References

Bank of Korea "Monetary and Fiscal Policy Interactions in the Wake of the Pandemic in Korea" BIS paper no. 122, March 16, 2022

Brown, Brendan "How the Fed Helped Create the China Bubble and Bust" Mises Wire, May 21, 2024

Jordan, Thomas J "Monetary Policy under New Constraints: challenges for the SNB". Contribution to Jackson Hole Economic Policy Symposium Session on "The Outlook for Policy post pandemic" August 27, 2022

Zongyuan, Zoe Liu "China's Real Economic Crisis: Why Beijing won't give up on a failing model"Foreign Affairs Sept/Oct 2024

PART V

Waging War with Bad Money

CHAPTER 12

Bad Money in War, Proxy War, and Economic War

The laboratory of history provides evidence on waging war with good money and also with bad money. And there is a whole area of grey in-between, ranging from money which becomes degraded but with full realistic intention of restoration once the war is over to others where wartime debasement is so severe as to make their peacetime renaissance impossible. We start with examples of where money remains good throughout the hostilities and beyond.

France, Russia, and Japan Fight Wars with Gold Monies 1780–1905

In the Napoleonic wars from the late 1790s to 1815, France from 1803 onwards was on a full gold standard as established under Napoleon (see Bordo and White 2009). Britain, by contrast, from 1797 onwards suspended gold redemption during the war (see Duryea 2010). There was a pervasive and dominant expectation, however, albeit short of complete certainty, that gold convertibility of Sterling would be restored once the war was over and this occurred in 1819. The expectation had been realistic given the only modest excesses in money creation for the purposes of war finance.

The French decision to stay on gold was not simply virtuous but expedient because recent debt defaults (in the aftermath of France's war

B. Brown and P. Simonnot, *Bad Money*,
https://doi.org/10.1007/978-3-031-95425-2_12

against Great Britain on the side of the American) had made French citizens cautious about being caught out a second time. Hyperinflation during the French revolution had added to caution. Prospective inflation tax revenues were not worth the candle (given that the French would now hold very little paper cash unless fully backed by gold), and moreover the Napoleon regime obtained vast tax revenues, most of all from Prussia, during the conflict (subsequently the subject of reparations as stipulated in the 1815 treaty—see White 1999).

It had been very different during America's revolutionary war. Then France had provided large financial and military aid to its US ally (first as a participant in proxy war and then full war against Britain) on the back of a bad money system. This had culminated in the bankruptcy of the French sovereign in 1789 on the eve of the French revolution. Louis XVI had rejected the warnings in 1776 of his respected Finance Minister Turgot against the costs of France's participation in the Revolutionary War; replacing him with Jacques Necker (a protestant and banker with Swiss citizenship) who maintained he could finance the war with bond issuance (largely to fellow Swiss bankers) and was successful in this at first. He had taken the novel step of publishing the finances of the King, and this gained him some political popularity, but not with the King, even though the document contained what we would describe today as much "massaging". The King had fired him in 1781. In desperation and under huge political pressure, Louis XVI had taken Necker back 7 years later as state/royal finances were tottering in critical condition (see Harris 1976). France now formally defaulted on the debt (in the name of the King). Necker was again sacked by Louis XVI in early July 1789, and this was a catalyst to the storming of the Bastille, given his popularity as a reformer.

The Russo-Japan war (1904–5) provides another example (on top of the Napoleonic wars) of waging war with good money on both sides. There had been the counterexample of Italy suspending the gold standard in its 1866 war as an ally of Prussia against Austria-Hungary (see Tattara 2003); the Austrian-Hungarian currency was then fiat, inconvertible into gold or silver [see Schneider 2021]). Both Russia and Japan remained on the gold standard throughout—and in the case of Russia on into the sequel of revolution (1905/6). How was this possible? Japan benefited during the conflict from deep access to US loans (in the private capital market), with US opinion (and politics) favourable to Japan (see Best 1972).

Japan had come onto the gold standard in 1897. Russia had joined the gold standard under the guidance of Count Witte in 1893. Its ability to sustain convertibility of the rubel into gold through defeat by Japan and the subsequent 1905 revolution can be attributed variously to huge financial support from its ally France (as illustrated by a giant loan issues of Russia in the Paris market in 1906). Also Russia had joined the gold standard with gold reserves far above the legal minimum ratio, and this ratio was reached only briefly in late 1905 (the suspicion here is that Count Witte deliberately fixed a gold content for the rouble which meant that at the start of the Russian gold standard this currency was seriously undervalued—a bonus for rapid Russian industrialization. Finally interest rates in Russia were far above those in Berlin and London throughout its membership of the gold standard (until 1914)—as would have been consistent with the rapid economic growth in Russia during this period and its attraction to foreign capital as such (see Drummond 1976; von Laue 1953; Spring 1988).

Earlier there had been the example of France "staying on gold" throughout the Franco-Prussian war (1870-1) and into its aftermath of defeat and revolution (the Paris commune) and a reparations bill to Germany which far exceeded (in terms of what was actually paid and relative to economic size) anything that latter country paid after World War One; the intend of Bismark had been to crush the French economy (see Wiegand 2019).

France on the eve of the war had been the long-established pivot of the bimetallic monetary system, with gold and silver exchanging at a fixed ratio. French post-war stabilization actions included the floating of a huge loan in 1871/2 which as well as large domestic subscription was widely bought in Germany, offering an attractive yield. In Prussia and most of the other German states silver coinage had been predominant. France was able to inflict a "sting of the tail" on Germany. Having paid all reparations ahead of time by 1873 France promptly exited bimetallism contributing to a plunge in the silver price. The new German empire, though having now transitioned to a gold standard (with the benefit of France's reparations paid in gold) still held vast amounts of silver and suffered loss accordingly.

US Gold Inflation During Proxy War Against Germany 1915–17

Fast forward to the First World War. We have already discussed (see p.) the Great Inflation which took place in the US during the years of neutrality, say 1915-1917Q1. "Neutrality" in effect meant the US waging a proxy war against the Central Powers via huge financial and commercial support for the Entente Powers. A key form of support was the access which Britain and France had to the US loan market; and this included trade financing growingly for US exports of armaments to Britain. Trade financing for armaments was against the principles of strict neutrality. The newly created Federal Reserve (which opened its doors in November 1914) was an arch facilitator of such trade financing by its readiness to discount these trade bills, in effect turning them into a liquid and secure market.

Opponents to this within the Federal Reserve (notably Paul Warburg), arguing that such financing was flagrantly against the principles of neutrality, supported by some other figures in Wall Street emanating from Germany (for example, Jacob Schiff at Kuhn Loeb) were repeatedly overruled by the Wilson Administration, most particularly in a 1915 stand-off when Benjamin Strong had been absent due to ill health. Strong, effectively the top Fed policy-maker, was the New York Fed President an ex-Morgan "guy" (JJ.P. Morgan then the principal fund-raiser for Britain in the New York bond market), and Anglophile. Strong coordinated his moves (on financing) with the Administration (see Brown 2013) in which friendly towards Britain (and against Germany) attitudes were dominant, including key Wilson political advisor "Colonel" House (see Neu 2014); in these early years the Treasury Secretary was on the Board of the Federal Reserve. Alongside the financing issues, proxy war-waging against the Central Powers and in favour of Great Britain included the shipments of vast supplies of munitions and armaments, paid for by Great Britain. Those were allegedly sometimes packed into passenger liner-boats which in turn became the object of German torpedo attack. This had been the widely suspected background to the Lusitania disaster in May 1915 (see Press Association 2014). German commercial access to US suppliers was in any case impossible given the British naval presence in the Atlantic. And British forces had cut direct telegram and telephone wires between Germany and the US beneath the ocean, meaning all communication had to be through third-party neutrals (see Zelikow 2022).

The observation that the US did not provide directly financial aid to Britain and France (other than via the financing routes as described above) is in effect far from the mark. In effect the US provided huge direct aid via massive monetary taxation—otherwise described as inflation tax—imposed on the US population in general. The US authorities continued operating the free minting procedures of the gold standard—meaning that bullion presented to the relevant authority (working now together with the Federal Reserve) stood ready to take in gold bullion and exchange this for coins of the same value (as assessed at gold parity) or banknotes (now Federal Reserve notes) or designated bank deposits (now reserve deposits at the Federal Reserve). This free minting provision is a key component of the international gold standard mechanisms. But now the international gold standard had become kaput—in August 1914.

Under these circumstances, by keeping coin minting in place in the face of huge gold amounts presented by Great Britain and France to pay for their war expenditures, the US authorities in effect abetted the generation of severe monetary inflation. This showed up both in asset markets (virulent speculation for example in "war stocks", which collapsed briefly in late 1916 when rumours circulated that President Wilson was pressing the Entente and Central Powers to make peace (see Baruch 1993) and in goods and services markets (where consumer prices soared overall—doubling over the duration of World War One. The gold presented by the Entente Powers included vast amounts of gold sequestered from its banks and citizens.

If the Wilson Administration and Fed together had resolved not to allow the US population to be taxed in this way they would have had to break transitorily the provision that the authorities would buy gold at par value; most efficient would have been a cessation of purchases. If they had taken such action, the dollar price of gold in the US would have collapsed. The Entente Powers would have got much less for their gold. So as to sustain their US purchases, they would have had to levy much higher taxes on their citizens; the alternative would have been to cut their spending alongside a weakening in their potential for fighting the war. The records do not show any such proposition for suspending US official purchasing (minting) of gold having come up for discussion. In general, Benjamin Strong with Administration backing took a position in favour of continuing with the unadulterated and expanded gold buying procedures, sometimes extoling how the US's new huge roles in international financing and gold transactions would benefit New York as financial capital of the world (see Brown 2013).

As regards the European belligerents, Great Britain may well have been trying to copy the example of a transitory departure from the Gold Standard during the Napoleonic wars with a highly plausible though not certain return in the eventual peace. But all of that was pie in the sky given the sheer extent of monetary degradation (especially sequestration of the gold monetary base).and the post-war political realities in Britain where a "return to gold" at least in its full pre-1914 sense, was opposed by broad sections of the new political mainstream (including now the Labour Party). We should also reckon with the impact on opinion of that arch economic polemist, John Maynard Keynes. At this stage he had not renounced the gold standard, but was opposed to a full restoration of the pre-1914 regime (favouring the so-called gold exchange standard and possible returns to gold at a devalued parity compared to 1914) (see Hawkins 2023; Brown and Simonnot 2020). Keynes also advocated that the Federal Reserve pursue radically easy monetary policy so as to contribute to a re-balance of gold stocks away from the US. Keynes ignored the fact that Fed policy was already inflationary and generating the great asset inflation which culminated in the Crash of 29 and the Great Depression.

Gold Policies in Aftermath of World War One

As a theoretical exercise, a return to gold, meaning a restitution of a full gold coin standard, at pre-war par was possible for Sterling. A period of intense monetary shortage (reflecting the depleted gold reserves) would have brought severe downward pressure on prices. Trade and capital account surpluses for Great Britain would have reduced in turn the extent of gold shortage. An associated drain of gold from the US could have forced the Fed to abandon its easy policies at the time (in fact inflationary)—a course which would have become politically tenuous there (in the US). The Great Recession of 1919–20 that had been triggered in part by an eventual sharp post-war monetary tightening of the Federal Reserve surely played a role in the Democrats defeat in November 1920, although historical commentaries suggest other factors were more important—in particular a mood of isolationism after disillusionment about Wilson's policies of war and peace. Anyhow the new Congress where the

Republicans now commanded huge majorities proceeded to "audit" the new Fed including its role in the 1920 (Jan)–21(July) great recession. The Congress to which the Fed is answerable made it clear that this institution should steer a path of stable prices and counter deflation (see Meltzer 2003).

All of this was at a time (the early/mid 1920s) when the second industrial revolution came into full swing (the mass assembly line, telephones, radio, electrification); and the commodity booms/bubbles of the war were unwinding, both meaning large downward pressure on prices under a sound money regime. But money was not now sound. Yes the US was on a full gold standard. But the innovation of the Fed in itself led to a large shift downwards in the demand for monetary base (relative to what it otherwise would have been) and though this had still a considerable gold content, there were now large margins of discretion in how monetary base grew (or shrank) relative to gold in the monetary system (the Federal Reserve Act set minimum legal ratios of gold backing for Federal Reserve notes and for deposits of the banks at the Federal Reserve); but in practice the gold position only influenced Fed policy when this reached near the gold limit. In general, the political forces described operated so that the Fed steered monetary policy so that money was more plentiful than under sound money and this showed up as severe asset inflation—already evident in 21–2 and then again from 24 (storm in Europe in 1923, featuring most of all the French-Belgian occupation of the Ruhr and the German hyperinflation had caused a pause in the asset inflation).

In this climate, a return to a full gold coin standard by Great Britain would have meant tight money there during an adjustment period. Gold inflow to Britain, primarily from the US, would have had a counterpart in a tightening of US monetary conditions. The diminution of excess gold reserves within the Federal Reserve (measured relative to the legal gold backing of Federal Reserve notes) would have constrained US monetary policy. Perhaps incipient asset inflation in the US would have gone into reverse very early. In itself that would have been a Good Thing.

Given the protectionist tilt of US policy under the new Republican Administration (and Congress), away from the trend to lower tariffs under the Democrats, as illustrated by the Fordney McCumber Tariff Act of 1922 (see Bartlett 1998), Washington would have not welcomed Britain re-gaining lost gold reserves via a long spell of super competitiveness.That would have translated into a huge British trade surplus (and note at this time the importance of the British economy together with the so-called

Sterling Area in world trade was much greater than today) which would have had a counterpart in intensified competition for US exporters and industries competing with imports.

We should also appreciate that the British Treasury had played a lead role within the newly founded League of Nations in promoting the idea of an international gold exchange standard, where countries re-joining the gold standard after the war would do so by effectively pegging their currencies to the US dollar whilst restricting convertibility to paying out bullion at a fixed price against a large minimum amount. This standard was agreed as the way forward at the Genoa Conference in 1922 and the guiding principle was to "economize on gold stocks which had become scarce outside the US". Such a standard was essentially lacking most of the automatic mechanisms responsible for gold money functioning in a sound way whether within the country signing up to the gold exchange standard or from the viewpoint of the system as a whole.

These concerns did not enter the UK political debate. The "return to gold" was enacted under the then Finance Minister, Winston Churchill, whose Conservative Party had won a landslide victory in the General Election of 1924, defeating the outgoing minority Labour government. Criticism of the move came from a different standpoint, made notorious by Keynes, that the pound should have been devalued first, meaning a gold parity well below that on the eve of the First World War. That would have been in the context still of a gold exchange standard internationally. Neither in the official discussions surrounding "Sterling's return to gold", nor in the writings of Keynes, is there any mention of the problem of US protectionist pressure which could have materialized in response to a pound devaluation. (see Moggridge 1972) And there is no mention of the possibility that such a move could have punctured that asset bubble globally that was forming and especially in the US and Germany from 1924 onwards. (In the US it is possible to make a diagnosis of asset inflation as far back as 1921/2—see Brown (2017).

Gold, Dollars, and Swiss Francs in World War Two

Forward to the Second World War, on the eve of this, the gold standard had long disintegrated—the first mega-blow in 1914 and then during the Great Depression (British exit from gold 1931, US exit 1933, Gold bloc disintegrates and off gold 1936, Switzerland suspends minting of gold coinage 1936). Yes, from the Tripartite Agreement of 1936 onwards the US Treasury remained committed to converting official foreign holdings of dollars into gold on demand at the price of $35 per ounce. And this commitment continued to be honoured in principle throughout the war and its immediate aftermath, but only with respect to friendly and strictly neutral nations (Switzerland came to be treated as hostile neutral -partly on the basis of intelligence that the Nazis were using Swiss banks for international payments, hence Swiss dollar balances held in New York became restricted—see Brown [2019]).

Both the US and the UK governments in their war financing were influenced in varying degrees by Keynes's pamphlet/book on How to Pay for the War (1940). Implicit in the pamphlet was the contention that inflation tax would pay a role in the financing of the war. But that was not the main contention of the pamphlet and as such on its own it would not have brought anything new "to the table". There is absolutely no consideration in the pamphlet about paying for the war by adhering to sound money. Under such a regime, prices would rise to a higher level on average during the war—as demand for money fell in line with diminished real incomes in aggregate and shortages of some goods and services were reflected in businesses raising prices of these. But this would go along with strong expectations that prices would then fall back to pre-war levels in the eventual peace. As we have seen (see chapter 4) earlier in this volume a built-in expectation amongst the public about price falls post-war would be an important element in convincing them to delay consumption during the war.

The alternative idea in Keynes's pamphlet was to hold back household consumption during wartime—essential to freeing up resources for the military by means other than an immediate levying of inflation tax (sharp fall in value of money)—was to trick the public into saving more than they intended in the first place. The monetary policymakers were to spread "money illusion", given a helping hand by price controls supplemented by rationing during the conflict. The government's bond salespeople should evoke patriotism as well as providing arithmetical examples of nominal income and capital accumulation possible (without highlighting erosion in real terms by inflation) to sell massive quantities of war bonds to a public which was not calculating inflation risks appropriately. The record shows there was much new in any of this pamphlet about essentially running wartime finance based on bad money. The war was paid for in large part by a big dose of post-war inflation. War bonds eventually recorded large real losses for their holders—a big factor in catapulting the Republicans under Eisenhower back into the White House and control of Congress in 1952 (see chapter 13).

Bad Money in Korean War and Vietnam War

When it came to the Korean War (1950–2), the supply of new suckers for potential War Bond Issues at low coupons was running short. In a political climate now more hostile to inflation, and the Conservate Coalition (of right-wing Democrats and Republicans) having made substantial gains in the 1950 mid-terms (see chapter 13 and Brunnet et.al 2023)—sufficient to block Truman from implementing his "Fair Deal" program, the Federal Reserve shifted policy framework. In an accord with the US Treasury, a new active era for monetary policy. Price-fixing via Fed interventions in the US Treasury bond market was now at an end. But this was far from ushering in a new sound money era.

Anyone who read seriously the Republican manifesto of 1952 could find plenty about the ills of inflation and how the Democrats were responsible. But there was no new regime on offer—just an affirmation that a one-day (not now) return to gold convertibility internationally would bring new monetary discipline to bear, which would mean stable prices. And there was no attempt by the Fed under its new Chair, McChesney Martin, (nominated by President Truman in April 1951) to seriously allow prices to fall back in the aftermath of the Korean War as they should have done under a sound money regime once the war shortages had faded. Instead Martin and his colleagues took credit for a few years of stable prices, followed by a rise of consumer price inflation to 2% or more during the second half of the 1950s, which Arthur Burns complained about as unacceptable high (see Burns, 1957; Hetzel 1998); Burns from 1953 to 56 had been Chair of the Council of Economic Advisers under President Eisenhower.

In fact, the story of post-Korean War inflation in the US through the rest of the 1950s was essentially monetary, in contrast to Burns' account which was largely institutional. The Martin Fed failed to follow a sound policy which would have seen prices falling after the Korean War and beyond its aftermath given the rapid productivity growth occurring worldwide including the US and the economic miracles in Continental Europe and Japan. Instead, the Martin Fed in reality was pump-priming the monetary system and this was showing up in fairly persistent asset inflation (what Martin described as the punchbowl) and significant consumer price inflation alongside as already described above. Yes, Martin periodically decided to embark on a snap tightening (taking the punchbowl away) which in turn became the cause of the apparent stop–go cycle with three recessions (the mildest of these was the 1953 July to 1954 May downturn called the "post-Korean War recession" which included a big fall in military spending) during the Eisenhower Administrations interspersed with impressive booms. That stop–go sequence was to become the fodder of the Keynesian economists galvanizing behind a new approach to policy (perpetual pump-priming) taken up as an election theme by the Democrats and their 1960 presidential candidate John Kennedy.

Fast forward to the Vietnam War. In terms of the actual budget arithmetic, the expenditure totals and deficits were less daunting than the Korean War and of course much less so than the world wars (see Cordesman 2017; Daggett 2010; Srinivasan 2024; Vandebrouke 2020). Symptoms of monetary inflation in the goods and services markets (especially consumer price inflation) did become more menacing from the mid-1960s just as the US involvement in the war intensified. The actual budget deficit peaked at 2.3% of GDP in 1968 then fell sharply. There is no simple story which fits that fact where the Federal Government printed money to finance expenditures, and this generated inflation. The contribution of the war to monetary inflation must involve more than simple money-printing.

We could say that despite the growth of government spending, both military as related to Vietnam, and social as related to the Great Society Program (see Shlaes 2019), the modest size of the fiscal deficit demonstrates that taxation also rose in big steps. Inflation was plausibly an important factor given the as yet largely non-indexed structure of taxes (It was only in the early 1980s that tax brackets were adjusted in line with the CPI, so as to prevent "bracket creep"). And the Fed's efforts (see below) to hold down rates especially in the bond market to contain the cost of government borrowing meant in effect a greater revenue from inflation tax (though this does not appear in the conventional nominal accounting of government). These points are unrecognized by some authors (for example see Garrison and Mayhew 1983) who dispute that the Vietnam War was a key factor in the Greatest Peacetime Inflation.

Even so we should recognize that the build-up of monetary inflation far preceded the war (with antecedents as described in the 1950s followed by the whole ethos of Keynesian growth stimulation (even though Fed Chair Martin not himself at all converted to this) based on a supposed trade-off between unemployment and inflation (the Phillips curve) (see Brown 2017). The outbreak of high goods and services inflation in late 1965 and 1966 preceded the most intense phase of US involvement in the war though after that the two (war and high inflation) accompanied each other in broad terms, with some considerable fluctuations (of the inflation).

There was an indirect impact of the Vietnam War on US inflation and indeed global inflation which transcended mechanics of money printing or not. Fed Chair Martin's view was that his institution had a role to play in holding down the cost of government funding. War expenditures together with the new Great Society expenditures did add to widespread concerns about inflation danger (see Higgs 2011). Yes, these could have been soothed and contained by a show of firmness on the part of the monetary regime. The Fed would have demonstrated that it was in control and pursuing zealously monetary stability whatever the state of the budget due to the military and social expenditure pressures. But Martin was not the man—and nor was his board—to pursue such an independent course. It is a matter of counterfactual speculation whether they would have survived for long in their posts under intense pressure both from the White House and Congress.

The Fed for Martin was an institution in government not independent of government (his well-known phrase that the Fed must retain its independence within the government but must not be independent of the government". And he was sensitive to though not a push over to arguments from the President downwards within the Administration that it would be "unpatriotic" to drive up interest rates in any pre-emptive fashion. Already in December 65 according to oral history Johnson in anger had pushed Martin up against a wall with the refrain "Martin, my boys are dying in Vietnam and you wont print the money I need". (McMaken 2018) Implicitly, the Fed Chair was going along with the White House view that without the war there would be no need to push interest rates up to abnormally high levels and that as regards war finance the Fed would give time to the fiscal restraint option which did indeed materialize to a significant degree. There should be some wait-and-see and some accommodation for gathering intent to tighten fiscal policy even if this were to be done only on a transitory basis. The sound money critics would say that by 1968 and indeed much earlier (as far back, for example, as the gathering symptoms of asset inflation in the early 1960s) there was justification for a much tighter monetary policy which did not depend essentially on the bulging of war expenditures though that would argue in the same direction.

The narrative about the Vietnam war and its role in inflation also got a big boost from the campaign of French President de Gaulle to dethrone the dollar standard and incentivize a move of the international monetary system towards gold having an anchor role. The upward pressure on the gold price evident especially in early 1968 when the major central banks suspended the gold pool arrangements under which they intervened to prevent the market price of gold rising above its official dollar price all fitted into this. The Gaullist narrative linked the military escalation in Vietnam (as became evident following the North Vietnamese so-called Tet Offensive launched at end-January 1968) and the internal related US social turmoil with a bleak prognosis for US inflation. In turn de Gaulle, prompted by his chief economic adviser Jacques Rueff, called for a world monetary system based on gold rather than on dollar hegemony (see Chivvis 2010).

The Gaullist narrative connecting the war and inflation was not robust. The US could have waged war in Vietnam whilst under a sound money regime as the history of other wars in this chapter has illustrated (for the case of sound money in the form of gold). Growing unsoundness was not a direct inevitable consequence of the Vietnam war though it may well have suited the political trade-offs (lower taxes now, greater inflation dangers into the long-term) as perceived by the Johnson Administration.

Bad Money Financing of the War on Terror

Fast forward to the war on terror, including all its aspects both in terms of civil defence, regulatory offensives, and the wars in Iraq (including ISIS) and Afghanistan. We could say that this war was concentrated in the first decade of the present century, albeit that high direct military costs continued beyond then with military operations in Afghanistan and regarding veteran affairs. The total cumulative real military cost including these has been put in a wide range; an estimate from the Watson Institute at Brown University (see Crawford 2021) puts the cumulative cost up to end-2020 at $8 trillion in current dollars. In broad terms the estimates (cumulative) are of a similar order to the Vietnam War (spread over a longer period).

Neither the Vietnam War nor the War on Terror were the route cause of the monetary inflation which accompanied them. And the inflations had different characteristics. By the time of the Vietnam War escalations (say 1966 onwards), the US was transitioning into an inflation in which goods and services markets had taken over as emitting the strongest symptoms (of monetary inflation) from asset inflation (which had been in the early/mid 1960s). By contrast, the War on Terror started (with the 2001 attacks on New York) in a period of US recession when monetary inflation had not yet got underway. The war on terror was a catalyst to the Bush Administration orchestrating a giant monetary stimulus through 2002–4 in the run-up to the November 2004 election.

How did this catalyst work? First there was the resignation/sacking of Larry Lindsey as chief economic adviser to the President. His insistence that the cost of the Iraq war would be $200bn or more was unacceptable against the alternative estimates of $50bn or less from other Administration officials including the defence secretary who maintained that oil Iraqi state oil revenues would finance most expenditures. It should be said that final post-fact estimates put the costs at between $2 and $4 trillion. The exit of Lindsey had wider implications. He had been a strong voice when at the Fed warning of the bubble economy in the mid/late 1990s. He would plausibly have been a brake on the extension of the bubble economy beyond the pause of 2001–2, which was now being put in place.

War is in general unpopular and registers as such in elections. And there was the question of competence. Was the Bush Administration responsible via intelligence failure or how it reacted to such intelligence for the disaster which had occurred? Even more important from an electoral standpoint to get on with the job of reflating. As regards Fed policy, renowned inflationist Professor Bernanke was nominated in mid-2002 to the position of Governor in the Federal Reserve Board with plausible indication that he would be the academic eminence grise (see Brown 2022). The financing of the war on terror (already a military intervention in Iraq was well within the "radar screen", and the priority of a good economy ahead of the crucial 2004 elections, are obvious factors might well have weighed on the minds of those (including ultimately the President) behind the nomination of Professor Bernanke. Alan Greenspan had his chairmanship renewed eventually for a half term (2 years) from January 2004.

We don't know the substance explicit or implicit of the negotiations between Greenspan and the White House (President George W. Bush) behind that extension, but surely accommodation of pre-election monetary "accommodation" and smooth financing of the war on terror (including Iraq) (smooth here should not be interpret as explicit monetization) was at least an implicit part of the story. The Bush Administration was no stranger to making trade-offs in the course of the war. On the geo-political stage, the key trade-off with hindsight may well have been the negotiations with certain East European nations to get their participation in the Iraq military operations, either at the start or subsequently in a peace-keeping role. Was US support for a subsequent bid for NATO membership plausibly the sought after and offered prize? (see Spetalnik 2008).

In sum, the resumption in 2002 (after the September 11 terror attacks on New York City) of the great monetary inflation, which had started in 1995—after the 1994 monetary crackdown on resurgent CPI inflation—and then paused during 2000 and early 2001, was in no way essential to financing the war on terror. But that war set off political forces which drove the Bush Administration and the Fed (staffed increasingly by its appointees) into an effective aggravation of monetary inflation, albeit that all its officials from top down would have denied that.

We should also note that the war on terror became the catalyst to vast-ranging legislation both in the US and outside ostensibly to clamp down on terror financing. Under that banner a whole range of interests entered the legislation. In general, the range and power of the "surveillance state" in the global and national (including US and EU) banking systems increased. The way in which these additional controls were administered - for example the "war on cash" and the curtailment of client-bank confidentiality - further eroded the vital potential role of the monetary base as anchor to the monetary system (see Brown 2023).

Postscript: from Ukraine War to US-China Economic War

As a postscript to this chapter, we move forward to the Russia-Ukraine War and then to the US-China economic war. These cannot strictly be part of a history chapter as they are still being waged at the time of writing. But we can make a few observations which fit in with the themes of the chapter so far.

During 2023–4, we could say that the US was leading its NATO allies in a proxy war against Russia—providing together huge military and financial aid to Ukraine subsequent to the Russian invasion launched in February 2022. As of the time of writing (summer 2025), estimates of cumulative US aid are at just short of $200bn (including interest taken from frozen Russian assets in the US) (see Masters and Marrow 2025)—around 0.7% of annual GDP. So not as yet at all comparable to cost of war on terror or the Korean war. And of course, so far, no boots on the ground but active and key involvement of US military forces without boots. Through 2025 the US has been pulling back in various respects from the proxy war but not exiting. Correspondingly the financial costs to the US of its participation have been diminishing.

There has been a largely spurious discussion in the political arena seeking to distinguish that part of military spending which was given directly to Kiev and that part which in fact was spent on US providers at home of military goods and services for Ukraine. Both weigh on the budget and both ultimately mean a diversion of goods and services away from other destinations to which they would have flowed (without the aid operations) under the direction of free market forces, meaning ultimately less investment and consumer goods and services available to the US population in aggregate. It is only in the largely flawed models of the Keynesian under-consumption theorists that more guns produced in the US and delivered as a gift to a foreign power mean higher rather than lower economic welfare in aggregate for the domestic population. It is deifferent where the foreign power, in this case Ukraine, obtains the US guns (or equivalent) thanks to financial aid from a non-US source. That type of arrangement became a prospect in Summer 2023.

Even so, the actual size of the aid whilst huge in absolute terms is not over-powering. But the waging of the proxy war and the US participation in that has had economic impact which transcends the budget arithmetic. First, it may have made it politically harder to cut back elsewhere in the budget: why exacerbate poverty or illness is as to pay another $200bn to Ukraine; so let's just keep with the budget deficit numbers in prospect, albeit massaging them as much as possible with inputs such as optimistic growth assumptions or ambitious cut-backs in waste. Second, the alignment of China with Russia in the war (providing, for example, dual-purpose technology and buying energy) was a catalyst to a gathering economic war between China and the US.

China now, according to the US economic warriors, was not just guilty (as before) of offences against the principles of global trade (most particularly by its dispensing of vast state intervention in all its forms) but was a danger to world peace amidst heightened concern about Taiwan, its alliance with Russia, and its close ties to Iran. Understandably, all this contributed to a plunge of confidence amongst the Chinese in the dollar or fiat monies of countries allied with the US (including European and Asian). Already smarting terribly from the real estate market collapse and related financial stresses, Chinese savers had little reason to trust the Chinese state, especially given very unfavourable demographic trends. These factors help to explain their huge emerging demand for both gold and cryptos. The new freezing action by the US and its allies at the start of the war and intensified during it (also against third parties involved in various ways of helping Russia) scared a wide range of investors (including businesses) in the "neutral world" outside China to lighten up similarly on their holdings of the fiat monies.

The Washington warriors' concerns were evident about China's scope and intentions to act aggressively in ways which would hurt US interests. The fundamental consideration, however, for many warriors was still that China's entry into the WTO (as agreed and promoted through Congress by the second Clinton Administration) should never have happened: China had consistently broken the rules of a free trade system, most evidently via the channels of massive state intervention in industry and financial repression including extensive exchange restrictions. Yes, there had been benefits for US consumers from access to cheap goods with their origin in China; and yes, some US businesses both in the financial and non-financial sectors had made massive riches out of their involvement with China and its regime, strengthening their overall monopolistic position globally in conjunction with their participation in crony capitalism at home. The contention of the economic warriors against China, though, was that US industrial economy had lost out seriously in consequence, meaning an overall cumulative loss of potential prosperity. The loss was skewed towards groups in key political bases.

Philippe Simonnot 1 considered critically Montesquieu's view that "commerce improves manners and cures the most destructive prejudices". Generously, he attributes this view as one factor in the advocacy of China's entry into the WTO in the 1990s despite the widespread wariness, especially on the part of the EU Trade Commissioner Pascal Lamy, in charge of the EU-China WTO "dossier", about the Beijing's extensive state intervention in industry. Philippe thought that Lamy feared that the French government could be accused of similar massive state intervention in its business sector. More broadly, Philippe was pessimistic about Montesquieu's view when it came to the power of international trade to wean China away from the communist dictatorship. Events since Philippe's passing would have surely increased his sense of despair on this issue.

Philippe's despair might not have been top of the narratives which circulated in markets in response to the Trump Administration's unveiling on April 3, 2025 its new trade policies. The narratives which did circulate were heavily entrenched in bad money economics combined with Keynesian fallacies. The big fear was that the tariffs would bring US recession and that stagflation would loom large in the US. We should note, however, that in a good money system—by definition—there would have been no overall monetary inflation and no stagflation. Base money would have continued to grow at a slow pace. Demand for base money (in real terms) would have remained broad, strong and stable, rooted in the exceptional qualities which it renders. No monetary inflation means no symptoms—when diagnosis made with appropriate skill rather than superficially—in the form of inflation in goods markets or asset markets.

Diagnosis of symptoms is especially tricky in the context of supply shocks and accompanying fiscal policy changes. Under a sound money regime, prices of goods and services on average would fluctuate under such circumstances (trade policy-induced supply shock) including a possible pervasive but cumulatively limited move in one direction, upwards or downwards. The shocks and accompanying fiscal policy changes can influence the demand for base money in real terms and so the path of goods and services prices on average given the tight constraints operating on the supply (in nominal terms of base money).

Suppose in the long run if indeed the economic warriors were correct that repealing China's entry into the free trade system would mean eventually greater US economic prosperity—in effect a productivity bonus at an aggregate level as resources including capital and labour shift between sectors in the US economy. Then there would be a related growth demand for money (monetary base) with resulting downward pressure on prices in general (as considered over the long-run). If the warriors are wrong and prosperity diminishes in consequence of their trade and related fiscal policies, then there could result some upward adjustment of prices on average—as the demand for base money in real terms would diminish in line with sunken real "permanent" incomes.

The levying of big tariffs, most of all on China, would mean less spending on imports. But US spending on domestic goods and services, especially those which are close substitutes for imports, could increase. Recessionary influences due to a fall in US import demand would be felt in the world outside the US. In principle though the invisible hands of market forces - including adjustment of prices both in absolute and relative terms - should generate there new economic activity. But would that happen?

Perhaps the biggest question of all was the potential adjustment within the Chinese economy in response to the new US trade policies. Could the big knock to US demand for Chinese goods and resulting business difficulties in China spur a move there towards economic and political freedom under which new more than offsetting economic activity would take off.

Finally, the outbreak of the US-announced tariff war under the actual bad money regime did carry considerable inflation risk under the monetary status quo. The monetary regime in place, encouraged by the dominant political forces operating, could respond to the feared economic weakness (whether as in the US due to trade war uncertainty and the actual supply shock or in the rest of the world as caused by shrinkage of export business with the US by stepped up monetary inflation. This would counter any tendency for the business downturn to lower the average price of goods and services. In the US, prices might rise significantly after an initial phoney stability reflecting the import surge ahead of the tariff imposition. This would be the "empty shelves stage" when retailers such as Amazon, Home Depot, Ikea, Walmart, whose business model featured largely the sourcing of cheap Chinese merchandise, had not yet managed to re-source lost supplies. There would also be the empty shelves explained by consumers and businesses switching their purchases to imperfect substitutes (whether imports or domestic product) for Chinese goods and yet production of these cannot be ramped up in the short run.

Later, as the supply shocks eased and even went into reverse—this would occur both in the US and in some foreign countries not subject to the full force of tariffs as expanded production would replace the goods now subject to high tariff—there would be some downward pressure on prices of goods and services in the US. A possible factor in supply shock easing would be substitution by both consumer and producers away from goods now subject to US tariffs. Another possible factor could be a future roll-back in tariffs as US trade policy adapted to forces in the political arena. Under the actual monetary regime, though, this downward pressure from easing supply shock could become the catalyst a new monetary inflation. Regime officials would justify an effective new monetary injection on the basis of resisting price falls and preventing a fall of inflation below 2% per annum.

Under a good money system, price rises early on when supply disruptions are greatest would result most likely in immediate shortage of base money. Higher money market rates combined with individuals and businesses cutting back intended spending on non-monetary goods/services so as to rebuild their balances of base money in real terms would tend to reverse some of the overall (average) rise in prices which had occurred on impact as the supply shock erupted. Under the good money system individuals know that average consumer prices in the most severe dislocation phase are most likely higher than later on when the supply shortages ease. Hence, it makes sense to delay consumption. The price fall would be all the larger if there were indeed eventually a productivity surge in the US in consequence of ending the deeply corrupted free trade US relationship with China under Beijing's repressive political, economic and financial regime.

References

Bartlett, Bruce "The Truth about Trade in History" Cato Institute, Commentary July 1 1998

Baruch, Bernard Mames "My own story" Buccaneer Books 1993

Best, Gary Dean "Financing a Foreign War: Jacob H. Schiff and Japan" American Jewish Historical Quarterly (June 1972) John Hopkins University Press

Bordo, Michael and White, Eugene "A Tale of Two Currencies: British and French Finances during the Napoleonic Wars" chapter 10 in "The Gold Standard and Related Regimes" Cambridge University Press 2009

Brown, Brendan "The Curse of the Federal Reserve" Palgrave 2013

Brown, Brendan "Book Review: "21st Century Monetary Policy—the Federal Reserve from the Great Inflation to Covid 19 by Ben Bernanke" Quarterly Journal of Austrian Economics, Vol. 25, Issue 2, 2022

Brown, Brendan "Goods Inflation, Asset Inflation and the Greatest Peacetime Inflation in the US" Atlantic Economic Journal, Vol. 45 pp. 429–442 November 2017

Brown, Brendan (2019) " The Flight of International Capital" Routledge

Brown, Brendan and Simonnot, Philippe (2020) "Europe's Century of Crises under Dollar Hegemony" Palgrave 2020

Brown Brendan (2023) "Qualities of the Monetary Base Essential to Sound Money: Fiat and Gold" Quarterly Journal of Austrian Economics, Vol. 4

Burns, Arthur F "Prosperity Without Inflation" Fordham University 1957

Chivvis, Christopher S "The Monetary Conservative: Jacques Rueff and Twentieth Century Free Market Thought" Northern Illinois University Press 2010

Cordesman, Anthony H "US Military Spending: the cost of wars" Center for Strategic and International Studies, July 10, 2017

Crawford, Neta C "The US Budgetary Costs of the post 9/11 wars", Watson Institute, Brown University, Sept 1, 2021

Daggett, Stephen "Costs of Major US Wars" Congressional Research Service June 29, 2010

Drummond, Ian M "The Russian Gold Standard 1897–1914" The Journal of Economic History Vol. 36, No. 3 September 19786 pp. 663–688 Cambridge University Press

Duryea, Scott N "William Pitt, the Bank of England and the 1797 suspension of specie payments" Libertarian Papers, Vol. 2, Article 15, Mises Institute 2010

Garrison C.B and Mayhew A (1983) "The Alleged Vietnnam War Origins of the Current Inflation: A comment" Journal of Economic Issues Vol. 17, pp 75-86

Harris, Robert D "French Finances and the American War 1777-1783" The Journal of Modern History Vol. 48 No. 2, June 1976 pp. 235–58 (University of Chicago Press)

Hawkins, John "One hundred years ago: Kaynes's "A Tract on Monetary Reform" History of Economics Review, Vol. 85, pp. 45-58 July 2023

Hetzel, Robert L "Arthur Burns and Inflation" Richmond Federal Reserve Quarterly, Winter 1998

Higgs, Robert "The Economics of the Great Society: theory, policies and consequences" The Independent Institute, February 1, 2011

Masters, Jonathan and Marrow, Will "Here's how much aid the US has sent to Ukraine" Council of Foreign Relations, March 11, 2025

McMaken, Ryan (2018) "When LBJ Assaulted a Fed Chairman" Mises Wire, July 31, 2018

Meltzer, Allan H "A History of the Federal Reserve" Vol. 1, 1913-1951 (University of Chicago, 2003)

Moogridge, Donald E "British Monetary Policy 1924-31: The Norman Conquest of $4.86" Cambridge University Press 1972

Neu, Charles E "Colonel House : A Biography of Woodrow Wilson's Silent Partner" Oxford University Press 2014

Saul David, "Lusitania Divers Warned of Danger from War Munitions" The Guardian, May 1,, 2014

Schneider, Sabine "Imperial Germany, Great Britain and the Political Economy of the Gold Standard, 1867-1914" Cambridge University Press, April 13, 2021

Srinivasan, Hiranmay "US Military Spending by War since World Way One" Investopedia 31/10/2024

Shlaes, Amity "Great Society: A new history" Harper 2019

Spetalnik, Matt "Bush to press for Ukraine and Georgia in NATO" Reuters April 1 2008

Spring, D.W. "Russia and the Franco-Russian alliance 1905-14: dependence or interdependence" The Slavonic and East European Review, Vol. 66, No. 4 October 1988 pp. 564–92

Tattara, Guiseppe "Paper money but a gold debt: Italy on the gold standard" Explorations in Economic History, Vol. 40, Issue 2, pp. 122–42 April 2003

Vandebrouke, Guillaume "Which War saw the Highest Defense Spending? Depends on how it is measured" Federal Reserve Bank of St. Louis February 4, 2020

Von Laue, Theodore H "The High Cost and the Gamble of the Witte System" The Journal of Economic History Vol. 13, No. 4 pp. 425 1953

White, Eugene N "The Costs and Consequences of the Napoleonic Reparations" NBER working paper 7438, December 1999

Wiegand, Johannes "Destabilizing the Global Monetary System: Germany's Adoption of the Gold Standard in the early 1870s" IMF Working Paper WE/ 19/32 2019

Zelikow, Philip "The Road Less Travelled: The Secret Turning Point of the Great War, 1916-17" Public Affairs, New York 2022

PART VI

Bad Money in US Elections

CHAPTER 13

A Modern History of Bad Money in US Elections 1890–2012

The question of whether to change the status quo monetary regime in favour of a new better monetary regime is rarely top of the agenda or on the agenda at all in the political arena where election campaigns are fought. But there are exceptions. In the US, these have included elections in 1896 (and again in 1900 and 1904)—William Jennings Bryan and the "cross of gold"—and in the mid-1970s to the early 1980s (Carter slamming "Republican monetary policies" in 1976 and then Reagan backing monetarism in 1980 and 1982). In Europe, we can think of Germany in 1969 (the Social and Liberal Democrats backed a revaluation of the DM as a means of freeing Germans from the inflationary dollar and getting immediate benefits of lower prices for the middle-class voters. A hard franc based on gold as a replacement of the dollar entered the French political arena under the De Gaulle presidency in the 1960s.

In this chapter and the next, the focus is on US elections since the last decade of the nineteenth century to the present exploring how the passage of the US through war, recession, inflation, and pandemic, has played out in terms of monetary issues entering the political arena as specifically related to the outcome of elections.

B. Brown and P. Simonnot, *Bad Money*,
https://doi.org/10.1007/978-3-031-95425-2_13

Monetary Populism—Bryan's Cross of Gold to Wilson's Federal Reserve

At the start of the 1890s, the US was on the gold standard (having returned to gold in 1879 after the suspension which started in the Civil War—see Mitchell 2022). But alongside that gold convertibility of the US dollar were episodes of monetary inflation (with evident symptoms of asset inflation) and related banking instability. The source of the monetary inflation was on occasion (as 1889–91 and in the early years of the first decade of the twentieth century) government interfering with the operation of the gold system without breaching convertibility. Such interference was possible for several years at some points though essentially self-limiting and ending in bust (see Rothbard 2002). Also sustained spurts in gold mining related to new technologies or new discoveries could feed monetary inflation (as in the first decade of the twentieth century) but to a degree much lower than experienced under the post-gold fiat money regimes. Banking crisis was endemic due in considerable part to a flawed and uncompetitive structure of the banking industry set up by the Lincoln Administration during the Civil War, which had replaced the so-called free banking "system" (see Richardson and Sablik 2015).

In 1889–92, a Populist Republican President Harrison had put in hand vast purchases of sliver at a fixed price against gold (despite global glut of silver) and big Federal spending packages to match. The driving force behind these silver purchases had been the glut of silver in global markets in part stemming from rapid technological change in mining. The glut had gone along with an end to bimetallism in the 1870s amongst the Great Powers in Western Europe including crucially France (see Chap. 12). In the aftermath of the Franco-Prussian War (1870–1), the new German Empire adopted a full gold standard terminating any monetary role for silver within its political jurisdiction (see Wiegard 2019). Under the bimetallist regime gold and silver coins had circulated at a fixed rate of exchange to each other.

In the US, a clear break with bimetallism had not yet occurred, in part because of the key political importance of the silver mining interests most of all in the South and West. The sustaining of some monetary role for silver as bolstered by official silver purchases as legislated under the Harrison Administration had been a source of monetary inflation showing up as asset inflation. There had been a first swoon in the stock market and pull-back of the economy in 1891–2 as overheated monetary conditions inevitably led on to a gold drain (both internal and external). Partly in consequence—another factor was discontent with the high tariffs favoured by the Republican Administration (and this helped protect silver interests)—the 1892 elections brought Harrison's defeat and victory for the Democrats. Grover Cleveland, a staunch monetary conservative, became 2nd time President (1st time 1885–8).

Cleveland was renowned as a sound money Democrat (a so-called "Bourbon", see below). And he had diagnosed that an important cause of the recent financial instability and crisis had been the shoring up of some monetary role for silver. Accordingly, he resolved to end the silver purchase schemes under the Sherman Silver Purchase Act (signed in 1890 by President Harrison); these silver purchases had been a form of monetization inconsistent with adherence to the international gold standard in which bimetallism (gold and silver at a fixed rate of exchange to each other) was no longer a feature (see Meissner 2015). Deep recession followed. And there was a backlash in the form of landslide victory for the Republicans in the mid-term elections of 1894. This was the background to Williams Jenning Bryan's ascendancy within the Democratic Party and his becoming the Democratic presidential candidate in 1996. In effect, Bryan's victory at the Democratic convention meant the end of monetary soundness as a defining doctrine of that party.

In our founding dialogue to this book, Philippe Simonnot viewed Bryan as a seminal figure in the evolution of soft money (bad money) doctrine on the US political stage—see Brown and Simonnot 2020). Bryan campaigned for ending the "cross of gold" and a monetary regime (including re-monetization of silver) which would promote the economic well-being of those outside the banking elites on the East Coast. Three years of cyclical weakness in the economy interspersed with two financial crises (1892 and 1893/4) had been the catalyst to Bryan's victory over the until now dominant "Bourbons" in the Democratic Party who supported laissez faire liberalism, fiscal conservatism, sound money—including now the gold standard rather than bimetallism, and against imperialism and high tariffs. Bryan's ideas were most popular in the South and West, both amongst indebted farmers and the silver mining interests. But also more generally, his ideas resonated amongst those resenting the East Coast elites and also those in a position to gain from some inflation.

Problem: the backstop of support for the Democrats from Catholic Germans in favour of sound money and by tradition Democrat voters eroded due to Bryan's monetary stand. Many of these switched to the Republicans, albeit contained in their enthusiasm by the strong support amongst the latter for Prohibition. Non-Catholic Germans switched in similar fashion. Germans traditionally liked free trade as favoured by the Democrats and were against the high tariff policies of the Republicans. Despite Bryan's landslide defeat in 1896 he went on to be Democrat Presidential candidate in 1900 and 1904 and 1908, always on a ticket of monetary populism, and always losing. Republicans presidents occupied the White House throughout the years 1897–1912.

Without delving into the detail of election results, the genie was out of the bottle. The cause of monetary populism had become an election theme, actual or potential. The monetary populists (Bryan people) were part of a broader Progressive coalition within the Democratic Party (not all Progressives supported Bryan currency populism, and of course, there was also a Progressive wing in the Republican Party as we shall see below). The sound money people amongst the Democrats, who belonged in general to the so-called "Bourbons" had suffered a fatal defeat at the Chicago Democratic convention (July 1996) which elected Bryan as the candidate. They continued to recede in importance even when the economy pulled out of its long and painful cyclical downturn of 1893–6. On the Republican side of the aisle, the sound money people had largely become eclipsed through the 1890s; the years when President/General Grant had towered as a sound money advocate within the Republican Party (taking the US back onto the Gold Standard with the signing into law in 1875 of the Resumption Act) were far behind. Now, in the last decade of the nineteenth century and first decade say of the twentieth century, the Republicans were not as unsound as to espouse like the Bryan Democrats a break with gold money. Adulterations of certain gold standard mechanisms—that was another matter. The Republicans had their own Progressive/populist wing, but this stuck with the gold standard.

It was Republican President McKinley who in 1900 signed into law the Gold Standard Act legally establishing gold as the sole metal base for the monetary standard. Theodore Roosevelt, a Progressive, on becoming President (previously vice-President, put on the joint ticket with Mckinley in 2000 due to the insistence of delegates to the convention from New York where he was Governor) in 1901 following the assassination of President Mckinley chose as his Treasury Secretary a political ally, Leslie Shaw. The latter had been prominent in the gold money camp during the crucial

1896 elections (where Bryan had been defeated). In sum, the Progressive/Conservative friction within the Republican Party had little to do with the issue of the gold standard.

Even so the Republican Progressives did not have a good reputation of keeping to the rules of the gold standard, though in the ultimate they were serious about the US remaining on it. We have mentioned already above the flaunting of the rules by the pre-Progressive Harrison Administration (1888–92). Then, Theodore Roosevelt's Treasury Secretary Shaw in the early 1900s distributed government cash balances amongst the national banks in a way such as to simulate the operation of a central bank and provide stimulus or liquidity as required (see Rothbard 2002). This had played a role in the asset inflation which got underway, and which went into reverse in the 1907 Crash. An additional factor in this boom-and-bust cycle was the increased supply of gold resulting from the cyanide technological revolution in the yellow metal's production and discoveries in Australia, South Africa and Alaska.

In 1912, the friction between Progressives and Conservatives within the Republican Party had worsened. Ex-President Roosevelt, having lost to incumbent Taft (the latter having broadly moved to the Right and the former to the Left in the previous two years or so) at the Republican convention in June (though winning in those states which held election primaries for the first time) campaigned as an independent under a new party (Bull Moose) banner. The split in the Republican Party in 2012 allowed Woodrow Wilson, the new Democratic Candidate for President, and endorsed by Bryan, to win the White House with barely 42% of the vote. Wilson made Bryan, now espousing pacifism and anti-imperialism (critical of the McKinley's annexation of the Philippines in 1898), his secretary of state (resigning as such in 1915 out of concern that Wilson's eschewing of strict neutrality in favour of Great Britain would drag the US into the conflict).

Wilson did not directly take up the issues of gold and silver; these were not at that time prominent concerns amongst the voting public. But Wilson was a staunch Progressive (see Ambar 2018). According to Rothbard (2007) the drive towards a Federal Reserve System, whether under the Taft Administration (1909–12) or later under Wilson, can be traced to the power of the Progressives, a biparty phenomenon, whose champions included Teddy Roosevelt: "This movement converted the US economy from laissez-faire to central statism". The Crash of 1907 and subsequent Great Recession had proved the opportunity for Progressives in both parties to work intensively in Congress on the setting up of a US central bank (see AIER 2017). President Taft as a Conservative (within Republican Party) did not hurry on this issue, allowing the legislative calendar by late 1911 to get bogged down on other matters despite subcommittee action.

The influence of Bryan and currency populism are traceable in the Wilson Administration's founding of a Federal Reserve System, both in its design and its winning of Congressional approval. The System gave less power to the bankers and more to officials nominate by the President and approved by the Senate than proposals which had made some way under the Taft Administration (1909–12). And there was a significant dilution of gold backing requirement for the new banknotes and deposits at the new interbank clearing house now part of the new institution. The Federal Reserve Act was passed and signed in the context of the US remaining on the gold standard, so the new institution's scope for initiating monetary policy was constrained, though not zero. The eruption of the World War when the Federal Reserve had barely opened its doors in 1914 meant that we never had a test as to how far the Wilson Administration would have "experimented" in continued peacetime with the probably expanded leeway for making monetary conditions easier (for some time—length unknown) within the ultimate constraints of gold. The new Administration moved forward with deliberation now after the delays under the previous Administration. The government and Washington was to be much more prominent in the System than under previous proposals (under the Taft Administration) and Wilson persuaded Paul Warburg (who built his ideas for the American Central Bank on German imperial precedent) to take a leading role in the new institution (subsequently to drop his re-nomination in 1917 amidst a wave of anti-German sentiment once the US had entered the war).

Franklin Roosevelt who in early 1913 became under-secretary of the Navy (and persisted in that role until becoming VP candidate in 1920), having been crucial as a 31-year old state senator to Wilson's victory in the Democratic Convention of Summer 1912 by winning over delegates in New York, cannot be viewed as a disciple of Bryan (who incidentally at that same convention had given his backing to Wilson). A key difference included Bryan's hostility to big business and his pacifism; in his two terms as New York Governor, 1928–32, Roosevelt had been ready to deal with the New York financial titans. And in the First World War, from early on (say the sinking of the Lusitania in May 1915) Roosevelt aligned with those arguing for both military readiness and intervention on the side of Great Britain. Franklin Roosevelt as a Progressive made his way skilfully through a party where currency populism ran deep. In any case there were overlaps and alliances in the Democratic Party between currency populists and progressives.

From Wilson's Proxy War Against Germany to Great Asset Inflation (24–8)

If in the future a progressive Roosevelt would see practical advantage in embracing currency populism (as he did once President in 1933) he should know that there was potentially broad support for this within the Party. His known admiration for his cousin, President Theodore Roosevelt, left no one in doubt about his commitment to the Progressive cause, albeit within the tent of the Democrats rather than the Republicans. Franklin Roosevelt as Governor of New York had been expert at avoiding the stirring up of trouble between the progressive and conservative wings of his party and had refused to act against known corruption scandals in New York for that reason (see Davis 1985). Early in his presidency (1934), President Franklin Roosevelt at a memorial service for Bryan had said "It was my privilege to know William Jennings Bryan when I was a very young man. Years later both of us came to Washington DC to serve under the leadership of Woodrow Wilson.—I learned to know and love him".

Of course, Franklin Roosevelt made no mention of Bryan's resignation from the Wilson Cabinet in June 1915 in disagreement with the Administration's handling of the Lusitania sinking crisis. Bryan had opposed Wilson's break with strict neutrality and effective entry into a proxy war with the Central Powers on Great Britain's side (see Chap. 12)—putting him on the opposite side to Franklin Roosevelt (see above), albeit then only a junior Cabinet member, previously New York state senator. The proxy war in effect became the key issue of the November 1916 elections. Both candidates—Wilson for the Democrats, Hughes (an ex-Supreme Court judge and Taft conservative) for the Republicans in effect promised a combination of military preparedness (a boost now to military spending in preparation for eventualities) whilst keeping the US neutral.

Hughes' position was compromised by his efforts (mostly successful) to mend fences with the Progressive wing under Theodore Roosevelt (who had again failed to win the nomination at the convention, but this time, unlike 1912, decided not to stand as an independent in the presidential election). Teddy Roosevelt's position on the war was that the US should enter on the side of the Entente (Britain/France) without further delay. Apparently (see Huston 1964), voters of German background particularly important in electoral outcomes in the Midwest brought a very narrow overall victory for Wilson (even on election night amidst early results, the Hughes camp was convinced they had won). These voters in the mid-West may not have trusted Hughes or Wilson to keep the US out of the war, but their distrust of Hughes was evidently greater.

The real perspective for these voters who thought about it carefully was that the Wilson Administration had taken the US into a proxy war with Germany on Britain's side. Even so by late 1916 Britain and France were struggling somewhere between possible defeat and stalemate. Top danger was that the US would drift or be catapulted from this situation of proxy war into actual war, rather than see Britain go into defeat. Alongside there was the danger of German submarine attacks on US vessels (including passenger) which contained armaments supplies and this becoming a provocation for US declaring war on Germany. These attacks had paused recently. Unknown to voters this pause accompanied secret efforts by the German Chancellor Bethmann Hollweg to persuade President Wilson to organize a peace conference (see Zelikow 2023). But the attacks could resume. Also unknown to voters was the refusal of the President to consider peace discussions until after the election. True an important hurdle to the US waging war on the side of Britain and France was that these countries were allies of Tsarist Russia, whose pogroms had made it a pariah with many US voters. But disasters of the war might stimulate internal forces in Russia which would triumph against Tsarist dictatorship.

Even so, a peaceful scenario with respect to the war was still possible. Germany, Britain and France (all having suffered huge losses and in stalemate) might be willing to come to the negotiating table chaired by the Wilson Administration. (in fact, President Wilson did travel down that road of seeking negotiations very briefly following the 1916 elections but in such a flawed fashion—see Zelikow 2023). Serious efforts would have included the US Administration threatening to abandon the proxy war on Britain's side unless that country joined the negotiations and dealt meaningfully. But how long or hard would the Wilson Administration go down that route; the present economic boom and financial boom on

Wall Street was based on the proxy war (including the gold monetization—see last chapter); a crash and recession prospect would limit how far the Wilson Administration would pull back from the proxy war; and there was the question of competence and divergence within the Administration; did Wilson know what his envoys were actually up to (some like Colonel House or Secretary of State Lansing vehemently pro-Entente). Despite all these reservations about Wilson's role or success after the elections in keeping the US out of boots on the ground participation in the war voters evidently decided that these scenarios of peace were even less plausible under a would-be President Hughes, whether taking account of the economic and financial interests dominant within the Republican Party, or the power still of Teddy Roosevelt supporters.

One final comment: though monetary inflation and its symptoms of asset inflation and goods/services inflation were strongly evident by Election Day 1916 and well before, these ills did not figure in the campaign. Why not? Neither side had any incentive to propose possible solutions—the most effective of which would be suspending the US Mint's purchase of gold from the entente or anyone else at the fixed price of $20.67 per ounce. Any such move would have meant ending or curtailing the proxy war on Britain's side as that country would no longer have the means from sequestered gold to pay for adequate war supplies. In any case, there was most likely a widespread understanding amongst voters that some inflation was the result of war in Europe; in that the US had stayed on the gold standard, surely things would return to normal after the war. And there were many gainers from the asset inflation.

Fast forward to the election of 1920. Already in the mid-term elections of November 2018 the Democrats had lost control of both chambers (a tiny effective majority in the House on the eve of the election being replaced by a near 50 seat Republican lead). The 1920 elections brought a massive landslide against the Democrats and a corresponding swing to the Republicans. One factor in the extent of the landslide was surely the depth and severity of the Great Recession January 1920 to July 1921. Benjamin Strong, President of the New York Fed (then the most powerful official in the system), had presided over a sharply disinflationary policy from late 1919 having failed to rein back persistent monetary inflation in the aftermath of the Armistice (November 1918). He and his colleagues had failed to realize the huge extent of money overhang in the system as created during first the proxy war with Germany (1915 to early 1917) and then during the full war. When prices failed to fall back through the first three quarters of 1919 as would have happened if a solid monetary anchor had been in place the Fed moved from October/November to implement a sudden and sharp discretionary tightening of monetary conditions = effecting a series of big discount rate hikes. It was not yet part of the Fed's reflexes to run policy in terms of the political cycle, and there are no grounds for believing that Strong ever had this in mind. This was an election of reaction against the Progressives across the board, given the depressionary economic situation and dissatisfaction with the failed war and peace policies of the Wilson Administration. The Republicans promised a "return to normalcy". German and Irish descendant voters were angry at the pro-British record of Wilson and his having taken the US into the war (already a factor presumably in the 1918 mid-term election defeats for the Democrats).

The Democrats could hardly have fought the election based on blaming the Fed for the recession; they had created this institution. Their shrunken numbers in Congress could participate in the vociferous committee hearing there into how the Fed had botched its immediate post-war policies (see Meltzer 2003). The upshot: the Fed through the rest of the 1920s came under considerable pressure from Congressional opinion to follow Irving Fisher's prescription of stabilizing the price level—ultimately a perverse rule at a time of rapid productivity growth such as was occurring during this second industrial revolution; the result, acute asset inflation and associated mal-investment. Some critics of the Fed's monetary inflation during these years (see, for example, Rothbard (2011) and Robbins (2009) make much of the decision by Benjamin Strong (Governor of New York Fed and effectively dominant personality within the system until late 1927) to cut the discount rate in July 27. They claim that this gave critical further impetus to the asset inflation. The justifications for action at the time included the contemporary mild recession (26Q3 to 27Q4), the corresponding setback in the stock market (Strong told Charles Rist, deputy governor of Banque de France, that he had given the market a "coup de whiskey"—see Rothbard 2021), and helping out the Bank of England which was coping with an incipient crisis of Sterling intensified by French withdrawal of official reserves in exchange for gold.

No one claims that Strong was politically motivated—in the sense of responding to some Republican anxiety about the looming 1928 elections given that the mid-terms of 1926, coincident with a mild recession, had brought some modest Republican setbacks (7 seats lost in the Senate meaning only a slight majority there now). And indeed well before Election day 1928. The Fed—by then under the effective joint leadership of Governor Young at the Board in Washington and George Harrison in New York—had more than reversed the rate cuts, raising the discount rate cumulatively to 5% by July from 3.5% at the start of the year—all out of concern at resurgent credit growth and the highly speculative climate in Wall Street. These policy shifts did not have any evident cooling impact by November (1928); the Republicans won the elections with an enhanced majority and a landslide victory for their Presidential candidate, Herbert Hoover (who in any case sided with those who were highly concerned about excess speculation on Wall Street and had been critical of Fed easing in 1927). Yes, with hindsight (and indeed some contemporaries had foresight), a looming global economic storm was already approaching, and, in the US, the fantastic real estate boom/bubble had already passed its peak. But none of this had a visible impact on the vote. One part explanation cited by historians is that the Democrats had selected as presidential candidate a catholic losing support thereby amongst some traditional voters in the South.

Political Triumph of Democratic Monetary Populism 1930–6

1930 was a turn election. The Wall Street Crash of October 1929 had proved to be an early episode in an emerging severe recession; there had been some optimism in Spring 1930 about a coming business cycle upturn later in the year, but by late autumn such hopes had died a death amidst a rash of bank failures. In the November 1930 Congressional Elections, the Republican majority in the House dived to one, and by the time this newly elected House convened for the first time in early 1931, the loss of seats in special elections had flipped the chamber to Democratic Control. The Senate remained in narrow Republican control. The severe recession was surely the dominant factor in the election results. There is no direct evidence as to how big a factor was the unpopularity of the big new import tariffs under the Smoot-Hawley Act signed in June 1930. Significantly, Franklin Roosevelt, who had won the November 28 gubernatorial election in New York, was re-elected for a second term as Governor in November 30. He was already widely viewed as the front-runner Democrat Presidential candidate for November 1932. There were not strong expectations as to what that would mean for policy, other than a tilt back to Progressivism, and he had a record for realizing public infrastructure spending projects and social welfare legislation as Governor. In January, 32 political commentator Walter Lippman had expressed a conventional view when he remarked "FDR is no crusader. He is no tribune of the people. He has no envy of entrenched privilege. He is a pleasant man who without any important qualifications would like to be President".

It is surely plausible that the US election results of November 1930 played a role when it came to expectations formation in financial markets through 1931, albeit that the shock result of General Elections in September 1930 in Germany (the Nazi Party emerging as the second largest party) ranked higher as a prime mover of international capital and credit flows through the first half of 1931. When the UK government broke Sterling's link to gold, in the wake of Germany's debt crisis and related standstill on short-term debts (and exchange restrictions), which in turn had triggered a run on exposed British financial institutions, domestic and international confidence in the dollar's continuing gold convertibility melted. Within 18 months, Roosevelt could be the US President as a result of a Democratic wave election in November 1932. True, President Hoover had become hyper-interventionist according to later critics (see Rothbard 2011, Shlaes 2009) and in his long political career, he had made passing alliances with Progressives. But Hoover's principled commitment as a thinker and constitutionalist (later substantiated by his authorship of conservative philosophy tracts (Cohen 2024) should have underpinned the view that he would not be taking the US off the gold standard.

The extent of the Roosevelt/Democratic landslide of November 1932 and the subsequent regime-changing monetary and currency policies could not have been taken reasonably as the central scenario back in Autumn 1930 at the time of the mid-term elections. It was the second back-to-back great recession of Summer 1931 to Summer/Autumn 1932 (in terms of US data) (the first recession was from August 1929 to April 1931) which was electorally decisive in the US, bringing about a sea-change—with dominant majorities for the Democrats in both Houses (reaching the key 60 seat level in the Senate). And through the campaign, one historian demonstrates that all elements of the New Deal were on display. True, Roosevelt's future gold and currency policies were not explicitly in the campaign—but big government and using government power to solve economic problems (especially depression) certainly were up front; that would have raised alarm bells about the sustainability of future gold convertibility for the dollar. This was the party after all of Bryan, who had departed this world 8 years previously. This was not the age of exit polls though. So, we don't know how much electors were responding to Roosevelt's possible policies on gold or other economic questions as against the more explicit hints about endorsing the end of prohibition (Hoover, the incumbent President, was equivocal on prohibition—at most suggesting that states should have a large role in the wet or dry decision).

The large further swing of support to the Democrats and Roosevelt in the elections of 1936 reflected strong economic recovery through 1934–6. The Administration seemed to be vindicated in its decision to reject any early normalization of monetary conditions, continuing with the massive monetary base which had resulted from the monetization of gold inflows in those years (the source of the gold inflows was largely the gold bloc, where fear of its demise drove capital flight out of the French franc most of all and into dollars. Monetary historians of whatever school have made much of the Federal Reserve's monetary normalization "campaign" of Autumn 1936 to Spring 1937 (see Brown and Pringle 2022). There were three increases in reserve requirements as mandated by the Fed (with respect to deposits outstanding)—August 36, March 1937 and May 1937—amounting to a cumulative doubling (see Friedman and Schwartz 1963).

The significance of these moves in total is in doubt, given the only very slight rise in money market rates by that last date (May 1937) and the huge starting total of excess reserves. Whatever the case, the pre-election move of August 36 (a first rise in reserve requirements) was surely trivial in the bigger picture—and maybe deliberately so given the looming contest. Pre-election political calculations could also help explain why the Roosevelt Administration turned down any suggestion from abroad (including the BIS) about cutting the gold price of the dollar (thereby revaluing the dollar against the gold bloc) to cool emerging inflation pressure in the first half of 1936. There was concern both in the US and outside about the US stock market having become frothy, commodity markets too hot, and actual goods inflation troublesome. But implicitly, the Roosevelt Administration was not ready to act pre-emptively. Welcome to fiat money and the conduct of now sovereign monetary policy becoming a tool of the government in seeking re-election.

The break-up of the gold bloc in summer 1936 (following the election triumph in France of the Front Populaire in the Spring) and the subsequent episode of flight capital returning to France, Switzerland, and Holland (all in gold bloc) could have exerted some disinflationary influence on the US monetary situation and from there on to the US economy, but not with a time line effective before the elections, which Roosevelt and the Democrats won even more overwhelmingly than in 1932. They now held more than three quarters of the seats in the Senate and House. Had the US become a one-party state?

Not so fast. The rampant asset inflation of 1936 was already starting to cool by Spring 1937. The cause of the cooldown was debatable—was it concern about heightened union power; or about the potential more broadly of Roosevelt to radically extend the New Deal; or was it simply the endogenous bust which follows great monetary inflation; or had the end of gold induced hyper-monetary base increases together with the three rises in reserve requirements been effective in inducing monetary tightening or at least lowering expectations about future inflation? (see Brown and Pringle 2022). And when the Japanese invaded Shanghai late that summer (1937), the US stock market crashed; the darkening geopolitical skies also in Europe could well have been an important factor behind that crash. Robbins (2009) notes that war risks were already a key influence depressing business confidence and spending in Europe. (Germany had re-militarized the Rhineland in Spring 1936 in contravention of its Treaty obligations, but bringing no response from Britain and France). The late summer 1937 crash occurred several months into a business recession, which now was deepening in a menacing fashion—the so-called Roosevelt recession (May 1937 to June 1938), on certain metrics more severe than the first recession of the Great Depression.

All déjà vu from the perspective of the twenty-first century. Asset inflations lead to busts and severe recessions. Even so the "lead on" was remarkably swift in 1936–8, consistent with the hypothesis that monetary conditions did indeed tighten eventually (let's say through the first half of 1937) even though the rise in money rates was remarkably small. And we should note the more significant rise in long-term rates (shake-out in the bond market) in early 1937 until the Roosevelt Administration pressed (successfully) the Fed to intervene with direct bond purchases. But this post-election shock tightening of monetary policy (in so far as it occurred) was totally avoidable—a cost of the new fiat monetary regime having lurched far into monetary inflation during 1936. One key factor in plausibly explaining that lurch was election calculations ahead of November 1936.

Turn Elections of 1938, 1946, and 1950 to Eisenhower Anti-Inflation Campaign 1952

The subsequent setback for the New Deal Democrats in the November 1938 mid-term elections, surely influenced by the reality and severity of the Roosevelt Recession, was stunning. The Democrats lost 72 seats in the House and 8 seats in the Senate: an end to those super-majorities and in fact a win for the Conservative Alliance spanning Republicans and conservative Democrats (the latter against most or all the New Deal but aligned with Roosevelt on foreign policy and defence as events unfolded). This important setback for Roosevelt on the economic policy front may have been a factor adding to the US dollar's appeal as safe-haven as the clouds of war darkened. An example was the wave of capital flight into the US from Europe when in March 1939 Nazi Germany abrogated the Munich deal and German troops entered Prague (see Brown 2019).

The passage of elections in 1940, 1942, and 1944 through the Second World War did not change in any significant degree the political map. The next big shake-up was 1946—a new President, Harry Truman, disgruntlement at the immediate post-war US economy (continuing very high inflation), the bitterness and length of the US automobile strikes, alarm at failures in foreign policy (as evident in the global and especially European ascendancy of the Soviet Union) all took their toll, with the Republicans as result winning majorities in the Senate and the House. There were ensuing expectations that the Republicans would consolidate their position in 1948, even possibly gaining the White House. This totally failed to occur with the pendulum swinging then back to the Democrats. Ostensible economic factors in that outcome included the apparent stop to CPI inflation (no retracement though of previous cumulative price rises through the war and its aftermath). The Federal Reserve had tightened monetary policy in 1948 via hiking reserve requirements. A mild recession did set in (November 1948 to October 1949) but its start is dated around Election Day.

The mid-term elections of November 1950 brought significant reversals for the Democrats. Though they retained majorities in both Chambers, the Conservative Alliance in Congress now could effectively block

Truman's pursuance of the "Fair Deal". The outbreak of the Korean War (in June 1950) and the related jump in CPI inflation took their toll on Democrat support. The way ahead to the Republicans returning to power in 1952 was open. The history books do not give an account of the extent to which Fed officials and the Treasury in concluding the Accord of March 1951 (Fed no longer effectively set policy to peg government bond yields at ultra-low levels) were influenced by the 1950 election outcome. The top channel would have been Congressional opinion as reflecting the changing composition of the money/banking committees and the perception in the political arena that a re-bound of inflation would be unpopular with voters. We can assume that the political antennae at the Fed were well out.

In any case, the surge of inflation during the Korean War and the related emerging huge losses on government debt (as long-term interest rates rose, no longer pegged at low levels since the Accord had come into effect) arguably contributed to the landslide gains of Eisenhower and the Republicans in the November 1952 elections. Big losses on the holdings of war bonds have been identified by researchers (see Brunet et al. 2023) as an important factor in the public's anger at the Democrats. The Korean War was still raging and extensive Congressional hearings and criticism of Truman Administration's conduct of this war had rubbed off on public opinion. True, the Republicans in their manifestos (for the 1952 elections) had no convincing agenda on monetary matters; They did not indicate any intention of allowing a future peace and related fall in commodity prices to be reflected in a serious fall of consumer prices on average back to pre-Korean war levels. Still, the voters perceived a higher degree of inflation danger under the Democrats than the Republicans.

Republicans Pay Price for Stop–Go Monetary Inflation 1952–60

Trust in Republican economic management eroded somewhat as the US descended into its first of three "Eisenhower recession" (from July 1953 to May 1954). This succession of recessions can be attributed to flaws in the actual monetary regime even though reformed in line with the Treasury-Fed Accord. Symptoms of monetary inflation in the goods and services market were camouflaged (to a varying degree) in the reported CPI data by increased supply in the aftermath of the Korean War and by strong gains in US and global productivity which continued through the decade and into the next. Symptoms of monetary inflation by contrast in asset markets were not camouflaged (though in some degree repressed by extensive financial regulation). In the total picture, the crescendos of asset inflation and periodic run-ups of CPI inflation until the Martin Fed decided with its customary lag to suddenly "remove the punch bowl" were the cause of the notorious "stop–go" economy in the Eisenhower years (albeit average growth in prosperity though the two Administrations was impressive). And the first of these stops (the least serious) brought modest losses for the Republicans in the mid-terms of 1954 exacerbated by public disquiet at the way in which the McCarthy witch-hunts and denunciations (against communists) were conducted. The losses were sufficient, however, to mean that the Republicans lost control of both Chambers.

A subsequent boom extending through 1955 to first half of 1957—over the Eisenhower Presidency 1953–60 economic growth and living standard growth was good by historical comparison though plausibly below where it would have been with sound money—coincided with the 1956 elections (The next business cycle peak was in mid-1957). Eisenhower scored a landslide election victory, slightly larger than in 1952 (against the same opponent Adlai Stevenson). Voters seemed to approve of Eisenhower's handling of two geo-political crises in 1956—the Suez War and the Hungarian uprising—though there was much to question in both (see Hybel 2014; Marcetic 2022). The stock market had soared through 1954–5—consistent with asset inflation as a symptom of monetary inflation. In the Congressional elections of 1956, there was little change (in overall seat tallies) from 1954.

The next election "wave" was not far off, though. The mid-term elections of 1958 brought huge majorities for the Democrats in both Chambers—64–34 in the Senate, 283–153 in the House. Explanation: a severe economic downturn 1957 August–5 April as the Fed had belatedly removed the punch-bowl. A flu pandemic had added to the woes especially through Autumn 1957 and Winter 1957/8. Also there was the alarm about the Soviet Union's success with the Sputnik Program (exploration of the Moon). Unemployment had risen from a low of 3.7% in early 1957 to a peak of 7.7% in August 1958. True the stock market had soared through 1958 reflecting no doubt the Martin Fed now having switched to monetary "stimulus" and related expectations of strong rebound ahead. But evidently that optimism did not permeate through to voters in general. In Europe, the Deutsche mark had led the way in becoming fully convertible (meaning the scrapping of all exchange restrictions including those with respect to resident and non-resident capital flows) in 1958. Some downward pressure on the dollar against the Deutsche mark did become apparent in 1959–60 especially in the run-up to the 1960 elections. There was speculation that the Democrats would re-gain the White House with an occupant (John Kennedy) who might be less orthodox with respect to budgetary discipline and the commitment to the Bretton Woods Monetary System (and the role of gold convertibility—albeit highly curtailed—there).

In fact, all these suppositions were quite vague and without much evidence to back them. Yes Kennedy was likely to be in favour of targeted public works spending; but on no grand scale and though close to some Keynesian economists was not inclined to run large deficits. And it was far from certain that Kennedy would win the election (1960); and amongst the possible presidential candidates for the Democrats Kennedy had not stood out as radical. In February 1963, he re-nominated McChesney Martin as Fed Chair against the initial advice of his Keynesian advisers, taking heed of his strong support amongst the "financial community".

The Democratic Inflation Wave of 60–8 and Its Republican Sequel 69–76

Back to the election and business cycle. A new business cycle downturn had started in April 1960, continuing into early 1961(February)—clearly favourable to a change in the party controlling the White House, away from the Republicans whose presidential candidate was then Eisenhower's Vice President Richard Nixon. In the Congressional elections, there was a slight swing back to the Republicans from their landslide defeat in 1958 but still with huge Democrat majorities; that was consistent with the Democrats (John F Kennedy) winning the White House. The subsequent build-up of monetary inflation through the years 1961–4, which showed up mainly at first in asset inflation with symptoms of inflation in goods and services markets well camouflaged (rapid productivity growth a key factor here) helped bring a landslide election triumph for the Democrats in the White House race (Lyndon Johnson President defeating Republican opponent Barry Goldwater) in 1964. They achieved a rare two-thirds majority in the Senate.

As monetary inflation started (abruptly) to mutate into visible high CPI inflation from 1965 onwards, a political backlash built against

Democrats. In the 1966 mid-terms they lost their supermajorities in Congress but were still in a big lead. Even in 1968, amidst record CPI inflation (excluding the episodes of World War and their immediate aftermath) and the Vietnam War, the Democrats retained their majority in Congress, though this shrunk (in both Chambers). But the Democrats lost the White House to Richard Nixon. The apparent recession of 1969/70 (since ironed away by subsequent data revision over many years but still featuring a weak phase in the economy) explained new Republican losses in the mid-term elections of 1970, to which Nixon responded by appointing a Democrat, ex-Governor Connolly of Texas, as Treasury Secretary. Subsequently, he and his under-secretary for international affairs, Paul Volcker were key players in the August 1971 "closing of the gold window"—the finishing blow to the Bretton Woods international monetary system—and the subsequent US dollar devaluation policy.

The cocktail of monetary inflation and dollar devaluation policy as then promulgated by the Nixon Administration through 1971–3 may have seemed at odds with "Republican tradition" (evidence though not clear here given Republican episodes of policy excess as far back as the late nineteenth century—for example 1888–92 and 1901–4 as mentioned earlier in this chapter). In any case "Republican monetary policy" could now be branded as potentially inflationary and unsound—as Democratic President Candidate Carter was to argue in the 1976 election campaign (see Grouse 2018). Of course, "Republican Monetary Policy" had been unsound in its own ways in the 1920s or 1950s—but the role of the White House in the conduct of monetary policy had been less obvious or strong. As we have seen , evidence is lacking that Benjamin Strong in deciding to give the stock market a coup de whiskey in 1927 was seeking to promote re-election of the Republicans; maybe he was responding in part to opinion in Congress about stabilizing the price level. (see Meltzer 2003). And the monetary inflation policies of the Fed under the Eisenhower Administrations were not carefully calibrated with the election timetable, though there was the coincidence (some might say more) of no action to remove the punchbowl during the economic and financial boom which was in full swing in 1955 (a year ahead of the next Election).

The inflationary policies of the Nixon Administration (as carried out by the Burns Fed) did go along with the landslide presidential victory of 1972. The reckoning for the Republicans came in the subsequent mid-terms (November 1974)—3 months following the Watergate resignation of Nixon and well into the severest recession since the 1930s as the Fed had eventually cracked down on inflation (from early 1973). A landslide victory for the Democrats in the 1974 mid-terms meant they now controlled over two thirds of the seats in the House—moreover, the new members were concentrated amongst Liberal Northerners, meaning a loss of grip of the Southern Conservatives who still controlled many committees. Even though the Burns Fed implemented a second great monetary inflation impulse through 1975–6 (continuing in 1977–8) it was not sufficient to gain the re-election of President Ford, who lost to President Carter in November 1976.

How Monetary Instability Powered Election Swings 1980–92

There was no quick monetary action to reverse the inflationary build-up; a new economic boom had emerged. Accordingly, the Democrats did fine in the mid-terms of November 1978 (only a small swing away from them, less than typical for a first mid-term under a new President). Having failed to nominate a "hard money guy" in early 78 to succeed retiring Arthur Burns at the Fed, President Carter seized a second chance to implement his election pledge of ending "Republican monetary policies (of inflation") with the appointment of Paul Volcker in late Summer 1979, with a mandate to crack down on inflation. In his first year in office, the run-up to the November 1980 elections, Volcker did implement at the start his "experiment in monetarism"; there was some notable discretion in interpreting and treating money supply targets strictly during summer and early autumn 1980 amidst weak economic data (see Hetzel 1984). But as this gave way to evidence of strength, Fed tightening action followed in the final quarter of the year.

The sea-change election of 1980 did have an inflation narrative amongst others, though mixed. Paradoxically the anti-inflationary initial medicine of the Volcker Fed and the accompanying recession of 1980H1 hit Carter and the Democrats; they got the blame for the re-bound of reported inflation through 1977–8 though much of this had its origin in the Burns Fed's second program of monetary inflation injection which had started in 1975–6 under President Ford. And the economic downturn during the first half of of 1980 also took its toll on support for Carter seven though this could be viewed as carrying out of his due to a belated carrying out of his campaign promise to end Republican monetary policies. The Republicans were not promising easy money—and in fact had endorsed the Volcker monetary experiment at this stage. But with Reagan as presidential candidate they won the popular mind with promises of tax cuts and less state intervention/regulation in the economy. And the continuing Teheran hostage crisis took its toll on support for Carter and the Democrats. The Republicans won control of the Senate (the Democratic majority in the House persisting, albeit subject to a group still of conservative representatives from that party).

Fast forward to the inflation which emerged during Reagan's second term and the election cycle. A severe growth cycle downturn through 1985–6, following on a sudden sharp tightening of monetary policy through late 1983 and first half 1984 (in response to new concerns about CPI inflation in the context of the Reagan boom and the large budget deficit), took its toll on the Republican fortunes in the mid-terms of 1986. And that was despite the switch towards monetary ease/inflation/dollar devaluation through 1985/6 as highlighted by the Plaza Accord in early Autumn 85. James Baker, now Treasury Secretary in the 2nd Reagan Administration, had become ensconced as the top power-player. The monetary inflation was camouflaged in goods markets by a collapse in the oil price on speculation that the OPEC cartel was falling apart. In global asset markets, though, inflation symptoms were becoming stark.

Already in 1982, two conservative Republicans had authored a joint letter to President Reagan imploring him to dismiss James Baker who they wrote was consistently thwarting implementation of the free-market policy agenda which they had backed and helped fight for in the Campaign. But the President had adamantly refused to follow their counsel see Baker and Glasser 2021). Now Baker was visibly determined to bolster the Republican prospects for 1988, where the Vice-President HR Bush, a close friend (of Baker), was a highly plausible candidate (though not selected yet). At first, Volcker's ideas on monetary policy coincided with James Baker's wishes (given the Fed Chair's concern in particular about the trade deficit and dollar overvaluation. That had changed by Spring 87 when Volcker became concerned about the inflation he had unleashed (including both consumer price inflation and asset inflation). In February (1987) the US had entered into the Louvre accord (a G-7 deal) whereby the US, Germany and Japan would cooperate to prevent further decline in the US dollar. At that stage presumably both Volcker and Baker were on the same page about inflationary danger of continuing dollar devaluation. By late summer Volcker was out (his term finished) and Greenspan was appointed in his place. The change at the top was consistent with Baker's concerns that further "hawkishness" by Volcker could jeopardize Republican victories in November 1988. Even so, in October 1987 the sock market suddenly had a panic attack. Was Greenspan pulling back from monetary inflation? One factor here was speculation that the Bundesbank would soon be abandoning its monetary stimulus policy, responding to a recent sharp acceleration in the German monetary aggregates and a strong re-bound of the German economy? In the context of dollar stabilization that would mean higher US interest rates. The Crash was the catalyst to the Greenspan Fed leading central banks globally into a new phase of strong monetary inflation.

Election outcomes were in line with the economic cycle, also taking account of particular economic pain in the "rust belt" now subject to intensified competition when the dollar was at peak valuations (1983–5). In the 1982 mid-terms, the Republicans had lost 26 seats in the House—a bad result even taking account of the normal swing in the first mid-terms following a presidential win; that result surely reflected the severity of the 81/2 recession, which was not even definitively at an end by Election Day. In the 1984 elections, the Democrats had picked up two seats in the Senate (bringing their total there to 47) whilst the Republicans had clawed back half their mid-term losses in the House but still remained definitively the minority party there. President Reagan won a landslide victory in the presidential vote. That outcome was consistent with the economic boom which had emerged through 1983–4.

In 1986, the Democrats won a further 8 seats in the Senate, winning back control (and they controlled the House all along). It was by no means a wipe-out election for Republicans who only lost 5 seats in the House and did well in gubernatorial elections. The warning was enough though for the Reagan Administration with James Baker guiding the ship to be wary of any return to a strong dollar amidst "premature" Fed withdrawal of monetary stimulus. The political strategy was to aim for the centre ground rather than taking forks in the road favoured by conservative Republicans. And indeed, there was success for James Baker in terms of the political calendar—WH Bush elected president in November 1988—albeit that the Democrats in fact made slight gains in both the Senate and House races.

The Greenspan Fed delivered very late its disinflation policy reaction to the previous 4 years (1985–8) of monetary inflation. A recession got underway from July (1990) (according to NBER dating) lasting until

March 1991. Accordingly, the Republicans lost some (not a lot) ground in the mid-term elections (November 1990), held during the First Gulf War. The Democrats obtained an enhanced majority of around 80 seats in the House and increased their majority slightly in the Senate. Economic weakness persisted well beyond the end of the recession, which had been mild. In terms of the political cycle, Fed Chair Greenspan had been late and at first tepid in moving towards monetary stimulus ahead of the 1992 poll. The Great Asset Inflation of 1985–8/9, a global phenomenon including the Japanese bubble economy (we could call this the Volcker-Greenspan monetary inflation), had brought extended credit deflation in its wake.

That continuing weak economic picture (in the early 1990s) doubtless played a role in the election result of 1992, in which HW Bush was defeated by Clinton. But Ross Perot, an independent self-funding billionaire, playing the card (amongst others) of right-wing populist resentment against the centrism of Bush and Baker, creamed off 20% of the presidential vote, much more of which, according to the pundits, came from potential Republican than Democratic supporters. His key message (to the right of Bush) was the need to cut the budget deficit and the size of the Federal Government. In fact, in the House elections, the Democrats lost 9 seats to Republicans and Clinton won the presidency with only 43% of the popular vote. Some Perot supporters in the presidential election, disgruntled with the economy, did not switch from Republican to Democrat correspondingly in the Congressional races.

In 1993 and 1994, a powerful growth cycle upturn had got underway (reflecting exceptional monetary stimulus delivered by the Greenspan Fed through 92–3); but this did not prevent a political "earthquake" in the mid-terms of November 1994 away from the Democrats, replacing them with the Republicans in control of both Chambers. This sweep has been largely explained by popular revulsion against the Clinton/Democratic legislative plans for universal healthcare. Also, the nature of the "Contract for America" put together by the Republicans, and in conjunction with research at the Heritage Foundation, with its proposals for less government and regulations, hit a chord in popular opinion, already ripe as illustrated by the success of Ross Perot mobilizing in 1992 large shares of the popular vote. The big run-up of interest rates amidst a sudden jump in reported inflation through 1994 (from Spring onwards), all reflected in a sharp growth cycle downturn by Autumn that year may also have played a significant role in bolstering the Republican vote.

Greenspan Asset Inflations of 1992–2005

But as the economy surged through the mid and late1990s, accompanied by a great asset inflation, (under monetary conditions as pursued by the Fed which resisted any downward influence on overall consumer prices from the initial productivity growth bonanza of the IT revolution—see Wells 2024; Brown 2018), the Democrats failed to win back control of the House or Senate. They made only slight electoral gains in the 1996 Congressional elections as against a big win for Clinton in the 1996 presidential election. We should note, however, that even then Clinton's share of the popular vote was well less than 50% as Perot again took a significant share of the vote (well down though on 1992) presumably mostly from otherwise Republicans. In general, good economic times may well have bolstered support for Clinton and the Democrats but were not sufficient to push either into a majority of the popular vote. Other possible hypotheses to explain continuing Republican control of Congress through 1996 and 1998 elections: free market ideology might be a "good news good" which people are ready to consume more willingly at times of economic prosperity than in bad economic times; or the initial left-wing lurch of the Democrats through 1992–4 may have left many voters scared lest they again run an undivided legislature and executive. Yet in practice many conservatives were dissatisfied with the roll-out of "Contract with America" by the Republican majority in Congress through 1995-2000, complaining both about its content and its lack of implementation (see Nickanen, 1995).

In the elections of November 2000, the Democrats did make a little progress in the Senate where they ultimately secured a tiny majority (working with independent) but they lost the White House after a disputed poll. The role of the passing weakness in the real economy and financial markets is ambiguous. There had been the NASDAQ crash in the Spring 2000 and by Election Day some economic indicators were flashing weakness ahead of a mild and short recession, which the NBER dates as starting in the first quarter of 2001. In fact, subsequent data revisions have "ironed" that recession away. The Contract for America though made no effective progress despite the Republican win for the White House (George W Bush) and the regain of Senate control in the 2002 midterms (the terror attacks on New York the autumn before appear to have bolstered the electoral performance of the President's party).

There was an inability and unwillingness of the mainly Republican-controlled Congress from 2000 to 2006 to rein in this President from implementing non-conservative economic policies. Under President George W Bush, the Republicans eventually went down to severe defeat in the 2008 elections. Not all here was due to failures of the President. The Contract with America people had failed to implement the insight of Milton Friedman—economic and political freedom must start with sound money (see Friedman and Schwartz 1963). There was no serious thought or priority given to sound money in the Contract.

In effect, the Republican reformers failed totally to promote legislation let alone ideas that would bring the madness of the incipient 2% inflation standard and its associated virulent asset inflations to an end. It was the Great Asset Inflation continuing through 1995–2006 (with a little remission 2001/2), culminating in the Great Financial Crisis (GFC) which eventually sunk the Contract with America. In addition, there was the eventual unpopularity and perceived bungling of the Iraq military intervention, seen as related to the influence of neo-conservatives who had failed to think through the issues and likely scenarios. The first quake against the hitherto successful Congressional Republicans (in electoral terms) came in the mid-terms of 2006 when they lost their majorities in both Houses (Democrats winning 31 seats in the House). Dissatisfaction with the Bush Administration's handling of the Katrina Hurricane was an additional factor here—as was an emerging puncture of the long-running housing bubble.

Even so this setback for the Republicans in 2006, already reflecting in part the chickens coming home to roost from another "Republican inflation" (and CPI reported inflation surpassed 4% at this time, alongside an ageing asset inflation), was some considerable distance from the utter defeat which the 2008 Crash and onset of Great Recession produced. The Democrats now were within reach of a super-majority in the Senate, which in fact they obtained the following Spring (as a Minnesota seat election challenge was resolved in the Courts). This was still a long way short of the huge majorities which Democrats had obtained in the Roosevelt era or in the years after 1958 (though those majorities should be qualified by their inclusion of Southern Conservatives, now almost an extinct species).

An economic upturn through 2010—ostensibly accompanied by fiscal stimulus and Bernanke Fed radical policies but nonetheless weak by the standards of previous recoveries from severe recessions—did not prevent a setback for the Democrats in the mid-terms of November 2010, where the Republicans won control of the House. The Tea Party movement—opposing the high tax and high spending policies of the Obama Administration—were symptomatic of grassroots opposition to the emerging actions, including the introduction of Obamacare. But this was no new Contract for America, rather tired at best. And the continuing albeit lacklustre economic expansion together with Fed's radical policies of QE and rate manipulation may well have contributed to a modest Democratic victory in 2012 (re-election of Obama and Democrats gain seats, but not enough to re-gain control of House). In the international financial arena, the Obama Administration had cooperated fully and indeed led in some respects (with implicit or explicit US aid) the salvage mission for European Monetary Union, out of concern that a blow-up here could prove to be a new "Lehman moment".

The mid-term elections of 2014 coincided with a serious growth cycle slowdown (not recession) in the US, coupled with global slowdown; the triggers were some stepping back from radical ease by the Fed and combined with that a first puncturing of the long-running China economic bubble (from 2009). The Republicans gained the largest majority in the House since 1928 and a gain of 9 seats brought them a significant majority in the Senate, the largest since 1980. No wonder the political pressure from the Democratic side (who still retained the White House) was towards a monetary policy that would be stimulatory. Super-dove Janet Yellen, supported by the most "progressive" senators including Elizabeth Warren, an advocate of strict financial regulation, who had effectively vetoed the candidacy of Professor Larry Summers, had already been installed as Chair in February 2014 on a simple majority vote. The Democrats, who controlled the Senate, had repealed the filibuster rules (under which a candidate would have to get 60 votes to defeat a filibuster) the previous December with respect to all except Supreme Court nominations (see Burgess and Seung 2013). Now, through 2014–16, she accordingly kept Fed funds rate pinned down at zero despite rampant asset inflation and camouflaged inflation in goods and services markets (where the big fall in commodity prices pursuant to the first China bubble bursting would have meant some tendency of prices overall to fall under anything like sound money). The "resurgent" Republicans (on one of the lowest electoral turnouts ever at 35% of eligible voters) certainly did not coalesce around any monetary reform plan in the direction of soundness. A conservative message without any sound money revolution at its core was hugely flawed—and helps to explain the electoral and market cycle through 2018 and beyond, a subject treated in our next chapter.

References

Ambar, Saladin “Woodrow Wilson: Campaigns and Elections” UVA Miller Center 2018

American Institute for Economic Research) (2017) “The Panic of 1907: the short crisis that began money’s long fall” published June 16, 2017 (no specific author).

Brown, Brendan “The Case Against 2 Per Cent Inflation” Palgrave 2018

[11], Brendan “The Flight of International Capital” Routledge 2014

Brown, Brendan and Pringle, Robert “A Guide to Good Money” Palgrave 2022

Brown, Brendan and Simonnot, Philippe “Europe’s Century of Crises under Dollar Hegemony” Palgrave 2020

Brunet, Gillian and Hilt, Eric and Jaremski Matthew S “Inflation, War Bonds, and the Rise of the Republicans in the 1950s” NBER working paper 31969, December 2023

Burgess, Everett and Seung, Men Kim “Senate goes for nuclear option” Politico, November 22, 2013

Davis, Kenneth S “FDR: The New York Years 1928-32” New York, Random House 1985

Friedman, Milton and Schwartz, Anna “Monetary History of the United States” Princeton University Press 1963

Grouse, Eric R “America’s Failing Economy and the Rise of Ronald Reagan” Palgrave 2018

Hetzel, Robert L “Monetary Policy in the Early 1980s” Federal Reserve Bank of Richmond, May 1984, Working Paper 84

Huston, James A “The Election of 1916” Current History, Vol.47, No. 278, pp. 205–9 October 1964

Hybel, A.R. “Dwight Eisenhower and the Suez Crisis of 1956” in “US Foreign Policy Decision-Making from Truman to Kennedy”, Palgrave 2014

Marcetic, Branko “US deliberations during Hungary’s 1956 uprising offers lessons on restraint” Current Affairs, June 1, 2022

Meissner, Christopher M “The Limits of Bimetallism” Working Paper 20852 NBER January 2015

Meltzer, Allan “A History of the Federal Reserve” Vol. 1 1914–51 , University of Chicago 2003

Mitchell, Wesley “A History of the Greenbacks” Liberty Street Press 2022

Nickanen, William “Whatever happened to the Contract with America” Cato Institute, September/October Policy Report 1995

Peter Baker and Susan Glasser "The Man Who Ran Washington" First Anchor Books 2021
Philip Zelikow "The Road Less Travelled: the Secret Battle to End the Great War 1916–17" Hachette Books 2023
Richardson, Gary and Sablik, Tim "Banking Panics of the Gilded Age (1863-1913) in Federal Reserve History, December 4, 2015
Robbins, Lionel "Great Depression" Transaction Publishers, March 2009
Rothbard, Murray N "A History of Money and Banking in the United States" Mises Institute 2002
Rothbard, Murray N "The Progressive Era" Mises Institute 2007
Rothbard, Murray, N "America's Great Depression" Mises Institute 2011
Rothbard, Murray N "The Gold Standard in Operation 1926-9" Mises Institute, December 29, 2021
Shlaes, Amity "The Forgoteen Man" Pimlico 2009
Wells, William "The Origins of the 2 per cent inflation target", Richmond Federal Reserve Economic Focus, 1st/2nd quarter, 2024
Wiegard, Johannes "Destabilizing the Global Monetary System: Germany's Adoption of the Gold Standard in the early 1870s" IMF Working Paper WP/19/32 February 2019

CHAPTER 14

Malinvestment, Inflation, and Populism 2016–25

The bad consequences of bad money, when they arrive in a form which is starkly obvious, do have knock-on effects in the political arena including general elections. That is a far cry from saying that these bad consequences fortify and build the case for good money which then triumphs ultimately in a decisive election victory. Seldom. Rather in the murky history of bad money, there are plentiful surprises where the bad money culprits return to a towering position in human affairs even after the chickens have come home to roost.

A key issue in all of this is that elections are about much else most of the time than the monetary regime; moreover, there is often no consensus or dominant view about who or what is to blame for regime failures. Alternative models of the inflationary process come up with different culprits. Some monetary economists may have strong views on who is to blame—but other experts almost certainly disagree. Most people casting their vote are usually not enthusiastic to use this for approving or disapproving proposals on the monetary regime unless this coincides with other matters at stake about which they may care about strongly.

With these points in mind, let's re-take the narrative of US elections from 2016 onwards. All the efforts of the Fed under Janet Yellen to keep the economy stimulated (policy rate stuck at near zero despite some emerging consumer price inflation, despite a glut in commodity markets, despite evident asset inflation and despite the economy in a

B. Brown and P. Simonnot, *Bad Money*,
https://doi.org/10.1007/978-3-031-95425-2_14

growth cycle upturn - albeit tepid - since the second half of 2015) did not prevent the Democrats losing the White House in the November 2016 elections. They made slight gains in the House and Senate elections but not enough to regain control of either. Evidently, there was a range of non-economic factors which played into this result—including prominently the conduct of the Justice Department in the matter of the Hilary Clinton's telephone—and economic factors which transcended whether the Fed was achieving its dual mandate in terms of unemployment and "low" inflation.

Donald Trump made headway with the contention that the economy was working for certain elites but in general was under-performing. There were statistics to back up that claim. The median real income per head had advanced only slowly over two decades (2000–19 by 16%) despite all the buzz about the digital revolution, compared to 45% in the previous two decades (1980–1999). There is a tendency in popular commentaries to assess prosperity by a focus on labour market statistics or fulfilment of the Fed's dual mandate (low unemployment and low inflation as now interpreted). Prosperity, however, is a much broader concept.

How well-off do people feel, taking account of leisure and work conditions, and how fast have their living standards been improving. Understandably on this score, many US voters were not feeling well—and so the inclination to listen to the siren voices of populists who offered a sizable improvement in their condition with ready explanations as to how some elites had put themselves first before America. Some populist-nationalists focused on how a flood of cheap Chinese goods into the US, promoted by Beijing's industrial subsidies and made possible by financial repression which bolstered the level of savings surplus and the trade surplus alongside in the People's Republic to extraordinary highs) had squeezed important segments of the US industrial labour force out of their well-paying jobs.

There were many points to discuss about this message—industrial subsidies are a problem, but do they feature in the Chinese small business economic layer from which Walmart, Ikea, and Amazon buy their vast supplies? And yes, China should pursue liberalization. This would promote imports and work against endemic huge savings surpluses stemming from deep malaise in the Chinese political economy; but was the magic wand of US tariffs the best instrument for this? Perhaps a better idea was currency reform—to make the yuan a much more attractive currency (getting rid of exchange restrictions, adhering to sound money principles, competitive financial markets), which would attract foreign inflows and also be attractive to domestic residents—all meaning a much higher external valuation for the yuan. Yes, China's entry into WTO may well have represented a huge error of US policy (under President Clinton); but the reversal of that error required more than a simplistic solution. All such nuances escape the sharpness of populist recipes.

By the time, it came to the 2024 elections, there was even more cause for disgruntlement amongst important segments of the US labour market and their families. In general, since the peak of the long business cycle in 2008, average US real GDP per head had risen by barely 20%. That compared to a growth of 37% between the peak of the long cycle in 1990 and 2008 (see Brown 2024). In the election campaign, the Republican populists blamed the usual suspects including China, President Biden, illegal immigration and more generally the Democrats. According to exit polls, much of the voting public was dissatisfied due to the rise in the cost of living under the Biden Administration (2021–4). The Trump/Republican campaign maintained that this cumulative inflation had been due to out-of-control government expenditure.

At the level of economic doctrine, we could say that the Republicans were advancing a "fiscal theory of inflation" (see Chap. 9); large government deficits stretching from now into the future raise concerns amongst much of the public that they will lead eventually to a default in real terms achieved by sustained and virulent monetary inflation whereby the government levies inflation tax (collected as the real value of government debts including base money fixed in nominal terms falls in real terms). Individuals and businesses aware of this likelihood bring spending into the present, tending to drive present prices up in anticipation of this outlook unfolding. The Republicans did not in general stress the role of present and recent past monetary policy in the process. The omission was unsurprising given that it was in 2019/20 under President Trump that the Powell Fed in conjunction with Treasury Secretary Steven Mnuchin had launched a giant "monetary experiment" of zero rates, QE, and previously unheard-of massive purchases of credit instruments.

In any case, inflation tax was not the main complaint bugging the voter it seems. The 2024 election was not a repeat of the Eisenhower sweep of 1952 when voters were angry at the losses which they had suffered on War Bonds (see previous chapter). Over much of the labour market wages had risen together with prices and sometimes by significantly more. And many individuals were sitting on large gains in their investment portfolios (including homes and pension savings plans) as delivered by asset inflation over so many years. Evidently, there were nonetheless some heavy losers from inflation—savers who had most of their assets in money and bonds with little or no debt outstanding, pensioners or would-be pensioners with non-indexed future benefits or doubtful about claims that these would increase with prices, and in general recipients of income fixed in nominal terms over long periods. There were also many gainers whose debts (including mortgages) had fallen in real terms or were otherwise fortunate as already described.

The fact that inflation was falling towards target of 2% by Election Day—in fact still one percentage point above—did not mean any compensation at all for the recent near 20% loss of purchasing power of the dollar which had occurred through the pandemic and beyond (2020–24). Republicans pointed out that almost all this loss had been under the four years of the Biden Administration. As we have noted already in this volume, under a good money regime, there would have been no grounds for expecting any cumulative loss of money's purchasing power during the pandemic and its aftermath. A big fall in prices post-pandemic would have meant gains in money's purchasing power which would have compensated for earlier losses.

Perhaps these are all arguments which a re-incarnated right-wing (Cleveland Bourbons!) of the Democratic Party could have made. This group would have attacked both their own wayward leaders of the past and the Republicans for having presided over a rotten monetary regime, and offering instead an alternative ideology founded on good money. None of that was remotely feasible in terms of the political map in summer 2024! Some classical liberals may dream of that possibility in the future, not even so far distant.

Back to the world as it is and looking at the period, say 2016–24, we can say that of monetary inflation's two symptoms—asset inflation and goods/services inflation—it was the former which in fact was predominant in influencing the political arena, via its stimulating of malinvestment and thereby harming prosperity. Even so, the headline CPI inflation rate of near 10% in 2021–2 (peaking year-on-year at 8.5% in mid-2022) was important politically—albeit not provoking a landslide for either party.

In the 2022 mid-terms, the Republicans won the House by a very narrow margin (having lost control in 2020) and the Senate shifted into narrow Democratic control after having been tied (with Biden's vice president holding the decisive vote) in the first 2 years of the Biden Administration. That was not a bad result for the Democrats. Asset inflation and big public spending programs may well have pleased important groups of the overall electorate. And of course there were rival non-economic issues, such as abortion in the wake of a Supreme Court ruling in June 2022 to return authority on this to the states, which swayed voters. The long-run influence of asset inflation in determining political outcomes comes via the malinvestment which it stimulates, thereby slowing or even halting the growth of prosperity—never mind that voters in general would not easily recognize this concept or its practical occurrence.

Governments, in the expectation of large inflation tax revenues cumulatively in the future, could pursue spending and tax cut plans with very low potential efficiency gains and indeed potentially a drag on prosperity, but helpful towards winning the next election. That is one form of mal investment, as in the public sector. More generally, mal investment is a concept which refers to the private sector. It describes how prices in capital markets distorted by monetary inflation cause distortions (away from optimal) in the allocation of capital (see Sechrest 2006). These result in poor or even negative gains in prosperity from investment compared to the counterfactual situation where there had been a good money regime.

There are several channels between monetary inflation and the distortions. For example, monetary inflation is likely to feature interest rates well below (at least in real terms) what would prevail under sound money; this in turn triggers "hunt for yield", where investors out of desperation pay premium prices for assets which have a good potential for delivering steady and indeed growing income over time—think here of firms which are on their way to monopoly status, or even there already.

Desperation for yield may well also mean investors pay premium prices for a range of risky assets, some of the subject of highly speculative popular narratives which would not have spread if rational scepticism dominated the marketplace as under sound money. This follows on the observations of behavioural finance theorists that individuals if given the choice between certain loss or a bad bet (which nonetheless has the possibility of rendering a large return, even though unlikely) will go for the bad bet (paying well above its actuarial value). In the real world, individuals most likely tell themselves false narratives which make the bad bets seem good. And these narratives may become consensus in the marketplace (see Kahneman 2012; Brown 2019).

The fact that malinvestment is happening does not mean that financial and economic performance are continuously bad. General Luck plays a potentially important role especially over short periods of time. Projects adopted based on distorted prices and incorrect calculations can still hit the jackpot. Innovations and technological revolutions are full of unknown potentials and costs. Though malinvestment may feed unjustified (according to rational calculation) implementation—or unjustified speed of implementing—of new technologies, this may turn out to be highly successful whether at the level of the individual in terms of rate of profit. As illustration, once a monopoly has been formed with the help of extraordinarily cheap capital it then sets a "death zone" around itself preventing new entry by possible competitors (it does this for example by predatory pricing of by pre-emptive buyouts). The monopolist or oligopolist in command of the new technology may be able to effectively wipe out competitors who otherwise would have been cutting prices (but still covering variable costs) on old technologies. In consequence the journey into the unknown occurs quicker but in suboptimal fashion thereby compared to what happens under competitive conditions.

Malinvestment does not necessarily show up in a low cumulative rate of return to capital, though over long periods it should tend to go along with disappointing productivity growth and growth of prosperity at a macro level. We see this during the long span of digitalization. Overall productivity and prosperity growth has been anaemic by comparison with many periods in the history of previous technological revolution. This may be partly due to a mushrooming of related business expenditures which become must-dos; for example, for digital technology, there is the whole expenditure of combatting viruses and more broadly security threats (actual and potential). But these areas of defensive business activity can yield high rates of return and can spawn new monopoly. (Of course, we could discuss similarly how the innovation of the motor vehicle brought along with it the danger of road accidents and the need for road policing and auto recovery services; the issue is whether these flaws and extent of expenditures necessary to keep their effects within bounds are just so much greater in the case of digitalization).

In sum, malinvestment may take the form of a too rapid rate of technological progress relative to what would occur under sound money in the absence of monopoly power. In general, under competitive conditions and with substantial costs of equity capital reflecting considerable uncertainty about the new technology and its potential flaws, introduction and implementation of new technology might well be justifiably slow. This allows more time to discover flaws and either deal with them, or transition to better technologies. For example, back in the 1990s, the huge flaws now apparent in the internet were not fully grasped or even discovered; a slower pace of advancement might have given time for discovery and finding alternative paths forward. Some firms who were loaded up with previous generation state of the art technology might slash their prices below the level which could yield a return on fixed costs but still justify high turnover rates at covering variable costs plus a little more. But firms launching the new technology if they are already monopolists from previous technological change may have strong interest in clearing out potential competition whether using new generation or previous generation technology; and they may have access to funds both internal and external, which price in such monopoly promise.

A faster rate of introduction of technological innovation is not always better and may be a bad consequence of monopolization; indeed, principles suggest the faster rate would sometimes be worse especially if a sub-optimal path is taken into the forest of the unknown and the costs of going back to its beginning are high (see Parayil 2009); this could be the case in particular where there are important networking effects of the new technology. In the case of digitalization, we can think of many flaws which emerged in the technology which were not known at the time of its early introduction—especially related to viruses and more broadly insecurity. Yet there is a high degree of non-reversibility in this technology due to networking benefits already in place when the deeper flaws are discovered. Once far progressed, it is not feasible for the invisible hand to turn the clock back to the fax machine as a broad-based alternative and explore a better way forward alongside a slower pace of digitalization meanwhile.

Incidentally, economic data may well treat the costs of the innovation as additions to GDP. This applies for example to the output of the huge industry which safeguards now our journeys every day through internet transactions. Under rules of GDP accounting, a substantial amount of this is treated as output or income gains. But at the level of the individual citizen this is not a gain. Another reason here why voters might not feel as well off as the official data would suggest.

Of course, the argument that our justified disgruntlement as ordinary citizens at the disappointing increase in our prosperity over time is due to monetary inflation and its manifestation in asset inflation and from there malinvestment has not made its way into the political arena. It is not an easy concept to explain or rally crowds behind. And there is no simplistic empirical demonstration such as the monetarists were able to muster for example in the 1970s and which could be used on the campaign trail.

If there is a simple message at all it is about how monetary inflation has promoted monopoly and how monopoly power is damaging overall prosperity. But that is not a message which has yet permeated into the main political arena.

Rather, in the 2024 US elections, the dominant theme was how the jump in prices (and fall in internal value of the dollar) which occurred through 2021–3 at such a pace was due to the spending bonanza by the Biden Administration. The answer: cut waste in government spending (including unauthorized spending by government agencies) and role back the Inflation Reduction Act (IRA) under which much of the industrial policy (related to environmental issues) had been assembled. Flaws in the monetary regime and the case for monetary reform just did not figure as an argument on either side of the campaign trail. The case could have been made by the Democrats in attacking the giant monetary inflation which had already occurred under the Trump Administration (2019–20) whilst admitting that this had also continued under the Biden Administration (still under the stewardship of Fed Chief Powell, reappointed by President Biden in early 2022).

Suppose the idea ever gets on to a main campaign trail that the actual deeply flawed monetary regime is responsible for widespread and serious ailments in the US economy (monopolization, malinvestment), beyond just consumer price inflation. The idea could strike many voters with intuitive sense as obvious.

References

Brown, Brendan "Under Trump, Expect No Change in the Monetary Status Quo: Mises Wire, December 20, 2024

Brown, Brendan "Review: Narrative Economics: How Stories Go Viral and Drive Major Economic Events" (by Robert Shiller). Quarterly Journal of Austrian Economics, Vol. 22, No. 4 Winter 2019

Kahneman, Daniel "Thinking Fast and Slow" Penguin 2012

Parayil, Gavinder "Schumpeter on Innovation and Technological Change" Cambridge University Press June 2009

Sechrest, Larry J "Explaining Malinvestment and Overinvestment" Quarterly Journal of Austrian Economics Vol. 9, No. 4 Winter 2006 pp. 27–38

PART VII

Speculation, Havens and Gold

CHAPTER 15

Manias and Asset Inflation

Monetary inflation shows up as goods inflation and asset inflation. These symptoms require careful diagnosis. For example, we reviewed earlier in this volume (see Chap. 1) how a spurt in productivity growth or any other type of abrupt increase in the supply side of the economy camouflage the symptom of monetary inflation in the goods markets. Then recorded CPI inflation might seem benign—at say around zero—but the underlying condition be inflationary in the sense that under sound money prices should fall at such times. Similarly—and some would say more so—there are issues in identifying asset inflation. It is misleading to equate asset inflation with a general rise in the price of assets, as has occurred in some of the literature on the topic (for example see Schwartz 2002) or in the general dictionaries of definitions (but not in the glossary of Brown and Pringle 2022), even though episodes of asset inflation usually include a sub-period during which that occurs.

Rather, we consider that the essence of asset inflation is pervasive corruption of price signalling in asset markets, including credit and capital markets alongside a wide range of markets for real assets including equity and property, by money which has got "out of control" in the sense of J.S. Mill—see Friedman (2006)—"when the machinery of money gets out of control it becomes the monkey wrench in all the other economic machines". Often that means critically the authorities are highly manipulating

B. Brown and P. Simonnot, *Bad Money*,
https://doi.org/10.1007/978-3-031-95425-2_15

interest rates—and especially long-term rates. In turn, these manipulations cause other asset prices, which take their cue from the bond market, to become distorted to important degrees.

There are other potential channels from monetary inflation to asset inflation which do not go directly through interest rates and bond yields. The story of asset inflation might start with apparently buoyant business conditions in the economy as stimulated by monetary inflation—and in turn extrapolative expectations of further capital gains based on past gains develop; such expectations formation is one characteristic of "irrational exuberance" (see Shiller 2016). And the failure of monetary conditions to tighten—monetary inflation continuing—means there is no break on this process (a point not made by Shiller who does not link monetary conditions to the emergence of irrational exuberance). Then in many asset inflations, yield chasing sets in, of which an element is desperation for yield if indeed rates do not rise from an abnormally low level.

Price signalling in capital markets goes haywire in asset inflations. Rather than prices of assets reflecting a view of future income across a range of scenarios carefully constructed and with probabilities which reflect sober-rational calculation, they become heavily influenced by such factors as desperation for yield (meaning, for example, a giant-sized premium on businesses with any monopoly potential) and calculation driven by highly speculative narratives. The state of the marketplace under such conditions has been described as "irrationally exuberant "though the authors attributing that description do not mostly make the connection with monetary conditions—see Brown 2019.

So where does mania fit into this? In the literature, there is not a strict definition of mania. Here, the concept relates to the amount of price distortion and corruption being near the extreme end of a range, without precise measurement being possible. Asset inflations and the phenomenon of mania do not fit neatly into Friedman's ideal discipline of positive economics (see Friedman 1966). As a generalization from the historical record, we can say that long asset inflations typically spawn manias in one particular asset class, usually small, but not across asset markets in general.

We can illustrate the point. The tulip mania in Holland of the 1630 s was part of a general asset inflation there—whose origin was gold and sliver coming to Amsterdam and fuelling the growth of deposits at the Bank of Amsterdam (see French 2021). In effect, Amsterdam became the cheapest and most trustworthy centre in Europe for depositing bullion (properties included free coinage, supervision of the quality of coins, and high-quality bank deposits). But the growth in money supply empowered an overall monetary inflation showing up most of all in asset inflation. Noteworthy besides tulips and indeed on a much larger scale was the speculation in Dutch East Indian stocks (though the absolute peak mania episode in these was synchronous with the South Sea Bubble and the Mississippi Bubble more than a century later; and the source of monetary inflation then was quite different—see Garber 2000).

Even what we choose to categorize as mania is not totally devoid of rationality. There is a reasoned story put forward to justify the manic high prices and speculation. But in sober-rational mood most if not all of us would find this story full of extreme assumptions and not eligible for more than a small probability in assessments of future possible reality. That does not mean that a crash is coming in the next few weeks or months, even though the historical record is such that the manic stages of bubbles do not last for long (measured in years). And as widely realized and commented upon, the rational individuals who are dubious about the asset market in mania are wholly rational in not "going short"; they may be crucified if the mania goes even further before the crash comes. And in any case, "going short" may just not be technically possible.

The emergence of mania in one (usually small) part of the asset market can be regarded as evidence that asset inflation overall is present. Manias surely do not emerge without predisposing asset inflation. That hypothesis though is not universally accepted. Kindleberger wrote his epic narrative on manias through history without mentioning the theme of asset inflation (see Aliber et al. 2023). For him, the driving explanation was the Minsky model devoid of such input. Here, in this volume, the emergence of mania is a strong indicator that a key symptom of monetary inflation—asset inflation—is present. But how, some critics may retort, can we explain the manias which occurred under the gold standard regime in the nineteenth century. The answer here is that the manias referred to—such as the railway manias in the US—occurred during periods when either the gold standard had been suspended (as in the aftermath of the Civil War) or when the US government was definitely behaving in a way such as to defy and handicap the workings of the gold standard (as in the late 1880s early 1890s or early 1900s (see Chap. 13)—a practice which always ended in crisis if there was no suspension of the dollar's convertibility into gold.

In the Great Asset Inflation of 1924–8, where the US as the new hegemon of the global monetary system was in effect pursuing monetary inflation, an oft-cited example of mania was the Florida land bubble. This was in the context of a nationwide construction and real estate boom. But the speculative content in Florida stood out as extreme (see White 2008). The speculative stories were not all nonsense; air-conditioning was a key innovation as well as travel by car which opened huge new opportunities to escape the northern winters and enjoy a beautiful coast. The sale of underwater lots may seem evidence of hyper-irrationality, but the reality was that real estate development required first draining swamps, and it was possible to attach billboards to the sand floor below the swamp. Speculators' views about the long-run future of Florida (where such views existed) were substantiated; it was just the timescale which was out! The first crash which occurred in Florida in 1926 coincided with a general downturn in construction nationally and a peaking of prices (apparently in 1925).

There were other examples of particular asset market mania outside the US during the mid or mid-late 1920s. Germany was from 1924 to 1931 in effect on a dollar standard. The German equity market was soaring to the sky in 1926 and early 1927—alongside the real estate prices in Berlin were rising exponentially (see Bresciani-Turroni 1968; Kippenberger 2024)—until the Reichsbank under its Governor, Helmut Schacht, decided in May 1927 to cool speculation down by imposing tight restrictions on lending (including margin loans) to equity market investors (see Voth 2001). A crash followed. Again, the mania so-called here was not without some foundation in rational speculation (after all Germany was in an economic miracle it seemed and why could this not have lasted as was to happen through the 1950s and 60 s?).

Fast forward to the monetary inflation in the US through the 1960s (starting in say, 1962) to the severe monetary disinflation of 1973/4. We have already discussed the nature of asset inflation through the 1950s, and this gathered strength into the 1960s as the grip of monetary inflation became stronger, with a longer run before any serious pull-back than in the 1950s (see Chap. 13) when the Martin Fed applied the principle of "taking away the punch bowl". The first monetary pull-back in the 1960s did not occur until Winter 1965/66 (see Fessenden, 2016) and was quickly aborted before a bigger crunch in 1968/9 (see Meltzer 2014). Manias through the mid/late 1960s include the IOS of Bernie Cornfeld (see Aliber 2002) and the boom in franchises which in turn was accompanied by explosive growth in conglomerate formation (between companies where there were no obvious joint economies). The crunch in 1969 was not as severe as many contemporaries believed—the recession of 1970 has been ironed away if we look at the data revisions over the years since. In the further virulent monetary inflation led by the US from 1970–2, a mania of note was the real estate speculation in the UK culminating in the so-called secondary banking crisis (Reid 1982). Rapid growth of the euro-dollar market had some manic features terminating in the Herstatt Bank failure of 1974.

The great monetary inflation presided over by the Fed from 1985–9, getting an early lift-off from the dollar devaluation at Plaza in late summer 1985) (see Brown and Pringle 2022), spawned a notorious global asset inflation with manias alongside. These included several hot markets in the Japan bubble economy including golf club memberships (selling for several million dollars each). Japan's monetary inflation was directly triggered as part of the official response to the fantastic appreciation of the yen which occurred in the aftermath of Plaza as brought about by accompanying US monetary inflation (see Yaguchi, 1994). Rampant financial engineering (zai-tech) was used to sell the apparent earnings of Japanese corporations. And in the international art markets, Japanese investors played a key role in sending prices to unexplored summits. Outside Japan another bubble market of note, otherwise called mania, was Swedish property (Englund 1999). We should note that in both Japan and Sweden a simultaneous deregulation of the credit market played an important role in its generation.

We come next to the Great Asset Inflation which raged from the mid-1990s to the mid-2000s. This was led at first by the Greenspan Fed's policy of monetary stimulus in 1995–6 as the economy slowed (no recession) in response to the brief disinflation of the previous year (1994)—and the 1996 elections loomed. Then as the incipient boom came into full blossom, the Greenspan Fed did not allow monetary conditions to tighten, arguing that the IT revolution and related productivity surge were cooling down reported consumer price inflation compared to what conventional economic forecasts were heralding. This earned Greenspan the title of "Maestro" (see Woodward 2001). The sound money critic would argue though that under such circumstances, the Fed should not have stood in the way of declining prices which are natural at such a time and by doing so it empowered asset inflation—overlapping the "irrational exuberance" of which the Fed Chair notoriously complained about already in December 1996. Greenspan never progressed from that complaint to diagnosing the monetary ailment of asset inflation. In Europe, the newly constituted ECB (from 1997) copied Fed policies.

Manias during this period (mid-1990s to mid-2000s) included the "dot.com" bubble and bust (99–00)—NASDAQ rose 800% from 1995 to March 2000 then falling almost 80% by October amidst crashes/bankruptcies in online shopping companies and some tele-communication businesses; the Chinese mainland stock market up 400% in 2006–7; the bubble in US sub-prime mortgages and parallel bubbles globally in weak credits re-packed via financial engineering into apparently good quality paper—and alongside all this a bubble in financial equities especially in Europe where there was also the story of a bold new world of European integration; the oil and commodity bubble of early 2008; the Iceland mania from the early 2000s until 2008 (see Aliber and Zoega 2011).

The Iceland bubble was led by a deregulation/denationalization of Iceland banking at a time when hunt for yield was on strong in global markets given the Fed's efforts to stimulate the economy out of the stagnation of 2001–2 and in the aftermath of terrorist attacks on the US. Iceland's biggest bank, Kaupthung Bank, grew its assets 30-fold from 2000–8; Icelandic real estate prices soared; the driving story was global financial institutions pouring funds into Iceland, whether in some cases taking kroner exposure, or swapping their exposure into their base currency and enjoying a so-called attractive credit spread. Global bond investors were avid buyers of kroner paper issued by non-Iceland borrowers, which they had swapped into other currencies.

Less exotic manias than Iceland included the so-called currency carry trades (Polish and Spanish homebuyers funding themselves with Swiss franc or yen mortgages); the Swiss franc and yen as the two lowest interest rate currencies, became one leg (as borrowing currency) of a vast carry trade business whose other leg was investing in high-yielding assets including currencies. Yes, carry trades can make rational sense in some situations where there is strong reason to think that exchange rate trends will not cancel out savings (or gains) in interest cost. But in the irrational exuberance and search for yield which characterizes asset inflations, people overweight the likelihood of the big gain outcome and play down the risks of loss. In the case of the yen, where investors had long enough perspective (right through to the 2020s) and held on to positions, there was much profit to be made. But taking foreign exchange views over 20 years is not the bread-and-butter of investing and only rarely can be rationalized as strategy given the needs to finance uncertain streams of spending in the shorter term. Back to the 1990s and 2000s, the speculative expectations over say months or a few years ahead during this carry trade bubble were seriously flawed most of all in the case of the Swiss franc (see pp). Flaws, however, do not mean instant crash. And as in all manias, many of those involved somehow thought they would get out before the doors slammed shut. Both the Swiss National Bank and the Bank of Japan abetted the mania by keeping their monetary policies expansionary, arguing that CPI inflation remained below target.

There is little doubt about the Fed's strong monetary inflation at least until the second half of 2005. A key symptom of this was the Great Asset Inflation from the mid-1990s to the mid-2000s. There had been a brief intermission in 2000 when Fed policy tightened sharply—an end to the extra monetary injections implemented in response to the debt crises of Autumn 1998 (including Russian debt default and the LTCM collapse in New York). The Fed had delayed withdrawing this extra stimulus out of concern about possible digital chaos at the start of the new millennium. The monetary injections had resumed in 2001, the program of monetary stimulus going subsequently into over-drive. Then at some point in the mid-2000s, Fed policy moved to disinflation and by more than its top officials (Greenspan and later Bernanke) intended or realized. We cannot see this from simply studying changes in Fed funds rate which had already neared its summit by Winter 2005/6. The Fed funds rate had climbed at virtually constant pace—which was largely pre-announced—from 1% in July 2004 to 5.25% July 2006 and stayed there until September 2007. Alongside the money supply aggregates were slowing sharply. Whatever remaining significance monetary data then had in an already corrupted monetary system (in particular, base money already had suffered a loss of potential to deliver extreme monetary services—see Brown 2023—and the Fed was focusing on manipulating interest rates as its main policy tool) got submerged by the change of Fed practice in late 2008 (as made possible by legislation in Congress and implemented by Chair Bernanke) to pay interest at the policy rate on bank reserves held at the Federal Reserve [see Brown 2023]). These reserves had previously paid no interest.

The presumption of monetary inflation through the years 2010 to at least the mid-2020s cannot rest on any simple (or any!) interpretation of the monetary data given the further extent to which the US monetary system diverged from anything near the situation under a sound competitive regime. Rather the diagnosis of monetary inflation is based largely on symptoms (asset inflation and goods inflation—with the latter interpreted to allow for downward non-monetary influences on prices) and on aspects of monetary practice (QE, zero rate policies and intent). And there is also the symptom of suspected manias.

Let's list these.

There was the continuing and building up mania in Chinese residential real estate (including construction); a first pull-back/crash in 2014/15—then a new continuation with final crash starting 2020 and continuing since. Fuelling this mania at the end of the line was monetary inflation in the US hegemon which made it possible for Chinese authorities themselves to run policies under which mania could occur (see Brown 2024).

During the virulent monetary inflation of the pandemic, we had mania in many stocks whose business model was tailored to the new conditions of social distancing and stay at home working—the mania made possible by the zero-rate policy and QE of the Fed and foreign central banks following or accompanying its lead. And in real estate markets, mania enveloped some small segments where properties were meant to be ideal for these circumstances. Meme stock mania emerged from all those at home gamblers enjoying inflows of pandemic relief cash and fantastically easy money conditions.

Alongside the identified manias, there have been long—some monetary critics would say continual—episodes of large bubbles in credit markets where spreads on high-risk debt have been compressed to extraordinarily low levels. There has been the bubble of the private equity market. The highly questionable prevailing narratives circulating amongst a heavy weight of investors included the continuing magic (for private equity) of rising equity markets and repressed interest rates; the presumption that the crony links which win contracts especially in the public sector whether in hospital care or the prison system would endure; and that the private equity teams not subject like public companies to quarterly accounting reporting could deploy management skills that were unrivalled for publicly listed companies. These narratives are far from convincing, the critics of private equity say, especially given the large fees charged. And beware the illusions of liquidity: there is none, and transparency is very limited if present at all; under certain types of market climate private equity holdings could become totally illiquid. The opinion that private equity is a mania was not so rare at the time of writing.

And then we come to plausibly the biggest mania of all during this period—crypto assets including the leading crypto money, Bitcoin. On sober-rational calculation, there was much to be wary of as concerns these monetary innovations, whether as medium of exchange or store of value. As regards medium of exchange, a fundamental attraction to potential users is the quality of anonymity. There are other potential advantages in the future—ultimately lower transaction costs in their broadest sense. The use of the blockchain means no financial intermediaries are necessary who incidentally record details of the end-users. Yes, the blockchain is visible by all, but if the owner of the wallets into which digital coins are put takes care—for example eschewing public coin exchanges and using virtual private networks (VPNs)—outsiders (including authorities) would not be able to put a name to the code description of the transactor. Taking care, though, becomes increasingly difficult given the increasing ability of hostile outsiders to trace the names behind the crypto wallet code. For example, if there is any transaction between the owner of the crypto and a seller of goods, services, or alternative assets, there is the risk that the latter might come under investigation. The seller might feel pressure to disclose identity or help in finding identity of the given person. There is another danger with crypto as a medium of exchange—a mistype of the destination wallet (for payment) or a technical error may mean the wrong person gets paid and there is no way of retrieving this error; the overall dimension of this problem is not known.

It is rational to assume that the efforts of authorities and others to discover identity of anonymous wallets will increase over time. Weak links here include the transparency of the blockchain and transactions between the persons who own those wallets and other parties who ultimately can be identified in the widening span of the surveillance state. And there are all the unknowns as to how the advance of quantum accounting may affect this issue.

The Ukraine-Russia war has expanded the demand for the property of anonymity by state and non-state actors in countries under sanctions or sanctions threat by the alliance of countries against Russia (in the proxy war mainly). And so Russian, Iranian, North Korean and Chinese enterprises and state actors under threat of US or European freezing action have an interest in paying in crypto (including Bitcoin, Tether, and others) bitcoin. Sellers of commodities around the world—especially but not only where these are state enterprises—in many cases would accept crypto (especially sellers of commodities including oil based in those countries).

In turn, the recipients of crypto in these cases might have use themselves for these monies when buying goods—whether armaments or others. In some areas/markets sellers of gold are willing to take crypto and do not at present come under pressure to reveal identities. There are also possibilities of obtaining dollars for crypto in various exchanges outside the reach of the western authorities (this is suitable for recipients of crypto who are not themselves under any threat of investigation by western authorities especially in the US). This is an important consideration for Chinese citizens who are using crypto as a vehicle for capital flight out of their country—and once out it can be exchanged for dollars and then into other assets in ways which would not be reported to authorities back home. The issue for them is which holders of crypto would want to sell to them back in China in exchange for Chinese yuan. They must have a way of themselves getting these yuan out of China, perhaps via offshore markets in yuan.

Turning to the store of value function of crypto, much has been made by its promotors of the fixed boundary to the supply of each form, not far above the present in the case of Bitcoin (for which there is a high and rising cost of mining the remaining supply) (see White 2023). Much of this argument is phoney. The range of potential near substitute monies for any crypto currency is immense. As new monies are created this will potentially subtract from the demand for bitcoin or equivalent. And there is no anchor for bitcoin in the form of consumer demand for this on account of services which it renders non-monetary in form. The lack of supply elasticity means that fluctuations in the real value of bitcoin (or equivalent) are very large as reflects shifting demand. We should mention the significant risk of loss due to hacking and other forms of theft. Then there is the danger of loss from somehow losing the password to the wallet (5 per cent per annum of the stock of bitcoins are reputedly lost in this way—surely not a "quality" which makes for good store of value). There is the hazard to value from the quantum computer as already mentioned and from government action around the world to attack this form of money.

In sum, possible rationalizations of the astronomical rise in the price of crypto assets from say 2018 onwards included the surge in demand for anonymous forms of payment (and parallel with this the scope for secrecy in conventional financial system was growingly under attack) as explained; there was also the "better than gold" viewpoint—that gold is much more cumbersome as a money given requirements of storage and the costs/

difficulties of shipping to make payment compared to the digital counterparts. And yes, it is true that in shipping gold the shipper is likely/certain to know the name of the person immediately behind the gold transfer—but not much more than that; the ultimate owner might well be able to keep his or her identity off the shipping paperwork. Yes, there are "know your client" rules in the world of making gold shipments via well-trodden routes. But there are many gold shipments outside those routes and in any case the client need not be the owner. Moreover, state actors can arrange shipments without filling in the forms; rather they hire the planes or boats (or compartments) and arrange delivery direct to the other side without incurring reporting requirements. There is huge consumer demand for gold (in form of jewellery) which exerts a stabilizing or anchoring role with respect to gold (working against wild price fluctuations and helping to increase supply elasticity of monetary gold with respect to price changes (and thereby demand swings).

Evidence of simply wild speculation in Bitcoin and other crypto currencies is strong. Large gains made by speculators/investors who were early enthusiasts about the new money encouraged expectations that further large gains lay ahead and bolstered confidence in some or all of the above "plausible narratives". Narratives about the present and future wonders of blockchain-based money—crypto—have circulated in a state of high fever. But blockchain is an internet-based technological innovation and as such has joint exposure to the deep flaws in that—lack of security and hacking is one such prominent flaw. Yet again in February 2025, this was evident to all with the heist of $1.5bn worth of coins from the Bybit crypto exchange (albeit less than the $3.6bn heist from Bifinex in 2016).

References

Aliber, Robert, Kindleberger, Charles, McCauley Robert "Manias, Panics and Crashes" Palgrave 2023

Aliber, R.Z. "The New International Money Game" Palgrave 2002

Aliber R.Z. and Zoega, Gylfi "Preludes to the Icelandic Financial Crisis" Palgrave 2011

Brown, Brendan "The Qualities of the Monetary Base essential to sound money: fiat and gold" Quarterly Journal of Austrian Economics Vol. 26, Issue 4, 2023

Brown, Brendan "How the Fed helped create the China bubble—and bust" Mises Wire, May 21, 2024

Brown, Brendan and Pringle, Robert "A Guide to Good Money" Palgrave 2022

Brown, Brendan "Book Review: Narrative Economics: How Stories go Viral and Drive Major Economic Events" by Robert Shiller, Quarterly Journal of Austrian Economics, Vol. 22, No. 4 Winter 2019

Bresciani-Turroni, Constantino "The Economics of Inflation" A.M. Kelley (New York) 1968

Douglas French "The Truth about Tulipmania" Mises Daily, December 22, 2021

Englund, Peter "The Swedish Banking Crisis: roots and consequences" Oxford Review of Economic Policy, Vol. 15, No. 3, Autumn 1999 pp. 80–97

Fessenden, Helen "1965: The year the Fed and LBJ clashed" Richmond Federal Reserve Econ Focus, Third/Fourth Quarter 2016

Friedman, M "The Optimum Quantity of Money" Aldine Transaction, London 2006

Garber, Peter M "Famous First Bubbles: The Fundamentals of Early Manias" MIT Press 2000

Kippenberger, Suanne "Weimar Estates: What 1920s Germany Teaches us about the eternal banking crisis" World Crunch, December 12, 2024

Meltzer, Allan "A History of the Federal Reserve" Vol. 2, Book 1, 1951–69 University of Chicago Press, 2014

Reid, Margaret "The Secondary Banking Crisis 1973–5" Palgrave 1982

Schwartz, Anna "Asset Price Inflation and Monetary Policy" NBER Working paper no. W9321 November 2002

Shiller, Robert J "Irrational Exuberance" Princeton University Press (2016)

Voth, Hans Joachim "With a Bang, Not a Whimper: Pricking Germany's "Stock Market Bubble" in 1927 and the Slide into Depression" U. Pompeu Fabra Economics Working Paper no. 516 February 2001

White, Eugene N "Lessons from the Great American Real Estate Boom and Bust of the 1920s" NBER Summer Institute 2008

Woodward, Bob "Maestro: Greenspan's Fed and the American Boom" Simon and Schuster (2001)

Yaguchi, Yukin "The "bubble" and economic policies in the 1980s" Journal of Japanese Studies, Vol. 20, no. 2 Summer 1994, pp. 291–329

White, Lawrence "Better Money: gold, fiat or bitcoin" Cambridge University Press 2023

CHAPTER 16

Gold is Money First, Haven Second

Gold has the reputation of being a haven. First and foremost, though, gold is a money.

It delivers the essential services of money—store of value and medium of exchange—even though in different ways and in some respects less efficiently than in previous epochs when leading nation-states had their currencies fully convertible into gold. Convertibility meant that the issuer of banknotes would promise to redeem these at par on request in gold, and gold could be taken to the mint in exchange for gold coins of the same weight. Gold coins circulated widely in everyday use.

Today, gold money is mainly found in the form of base money (sometimes described as "high-powered money"—see Brown 2023). By contrast for the fiat monies, or for the historical (and now hypothetical) case of national (or supranational) monies convertible into gold, base money is the bottom of an inverted pyramid, with upper layers including a range of wider money categories (for example time deposits, certificates of deposit) not delivering the same degree of "moneyness" as the base. For contemporary gold money, these upper layers consist of a small market in bullion bank deposits (amongst authorized dealers in the London bullion market) and a borrow-and-lend market (for physical metal) amongst professionals. Base money in the case of gold money today consists of gold bullion and gold coin, whether held directly, or

B. Brown and P. Simonnot, *Bad Money*,
https://doi.org/10.1007/978-3-031-95425-2_16

indirectly as 100 per cent backing for gold-denominated deposits with private banks for example or for gold ETFs.

Conventionally, monetary base in fiat monies paid no interest as is the case for gold (in fiat monies base money consists of banknotes and deposits at the central bank). Non-payment of interest on base money is an essential characteristic of good money architecture (see Brown and Pringle 2022; Brown 2023). In a good money system, the monetary base is capable of delivering monetary services of great intensity thereby enjoying wide and strong demand despite being non-interest bearing. In today's fiat monies including the dollar and euro, the central bank pays interest on reserves at the policy rate, with seriously ill consequences for the monetary system—see chapter 2).

In a good money system, individuals are willing to hold large amounts of base money (either directly or indirectly as backing for other monetary assets) without any interest and at some storage cost (in the case of gold). Here, even at the margin base money components render monetary services which are intense and special—worth the sacrifice of interest income. These services can be as store of value or medium of exchange.

The sought after services as store of value of monetary base instruments (gold coin and bullion for gold money) include sustaining of real value in the long-run without the bearing of any default risk, high level of liquidity in sense that they (the instruments) can always readily be exchanged into at least some widely held assets (including other monies) or goods and services, privacy (its holding is not registered with compliance authorities or in other ways; its use in transactions ideally should not reveal any trace of where it has been circulating or held previously); availability in standardized physical amounts for which the value to volume and value to weight ratios are very high, and finally (not least) aesthetics (beauty to some beholders in different amounts).

Services of gold as a medium of exchange require that some sellers of goods or services or assets will accept payment in gold in its standardized units (whether small and large bullion bars or recognized coins). In the actual world where legal tender laws and convention protect national fiat monies (or fiat monies issued by a group of countries), the use of gold as medium of exchange depends on negotiations between buyer and seller and these occur mainly where the potential size of the transaction is large; then costs—including the discussions, the receiver of gold in payment checking the purity of the metal, any transport and safekeeping fees—can be held to only a tiny percentage of size in value. (Further reductions are possible in this cost where coins are in protective cases, which prevent any chipping off as used to occur when in widespread circulation). Negotiations may not be feasible where one or more of the parties is subject to tax authorities enforcing sales taxes or capital gains taxes on gold; these are a disincentive to gold's use as medium of exchange as against store of value (in so far as taxes are not in practice levied on unrealized gains or on gold just held in safes).

Many holders of gold may derive benefit in the form of perceiving it as a potential medium of exchange at any time when he or she would want to use it as such, even though the likelihood of doing this in the immediate or short-term is quite low. The holder can get reassurance (in the potential medium of exchange function when wanted) in that there are significant numbers of people for whom gold is part of their monetary portfolio or who are open to the idea of gold being proposed in settlement. We can think of there being a large community in today's world of actual or potential gold users for transactions—people for whom the cost of negotiating a particular payment would not be large (relative to the transaction in view). Gold as a medium of exchange gains acceptance from it being so much a part of human civilization; and the physical qualities of gold as described above make it so suitable.

Gold as a money does excite speculative holding—as do some fiat monies at times (when there are widespread expectations say of the fiat money in general appreciating versus other currencies and by more than any loss of interest income). But with gold today, the speculative element in holdings might be especially large at least in certain episodes.

Speculation would describe the phenomenon of individuals holding much more gold than they would if it was just a good store of value—in the sense of expected to sustain its purchasing power over the very long run plus the other qualities listed—and a small circulating medium of exchange (largely by negotiation each time rather than near-automatic). The speculators might expect its value to increase by large amounts over their relevant time horizon, perhaps on the basis that many other people will wake up to its advantages as a money—and also on the basis that current predominant bad monies will just get so much worse (and more so than generally expected) that gold's monetary advantages and thereby use as money increase in relative terms. Or some speculators might expect that in a climate of growing discontent with the national money, governments might offer the palliative to voters of removing tax penalties on the monetary use of gold. Accordingly, gold's role would expand as a medium of exchange—meaning an increase in demand say for gold coin and small gold bars (for example 1gm or 10gm bars).

Such speculative drive behind gold money holding should be distinguished from safe-haven demand. The latter is based on the idea that gold will retain value or even gain in value in certain bad states of the world (one factor in that gain might be increased use, which the metal acquires at such times as medium of exchange or as store of value). The holder in general does not have any particular clue about when these bad times are coming and whether worse than generally portrayed in scenario-building in the marketplace.

Gold may also have attractions in general to portfolio investors who are not especially interested in its monetary properties as described here. Rather they view it as a "bad news good"—an asset which generally rises in states of the world (scenarios which become reality) which are bad, meaning most assets including equities are falling in value—whilst conversely it falls in good states of the world. Such a negative correlation between returns on gold and on diversified portfolios of equities would mean that adding gold to wealth holdings overall would reduce its overall risk. The basis of the assumed negative correlation between returns from gold and from a well-diversified portfolio of risk assets (including stocks and real estate) is that in really bad states of the world the demand for gold as money would increase sharply. In consequence investors would be willing to hold gold at expected returns on average far below that on say equities because of this diversification property.

Superficially, at least there is a problem with this bad news good description: gold tends to do well during periods of asset inflation (for example the asset inflations of 1976–80, 1985–9, 2003–7) so then we find the stock market and gold often rising together as a trend. There are exceptions though. For example, during the first half of the long asset inflation from the mid-1990s to the mid-2000s gold did not perform well; in the second half (into the first decade of the twenty-first century, though, gold had a strong performance. Some would say though that this experience suggests that in the second half of the 90 s, asset inflation was not so virulent as in the first half of the 2000s. A lull or reversal in asset inflation does not necessarily bring a big fall in gold—that occurs where there is an obvious monetary disinflation underway, but in principle, asset inflation can come to an end without that (with endogenous forces more important).

Instead, the asset markets in that earlier period (2nd half of the 1990s) did have much apparent real good news to discount (both in terms of booming living standards and geo-political peace) with the extent of irrational exuberance correspondingly less intense than sometimes diagnosed including Fed Chair Greenspan in December 1996. Even so, we still have to reckon with the madness of the dotcom bubble in 99/00 and the phenomena including the bubble-and-bust of Enron and WorldCom—bankruptcies in 2001 and 2002, respectively). We could put forward the hypothesis that monetary inflation in general was less fierce in the period 1996-2000Q1 than 2002Q4–2006, citing evidence of mid-cycle crises in the earlier period—the Asian crisis of 1997 (see Borg 1999) and the emerging market/Russia debt crisis of the following year together with the then brief swoon (1998) in the US stock market (featuring also the crisis of LTCM). In effect, the Greenspan Fed of the 1990s did engage in stop–go monetary policy. By contrast from 2001-5H1, there was most likely unbroken monetary stimulus and then eventually an unintended hard stop from 2005H2-7.

Gold's performance is highly interconnected with monetary inflation. Sometimes monetary inflation goes along with powerful asset inflation and a veneer of great prosperity at the top of the wealth/income distribution, which is not accompanied by general economic boom in living standards. In that case gold could perform well. And there is also much room when considering gold's portfolio qualities to stress relative performance. The gold price might not rise in some bad states of the world, but it could do much better than the stock market or some other mainstream assets including fiat money (taking account of fall in its real value due to inflation).

The essence of gold's star performance in bad times—in so far as this occurs—is that the demand for it increases then. This increase in demand may well be related to fears of fiat money inflation in the future because of bad events occurring now. There may also be grown fears of sequestration of wealth by domestic or foreign authorities and of high taxes—including inflation tax—to come on declared or traceable wealth especially if dominated in fiat money. Gold, if well-stored, may appear relatively safe under those circumstances.

The effect of potential increase in monetary demand on the price of gold is held in check by at least two considerations—the potential for increased supply from below ground over the long-run at higher prices and in the shorter term the sale of jewellery (over 50% of the above ground stock of gold is estimated to be in the form of jewellery). And we should note that the gold price also reflects speculation about bad events ahead. When these ultimately occur, they may already have been fully discounted in gold's price. In the Paris gold market of Spring 1940, the gold price had already peaked in terms of French francs before the Germans entered Paris. (See Gallais-Hamonne et al. 2019).

The laboratory of history, with evidence from the far past to the near present, helps to illustrate gold's haven role and how this evolves according to the wider context—economic, political, and geopolitical. During a prevailing gold standard, physical gold holdings (so long as safe from sequestration by the authorities) can provide a safe haven against a break with that standard as in the event of war (civil or international).

For example, during the US civil war, holders of gold were safe against the devaluation of the paper dollar caused by the issuance of the Greenback and the suspension of the paper dollar's convertibility into gold (see Mitchell 2009). Sterling which was then fully convertible into gold would have been as good a safe haven for US holders as gold in many respects—but subject to additional risks (for example if Britain were to enter a proxy war against the North by providing aid to the Confederates that might have made Sterling an unsafe investment for US citizens in view of possible freezing actions by either side). Moreover, in that era trans-Atlantic holdings of money were rare given lack of telecommunications and speedy travel. Fast forward to World War one.

As it turned out, citizens of the "Central Powers" (Germany, Austria-Hungary, and their allies) did best (in terms of monetary assets) in safeguarding their monetary wealth in gold, or where possible the monies of the neutral countries (notably Switzerland, Holland). The franc and the florin in fact during much of the conflict rose above gold parity as the neutral countries in Europe restricted gold inflows so as to break inflationary trends (see Brown 2012). So, they were transitorily better "bad news goods" than gold itself (though at war's end and in its aftermath, they returned to gold par). The dollar was not a safe haven at all unless held in bearer form (most notably banknotes)—as the US would sequester enemy assets (and the US entered the conflict in March 1917).

We could say in a long-run sense that gold was ultimately the safe haven against World War One if we consider its long aftermath—the boom/bust and ultimately Great Depression of the 1920s and early 1930s. But none of that sequence was foreseeable in any detail or at all by citizens during World War One, and there was absolutely no inevitability about the actual outcomes. There were many counterfactual histories eminently plausible for the post-war decade and beyond.

As regards the actual history of that era, there is little evidence if any that physical gold was bought in the late 1920s on the possibility that the economic and geopolitical skies would darken soon. The German stock market bubble already crashed in 1927 and the US real estate market had peaked (see chapter in this volume). But there was no general stocking up with gold in anticipation that worse might follow. This was still the heyday of good economic times and world détente. Even the Wall Street Crash of October 29 followed by the first severe leg of recession through 1930 and the shock Nazi successes in the September 30 elections in Germany brought no reported surge in gold hoarding. This was all in the context of the US still being fully convertible into gold, whilst the mark was fully convertible into dollars (and other currencies) and the pound was on a truncated gold standard (no circulating gold coin or right to redemption in gold coin). The German banking crisis of spring/summer 1931 did trigger flight from Germany (and central Europe) into dollars, and after the German standstill, there was flight from Sterling into dollars. Confidence in gold-dollar convertibility remained intact. All that changed with the shock of Sterling's break with gold and floating (against the dollar) in September 1931. Gold hoarding both in the US and outside took off. The rest of that story is well-known; the US exit from gold in March 1933, the flight out of gold bloc currencies centred on the French franc until their floating of devaluations in Summer 1936.

Gold's haven role on the eve of World War Two and during the War are also well documented. In the year of so up until the outbreak of war it was the US dollar which saw huge inflows from Europe. Doubtless, there was some accumulation of gold in clandestine forms by anxious citizens concerned about looming war and worried that holdings in the US dollar could be subject to US asset freeze or confiscation by their own governments. The Swiss franc became the main alternative to gold most of all from the viewpoint of public authorities (including governments) and citizens in Europe; the franc's attraction was uppermost for those in Germany and Central /Eastern Europe. Yes, the citizens fleeing Germany or the German authorities (and Nazi officials) could hold gold instead in Swiss vaults. But there was the general question about how these would be accessed in wartime conditions. And until late Summer 1940 there was a real possibility that Switzerland would be occupied by Germany. Further into the war dollar deposits in the US held by Swiss entities/names became subject to various US restrictions as applied to hostile neutral powers and so those partially immobilized dollar deposits fell in value versus the franc in the market where the two were traded against each other. In German-occupied Europe, hidden gold was the safe asset, in the sense that in the aftermath of war gold would retain its international value.

Fast forward to the monetary inflation of the 1960s and 1970s. For those with access to the international gold market where gold traded at around par to the US dollar ($35 per ounce) gold was indeed a haven asset. There was plenty of speculative writing both in the media and the academic press about how US inflation could culminate in a revaluation of the official gold price or even a free gold market where the price fluctuated against the dollar. And so hoarding gold became a safety play. But through the first three quarters of the 1960s monetary inflation was accompanied by asset inflation—and so in general funds flowed into stocks and real estate.

At the level of official transactions though, the European central banks (not the UK) led the way in accumulating gold, partly out of concern that dollars would lose their value, and partly to simply reconstitute gold reserves which had been depleted during two world wars. By the mid-late 1960s gold was again emerging though as a private safe haven asset. The freeing of the gold price in March 1968, when the central banks stopped operating the "Gold Pool" which acted to keep the free market price of gold in line with the official price—see Bordo et al. 2017—brought a whole new type of private interest in gold as an investment compared to when the gold price was a fixed constant (but subject to a sudden freeing up and initial rise as in fact occurred). US citizens though were still curtailed in their operation there (in gold) until the mid-1970s due to the Roosevelt era restrictions still in place on US citizens holding gold in the US. Estimates by Friedman and Schwartz (1963) (Andrieu 2022) suggested that only 25% of private gold holdings in the US had been handed over to the authorities at the pre-devaluation rate of $21 per ounce meaning that gold in the US and of course outside continued clandestinely to play an important role in US citizens' wealth decision-making.

Through the late 1960s and 1970s, gold was indeed a star safe haven against global inflation led by the US hegemon rising to a price in constant purchasing power dollars at the peak in February 1980 similar to in early 2025. There had been a brief 35% inflation-adjusted fall in the gold price from early 74 to early 76 (monetary policy had been sharply tightened from Spring 1973 onwards and the great recession ran from late 1973 to early 1975). Then there was an over 4 times rise to February 1980. That included a hyperbolic rise in the year to January/February 1980 when the price jumped almost 250% in the space of a year. Events in Iran (the fall of the Shah, the taking of power by Khomeini, the US hostage crisis—see Zonis 1991) had played a role in the rise, together with a further worsening of the inflation climate in the US through the first three quarters of 1979 until the nomination of Paul Volcker as Fed Chair (August 1979) (and even then there was some scepticism at large as to how far the Fed would tighten in the run-up to the November 1980 elections—scepticism subsequently borne out by some easing of policy through Summer 1980 on the basis of transitorily weak date (see pp.) and then the Russian invasion of Afghanistan in December 1979 brought hot speculative conditions in the gold market (though not devoid of all rationality). The price halved in the subsequent 2 years. In early 81, it had become clear that the Volcker Fed was in serious disinflationary mode; it became possible that the fiat dollar unlinked to gold could actually become a sound money. A sideway move from mid-82 to mid-85 was followed by an almost 40% rise from mid-85 (eve of Louvre accord and Volcker Fed's embrace of devaluation) to end-87 (at which point the Greenspan Fed was pursuing monetary reflation to combat any recessionary influence of the October 87 crash). Then a new decline set in with the gold price falling by 60% to end-91 (coinciding with a sharp monetary tightening and the recession/stagnation of the early 1990s).

The gold price held steady from end 91 to 2000 during the continued stagnation of 91–2 and then into the two Clinton Administrations—despite the first lap (1996–9) of the great monetary inflation of 1995–2007 overlapping the second. In the second lap of that great monetary inflation, 2003–5/6 and its immediate aftermath through 2007 and the first half of 2008, though, the gold price tripled. (Note that both asset inflation and goods/services inflation, the two symptoms of monetary inflation, can lag the monetary inflation which in this case already started to fade most probably from 2006—but this fading was not perceived in general by contemporaries.

We could say that the fierceness of monetary inflation increased dramatically into the early and mid-2000s. That contrasted with less fierce monetary inflation through the mid and late 1990s; in 1994, there had been a serious tightening of monetary policy in response to emerging acceleration of consumer price increases but then there had been a small rate cut for Fed funds to 5% in 1996, staying there on a plateau until Autumn 1998 when there had been a small cut (amidst the Russia debt and LTCM crisis together with brief equity market swoon, rising again in early 2000. In some respects, the monetary inflation of the 1990s was similar to that of the 1950s—a lower order than what followed through the 60 s and 70 s or into the first decade of the twenty-first century. In the previous chapter (see pp.), we gave an account of the range of manias during the 2000s. There was not a return to the high reported CPI inflation of the late 1960s and 1970s. Real downward influences on prices in the early part of the first decade of the twenty-first century included digitalization and globalization—the latter including China's entry into the WTO; asset inflation, however, was severe. Also, into the first decade, hopes of an extended or permanent geo-political peace faded. In the 1990s, there had been so much optimism about geo-politics following the fall of the Berlin Wall. Under the George W. Bush Administrations, the budget situation in the US had deteriorated so much compared to the years of surplus under the Clinton Administration.

There was a further doubling of the gold price (in constant purchasing power) from 2008 until the end of 2011 (the nominal price peak was at around $1900 in September) some 10% below the all-time peak (in real terms) of 1980Q1. A key narrative which catapulted gold in those years (2009–11) included the story that QE—the innovation of the Bernanke Fed—was equivalent to money printing, and this in combination with the deterioration of the fiscal balance meant that high inflation lay ahead. The peak gold price in late 2011 occurred simultaneously with a downgrade in the credit rating of US government debt by one of the major credit-rating firms (S&P). The problem with the narrative about money-printing was its failure to reckon with the fundamental change in the nature of reserves in the banking system following the Autumn 2008 "reform" whereby reserves now paid interest at a full market rate rather than zero as previously. Accordingly, the demand for reserves by the banks had ballooned; and so the massive increase in the supply reserves such as occurred under the QE operations through 2009–11/12 did not have the same inflationary implications as under a system where they paid no interest.

The 35% fall in the gold prices (in constant purchasing power) to mid-2016 from the peak in 2011Q4 reflected the fact that consumer price inflation fell through this period rather than jumping ahead. Contributing to this was the puncturing of the commodity bubble as the Chinese bubble economy encountered its first implosion. Reported CPI inflation in the US fell to almost zero at this time (though that was consistent with monetary inflation overall as evident in asset inflation given the non-monetary downward pressure on prices which meant that prices overall would have been falling under sound money). Then there was the brief apparently disinflationary policy (most likely some monetary inflation still "on") in the first year of the Powell Fed (2018) when the Fed funds rate climbed in steps to a peak (wait for it!) of 2.4% staying there through the first half of 2019; correspondingly the gold price had fallen further by 5% in 2018. It then started climbing ahead of the Powell rate cuts, which came from mid-2019 amidst all the chatter foreshadowing these (including obvious pressure from the White House).

The apparent stepping up of monetary inflation by the Powell Fed in 2019 (we must always say "apparent" because in the contemporary broken monetary system it is very hard to diagnose monetary inflation ahead of or separately from the symptoms; and policy rate adjustments or levels are notoriously poor as an indicator of monetary stance) and then the vast monetary inflation which coincided with the outbreak of the Great Pandemic meant a 60% rise in the gold price through to mid-2022. Also relevant to that super-rise was the outbreak of the Ukraine-Russia war and the related freezes on Russian reserves in Western banks and more broadly on selected private Russian wealth (including oligarchs close to Putin); there was the related threat of freezing action on deposits held by Chinese or other firms and individuals identified as doing business with Russia. All of this contributed to a view in much of the neutral world (neutral in the conflict or allied to Russia) that gold had new safe-haven properties. Rapid growth in reported international reserves held in the form of gold bore this out.

There was a 33% pull-back in the dollar gold price during the period of the so-called Powell Fed pivot to disinflation through 2022H2; but this pull-back did not last long when It became evident that the Powell Fed had no intention of running policy so that mending of supply chains in the aftermath of pandemic would bring prices down to pre-pandemic levels as would have occurred under sound money. Instead, the Fed presided over continuing rises in the consumer price index of 3% year-on-year or more. Strong asset inflation through 23–4 indicated that monetary inflation was again "alive and well" and accordingly by Winter 2024/25 the gold price was up near 70% from the last low point in Q4 2022. In late summer

2025 (the time of writing) the gold price (in US dollars) is up more than 100% from that low-point. This further big rise has occurred in the context of widespread suspicion that the tariff-related supply shock to the US economy plus the degradation of already weak public finances will mean an intensification of monetary inflation given the lack of a solid anchor to the monetary system.

What general principles about gold's safe-haven role can be deduced from the history as presented here? In general, sharp tightening (for real) of US monetary policy accompanied or followed by recession does mean a fall-back in the gold price, though not necessarily by a huge margin. The gold market seems to look beyond the immediate tightening episode to contemplate its likely short duration and the revamped monetary inflation beyond that towards providing stimulus. In line with this stock market crashes do go along with pull-back in gold prices but not necessarily by large amounts for similar reasons. War and peace and more generally a swing in the geo-political barometer do have perceptible impact on the gold price. We saw that a decade of re-awakened world peace hopes contributed to a stability of gold prices through the 1990s despite a background of monetary inflation, though exceptional budget surpluses in the US played also a role. More generally, here the condition of the US budget is sometimes of crucial importance to the gold price.

The growth of the "surveillance state" as aggravated by digitalization has also been gold-positive. Individuals see physical gold holdings in safes outside the banking system as providing a refuge against intrusion whether by state or non-state actors. Relevant to the history was the curtailment and ultimate extinction of Swiss bank secrecy during the period 2010–18. And before that we had the "war on terror" launched after the September 2001 attacks on the US, and which in effect meant a vast extension of the surveillance state with respect to financial transactions.

References

Andrieu, Thomas "Confiscation of Gold in 1933: Behind the Scenes of a Disposession" Gold Broker, October 11, 2022

Bordo, Michael, Monnet Eric, and Nael Alain "The Gold Pool (1961–8_ and the Fall of the Bretton Woods System: Lessons for Central Bank Cooperation" Working Paper 24016, NBER, November 2017

Borg, Andrew "The Asian Debt Crisis: Causes, Policy Responses, and Outcomes" IMF Working Paper WP/99/138 1999

Brown, Brendan "The Qualities of Monetary Base Essential to Sound Money—fiat and gold" Quarterly*Journal of Austrian Economics* , Vol.*26* Winter 2023

Brown, Brendan "Monetary Chaos in Europe" Routledge 2012

Friedman, M and Schwartz, A "A Monetary History of the United States" Princeton 1963

Gallais-Hamonne, Georges, van Hoang, Thi-Hong, Oosterlink, Kim "Price formation in clandestine markets: the case of the Paris gold market during the Second World War" *The Economic History Review*, Vol. 72, Issue 3, 2019

Mitchell, Wesley Clair *"A History of the Greenbacks"* Bibliobazaar 2009

Zonis, Marvin "Majestic Failure: The Fall of the Shah", University of Chicago 1991

CHAPTER 17

Life after Death for the Swiss Franc Haven

The Swiss franc still enjoys some reputation as a safe haven asset. We see that at the time of writing when the franc is climbing, not just against the dollar but also the euro, as anxiety in the marketplace grows about a US-led tariff war of which the core is conflict between the US and China. The continuing haven role of the franc is an oddity at first sight given that important core elements in its attraction as haven have diminished markedly over recent decades.

Even so, amongst the fiat monies, the menace of purchasing power erosion for the franc does stand out as relatively low, with evidence from the last decade under-lining that point. Yes, some of this continuing advantage of the franc has been historical accident, but there is also more than that in play. We should consider the role of haven in relative terms. In Europe, the end of the hard DM and then the end of the DM itself left a vacuum amongst fiat monies, which the franc has filled to a small extent. Though the Swiss financial marketplace and more broadly the financial system has lost once-upon-attributes of soundness and secrecy, the franc haven is more than a relic or in psychological terms a subject of Pavlovian reaction (sense danger, buy the franc, even though it is not the same money in terms of quality as in times past).

It was the First World War which catapulted Switzerland into the role of premier financial refuge. Already in the years before Switzerland had some reputation amongst the French as a place to be safe from tax. We

B. Brown and P. Simonnot, *Bad Money*,
https://doi.org/10.1007/978-3-031-95425-2_17

can see that in history as far back as in the case of finance minister Necker of Louis XVI (see chapter 12). But all of this was transformed by World War One. Switzerland was the first amongst neutrals.

Refuge funds came in both (and mainly) from the Central Powers (Germany, Austria-Hungary) and the Entente (mainly France and Italy). Yes, the US was neutral until March 1917 but financially and commercially it was almost wholly already in a proxy war against the Central Powers as an ally of Great Britain. And it was a much greater risk (from the viewpoint of safe-haven seekers in 1915 and 1916) that the US than Switzerland would enter the war as a full belligerent.

Moreover, the US authorities took no action like Switzerland to restrict gold inflows during the period of neutrality and so its currency (the dollar) could not rise above par. By contrast, Switzerland suspended official purchases of gold in the face of massive capital inflows and so its currency rose to a large premium at times (especially when peace seemed a long time off) against parity. Yes, Holland as a neutral was in a similar position to Switzerland. But its activities were more subject to curbs from Great Britain, which growingly throttled traffic going into Rotterdam and other Dutch sea ports out of concern that these supplies would go into Germany (see Brown 2011).

The Swiss franc's refuge role did not wane after the end of the First World War. It was the hard currency that citizens from the countries now in monetary chaos (first of all the defeated powers which became submerged in high inflation and ultimately hyperinflation). In principle those citizens could have bought dollars—but given exchange restrictions in their countries and geographic distance there were obvious advantages to Switzerland. Also, the Netherlands performed an important refuge function with respect to German capital flight at this time. We should consider the huge speculative retail interest evident in the Netherlands and Switzerland in buying German mark banknotes at what seemed such knock-down prices compared to gold parity (see Brown 2011); this retail interest made capital flight from Germany possible without a total collapse of the mark already in 1920 (rather than later in 1922/23). Switzerland in 1920–23 was also the chief destination for French capital flight, especially when the French currency plunged in 1923 during the occupation of the Ruhr by French and Belgian forces. Switzerland also played a role with respect to receiving capital flight out of Austria and Hungary as their currencies hurtled towards hyperinflation. The Swiss franc like the dollar was fully convertible into gold at this time and not subject to any devaluation risk.

We hear and read less about the Swiss franc's haven role during the economic miracle and global asset inflation period of 1924–8 (asset inflation visible most of all in US and Germany). Indeed, Swiss banks and investors—much as at the end of the century (1998–2006) (see pp.)—were drawn into carry trades, whether the currency trade from low-interest rate francs into high rate reichsmarks or the credit carry trade out of low-risk bonds say in dollars or francs into high risk (of default) German bonds (banks and municipalities for example) denominated also in dollar or francs. When these carry trades started to reverse say from late 1928 onwards Switzerland as a big carry trade creditor became subject to large capital inflows.

The financial sector in Britain was incidentally also engaged in these same carry trades but unlike the franc at that time Sterling was subject to the ultimate risk of devaluation, given that the "return to gold" (in fact attachment to a "gold exchange standard") had not been embraced across the political spectrum and Britain struggled economically through the miracle years of the mid-1920s; the risk increased significantly with the General Election defeat of the Conservative government in 1929.

During the German banking crisis of Spring and early Summer 1931, capital flight from Germany by ordinary citizens—concerned by the alarming deterioration in the political, economic and financial situation there (especially after the shock of the Autumn 1930 general election where the Nazis became the second largest party; and then there were the knock-on effects of the Austrian banking crisis including the Kreditanstalt failure in May 1931)- headed for Switzerland. In summer 1931, Germany introduced exchange restrictions to limit capital flight and capital flight in the form of banknote transactions again emerged.

Swiss bank secrecy had not become enacted up until this point. That happened in 1934, influenced by attempts of large neighbours—both France and Switzerland—to get hold of data on their resident customers (see Guex, 2000). France had been swept by political turmoil including a nearly successful fascist revolution in February 1934. The turmoil and uncertainty had stimulated outflows to the franc haven, interrupted by the French authorities seizing records of a Swiss bank branch in Paris (see Jenkins 2006). And the Nazis, now in power in Germany, redoubled efforts to contain capital flight in whatever way possible, including severest penalties. The Swiss franc became the refuge national currency of choice (physical gold also an obvious haven) through 1932 and early 1933 against devaluation of the US dollar (Roosevelt suspended gold standard immediately following his inauguration as president in March).

Funds also in 1931/2 sought safety in the French franc; it had become convertible into gold again in 1928 under Prime Minister Poincare but at a parity only one fifth of that in 1914 (gold coins never came back into circulation though a new series was minted in 1935 and early 1936 at one fifth gold content of pre-1914 circulating coins; the government had these melted down following the French exit from the gold standard in September 1936). By 1936 though, given the election of the Front National in France, speculation against the French franc became virulent—on the view (or fear) that the gold bloc (of which the French franc was the leading member, alongside the Dutch, Belgian and Swiss currencies and a few smaller ones) would come to an early end—in fact in September 1936.

One element in the market pessimism concerning the future of the gold bloc had been the German re-militarization of the Rhineland in March 1936 and the view that France would have to step up military spending in consequence (see Hillwood et al. 2011). The Swiss franc was devalued by 30% (see Bordo et al. 2022). That date (September 1936) also marked the end of a gold coin standard in Switzerland, as Swiss gold coins until now circulating (the "Helvetia Heads") had risen in exchange value (in francs) to well above par; so the authorities no longer issued these coins at par and individuals pulled them into hoards rather than continuing to use them in payments (see Roth 2006). Into the late 1930s, the Swiss franc re-assumed refuge properties very quickly—especially with respect to capital flight out of European countries as war fears (and German invasion fears) crescendo. In the bigger picture though capital flight into the dollar was the dominant current, especially given fears that Switzerland would be occupied by Germany in the event of a European war. These fears first became widely apparent immediately following the entry of German troops into Prague in March 1939.

How good a haven the franc turned out to be and for who has become the subject of much historical investigation. And the notoriety of top Nazis gaining personally from that safe haven and the Nazi Government using "neutral" Switzerland for wartime financial transaction is known widely (see Volcker Commission report 2000). Through all this, the Swiss franc emerged as unchanged against the US dollar in the post-war period (from 1946 following a US-Swiss agreement on unfreezing dollar deposits) and at first alone alongside the dollar as a freely tradable money (no restrictions by the issuing country on its exchange for other currencies whether by residents or non-residents). So by the time we reach the modern era (say the mid/late 1960s) the franc had two great qualities underpinning its role as haven—first a history and present institutional/legal support (bank secrecy, neutrality, and until 2000 the legal principle that the currency be backed by gold on the basis of par values); second, a history of the Swiss authorities (as upheld by elections and constitution) following sound money principle.

The big challenge to the haven role of the franc that loomed by the late 1960s was the high and virulent monetary inflation in the US to whose dollar the franc like almost all other monies was pegged under the Bretton Woods monetary system. In assessing the franc's role as haven at that time the key question was how near a breaking point Switzerland had reached; specifically, would Berne (or Zurich) step outside the status quo order so as to prevent its money being swept into the US inflationary sea. And in the late 1960s, the speculative tide (and safe haven tide) was indeed in the direction that Switzerland might well make the break, most likely in conjunction somehow with Germany and possibly the Netherlands.

The basis of this view was in part the known fondness of the Swiss people (via the voting booth) for sound money and also knowledge of political and central bank actual currents. The Swiss National Bank was renowned for its independence from government and indeed its non-government ownership (only weak props on their own for monetary soundness as much later to be revealed both in Switzerland and outside). For those who looked forward, the high echelons of the Bank and its advisors (by the late 1960s and early 1970s) were advocates of the new so-called hard money doctrine, monetarism. Yes, there were unknown answers to questions about how a small country like Switzerland could anchor a money such as to prevent monetary inflation, either home-grown or imported; in particular how to limit the growth of the monetary base and how effective would such limits be? And the giant (relative to size of country) gold reserves were a positive factor (in perceptions as to whether Switzerland could pursue monetary independence of the US hegemon).

As regards other aspects of the franc's haven role—bank secrecy, neutrality (in the context now of the Cold War), and the Swiss political near-unanimity behind those constitutional pillars—nothing was in question at this point. Books were written about the attractions of the secret (sometimes "numbered") Swiss bank account, and the "gnomes of Zurich" were part of popular folklore.

As matters turned out, the Swiss franc delivered a roaring performance to investors globally through the years of monetary turmoil from the late 1960s to 1978. Even against the hard Deutsche mark, the Swiss franc delivered a high performance (of appreciation). In the generalized floating of exchange rate which proceeded in stop-start fashion from May 1971 to February 1973 followed by a completely free float of the US dollar, the franc was the star performer through to 1978. The Swiss National Bank seemed to be the purest practitioner of monetarism, allowing interest rates in the money market to float totally freely whilst it exerted strict control over the growth of monetary base. As regards consumer price inflation a virtuous circle set in; the rise of the Swiss franc contributed to holding down prices and so low inflation in the immediate contrasted with much higher inflation in the US, UK, and the other soft money countries in Europe—including France and Italy.

The first upset to Switzerland's sound money image came with the massive intervention to weaken and then hold down the franc in 1978 (see Pierdzoch and Stadtmann 2003). This involved "temporarily" fore-going monetary base control as massive foreign exchange intervention took priority (see Rich 2003). Subsequently, during the phase of a super-strong dollar from 1981 to the first half of 1985, the Swiss National Bank returned to its previous control of the monetary base. Then the "stuffing" started to fall out of its vision of monetarism in the second half of that decade (the 1980s). That decline of monetarism as an ideal in Switzerland coincided with the end of the "monetarist experiment" in the US: in Germany, however, practical application of monetarism continued until German unification in 1990.

A change in inter-clearing procedures introduced in mid-1987 (shifting to electronic settlement) between the banks disturbed the past relationship of monetary base to the wider money supply aggregates, but no-one knew by how much (see Vital and Mengle 1988). And in the second half of the 1980s when the US monetary hegemon again led the world into high monetary inflation (symptomized by raging asset inflation as described elsewhere—see pp. —and also upward pressure on goods and services inflation) Switzerland was no exception (see Rathke 2024). The monetarist "experiment" in Switzerland was near an end.

In 1999, the SNB dealt a death-blow to monetarism in Switzerland, joining the Federal Reserve, the new ECB (which opened its doors in 1998) and others which had implemented or were already well on the way to joining a 2% inflation standard. In that regime, the central bank strictly controlled the "policy rate" towards achieving the given target based on a neo-Keynesian macro-economic model. In Switzerland, the official aim was to hold inflation now below 2%, not very different from the Fed and ECB at that point.

So much for the independence of the central bank as a bulwark of monetary soundness. A senior member of the SNB directorate gave a celebratory speech welcoming the transition from monetarism to forecasting inflation (see Hildebrand 2004). Ahead of the formal scrapping of Swiss monetarism, the franc in 1995/6 had sprinted ahead in reflection of the decisions at a European level, which set a firm road ahead to European Monetary Union. Would not the looming death of the Deutsche mark and uncertainties about the European monetary experiment not re-awaken the hedge properties of the franc in the minds of investors? The lift did not last long.

And we can take the late 1990s as the start of a terrific wave of carry trade-related outflows from the franc. Everyone everywhere it seemed was borrowing low-interest rate francs and yen to buy higher yielding assets in other currencies—a principal feature of the gathering asset inflation which gained new momentum after the brief hiccup of disinflation in 2000 and the early 2001 (when the Fed and other central banks briefly sharply tightened monetary policy). Correspondingly, the real effective exchange rate of the Swiss franc fell from an index level of just above 100 in 1995 to a low of 80 in 2007. A further general factor in the weakness of the franc in those years (to 2007) was the wave of euphoria (one aspect of the global asset inflation) about European financial integration and the EU under the new monetary union, whose apparent successes were heralded by top monetary officials in the US and Europe (for example, see Bernanke 2008).

A background element in franc weakness was growing doubt about the safety of the franc haven as the "war on terror" (unleashed in response to the terror attacks on New York in September 2001) gathered momentum with its key financial component. Evidence already emerged that Switzerland was coming under new pressures to comply with demands of foreign governments and their tax authorities. For example, Switzerland accepted EU demands to levy withholding tax on EU resident wealth holdings at Swiss banks. This was in the context of Switzerland having come closer to the EU through its negotiated membership of the "single market"; in exchange for the benefits of this Switzerland had to deliver on compliance issues amongst others (see Wasserfallen 2023). And from 2005 onwards there was the ongoing saga of UBS and its negotiations with US legal authorities to reach settlement on its abetting of tax evasion by US clients (see Allen 2023).

Growing inroads and checks on Switzerland performing a safe haven role with respect to foreign grey or black capital did not have a direct impact on the franc given that much of such wealth though parked in Switzerland was in foreign currencies and other foreign assets, with Swiss entities being used as intermediaries and safekeeping agents in various ways. But there were important indirect influences of the role with respect to grey or black capital on the franc. For example, some of those foreign investors seeking safety had preferred to put a share of their wealth in the franc, believing that franc domestic assets in the ultimate would not be so penetrable by foreign authorities (for example, no clearing through the dollar payments system perhaps meant less access of foreign powers). Also, if reduced haven use of Switzerland meant less international business for the banks, especially those subject to potential huge penalties by foreign authorities, the underpinning of the Swiss franc could become less strong.

On the other hand, Switzerland offered the advantage of large denomination banknotes (CHF1000), and this became even more prized following the ECB's freeze on printing more of its 500-euro note (see Pedroza 2016). Inside Switzerland, there is considerable scope to use these notes for purchases of goods and services—no regulatory filing of reports on cash transactions under CHF100,000. We should also consider possible knock on effects to how safe wealthy foreign citizens who once upon a time would have bought Swiss residence/citizenship by setting up in Switzerland (and buying assets there) would be affected. Further, huge losses potentially at the banks, and bank runs could mean the Swiss National Bank had to finance these through its foreign exchange reserves.

The eruption of the Great Financial Crisis in 2007/8 went along with a violent reversal of the carry trades. This sent the franc soaring in the currency markets. And when the crisis rolled on to the European sovereign debt crisis, the franc reached new heights. In 2011, in the midst of the euro-sovereign debt crisis, attention also focused on growing sovereign debt risks in the US as highlighted by S&P's downgrade of US Treasuries. So, the 2011 peak of the franc coincided roughly with the peak of gold, which was also driven higher by those factors. During all these years of huge upward pressure on the franc– first and foremost from the reversal of the carry trade - there was continual heavy intervention (sale of francs) by the Swiss National Bank (SNB). Subsequently, however, the SNB did not enter into any program to systematically dispose of that "temporary reserve accumulation" undertaken to counter allegedly (according to SNB) disorderly conditions in the currency market. Quite the opposite; the SNB turned itself into a giant asset manager with respect to those bloated reserve holdings. The failure to reverse the build-up and the continuing albeit intermittent currency interventions as a component of monetary policy left Switzerland open to the charge of currency manipulation. Already in December 2020 Washington added Switzerland to the list of countries it charged with currency manipulation. Resulting uncertainty about an eventual push–back from the US is negative for the franc's haven role. That became apparent when in August 2025 Washington levied a 39% tariff rate on a large share of imports from Switzerland.

Here we encounter one fact which has remained solidly in favour of the franc as a haven—the low government debt to GDP ratio, which results from constitutional guardrails against government deficits in the Swiss confederacy and a totally funded pension system (no deficits). Other factors still supporting a hedge role for the franc included the fact that the SNB had not joined the ECB and Fed in 2003 in making its inflation target "symmetric"; the Fed and ECB had both declared that inflation would not be allowed to fall below 2%—as serious a command as not rising above 2% (so-called symmetry). And the SNB had not joined the Fed and ECB (and BoJ and BoE) in the QE experiment based on massive purchases of exploding government debt volumes—albeit that heavy foreign exchange market intervention did mean huge expansion anyhow in the Swiss monetary base, albeit camouflaged to some extent by issue of SNB "certificates".

As back in 1978, the upward flight of the Swiss franc towards the sky brought a Swiss government (together with the SNB) reaction in 2011—on top of growing and heavy intervention through the aftermath of the global crisis so as to contain the rise of the franc as carry trade positions were closed. The franc would not be allowed to rise above an arbitrary ceiling of 1.20 CHF/euro. The ceiling was abandoned in 2014 in the face of great speculative pressure and in the aftermath starting 2015 the Swiss National Bank joined the ECB in implementing a negative interest rate regime—a far cry from the one-time Swiss model of monetary soundness. This regime was not abandoned until September 2022 (see Revill and Koltravitz 2022) in the post-pandemic inflation (much less in Switzerland than in US and Europe—see pp). Even so through the interim years the franc did have knee-jerk safe haven reactions—rising sharply on the onset of the pandemic and later in anticipation and then actuality of Russia's invasion of Ukraine.

And in the interim, there was the repudiation of Swiss bank secrecy as regards non-Swiss clients. Already in the early 2010s, Switzerland had knuckled to the Obama Administration's campaign to get information on foreign accounts of US citizens, under the FACTA (signed in 2010) foreign banks had to report to the US authorities the details of income and assets of US citizens). In 2016, Switzerland joined in the automatic exchange of tax information with a whole range of countries including the EU, with the list extended in the following years. This was all in a context where Swiss banks had lost their reputation for discretion and dependability. There had been the near bankruptcy of UBS around the time of the Great Financial Crisis—staved off by the Swiss government setting up a bad bank to take over bad assets and essentially fund UBS back to health (see Morubelli 2018).

Then there was the revelation of how Swiss banks had aggressively competed during the previous decade and more for US non-tax compliant funds where previously they would have kept their heads down and hidden. The aggressiveness may well have stemmed from the raging asset inflation and the fact that in Europe bank equities were a focal point of that disease of monetary inflation (amidst euphoria about how European banks could perform under the tailwind of European monetary and more broadly financial integration). The pressure on bank management to produce strategies which would whip up their share price in this climate must have been fierce. Then on Russia's invasion of Ukraine in February 22, Switzerland abandoned strict neutrality and joined in EU/US measures to freeze assets held by the Russian central bank and designated oligarchs.

The safe haven role of Switzerland and the Swiss franc depends now (at time of writing in early 2025) on several considerations.

First, though Switzerland has joined in international tax and other types of enforcement, is it at the front of zealousness in all respects and what type of workarounds have been found there, if any? There is no international scoring on this. And indeed, on the basis of publicly available information, there could now be more doubts about the US given several large settlements with the US Justice Department or judicial enquiries still underway—mostly concerning large banks in New York who have been aggressively pursuing profit in the asset management business. Switzerland froze Russian assets as described at the start of the Russia-Ukraine war, but the total amount reported fell far short of some expert estimates of the total which tried to take account of offshore entities involved (see Revill 2024).

Second, Swiss large denomination banknotes and gold in non-bank safes in Switzerland remain important refuges. And besides, the popularity of those banknotes and the potential to spend these in Switzerland in large amounts should help broaden, strengthen, and stabilize the overall demand for Swiss base money—an important plus should Switzerland ever take the path back to a well-anchored monetary system.

And third, the internal purchasing power of the Swiss franc for whatever reason has evaporated by substantially less over long periods than the dollar or euro; that history is a boost to international confidence in the franc going forward (though it has to be continually substantiated!). From 1996 to 2025, the price level in Switzerland rose by just short of 20%. In the euro-zone, over the same interval of time prices were up by around 75%.

In effect, the SNB was "content" with price rises averaging 1% p.a. over the long run—none of the Fed or ECB mantra of taking measures to make sure that inflation did not fall below 2% p.a. on average over many years. Did the SNB achieve this lower inflation by skill and intent or luck?

The argument for skill is that its inflation target is expressed differently—and less radically—than the ECB or SNB; that was deliberate choice. And on occasion, the SNB has welcomed/invited Swiss franc appreciation as a means of holding inflation down. And in the skill box, we should also put the sound fiscal situation in Switzerland, which surely dampens long-run inflation expectations compared to the situation in the eurozone or the US.

The argument for luck includes that at critical junctures for inflation and inflation expectations globally there has been a rush of funds into the Swiss franc, and the appreciation has set off a virtuous circle of lower inflation than elsewhere. The start to that virtuous circle might not be strong fundaments but a Pavlovian reaction to trouble looming, let's buy the franc. And for the historical record the effective real exchange rate of the franc has been on a virtual flat trend since the late 1990s—so none of the effervescence about safe havens that we say in the 1970s.

What is the biggest potential upside factor for the Swiss franc overall? It is political, economic and financial crisis in Germany; or alternatively an existential crisis for the euro.

References

Allen, Matthew "How the US tax evasion crackdown impacted Swiss banking" Swissinfo.ch December 5, 2023

Bernanke, Ben S "The Euro at Ten" Speech at the fith European Central Bank Conference, November 14, 2008

Bordo, Michael D, Helbling, Tomas, James, Harold "Swiss exchange rate policy in the 1930s; was the delay in devaluation too high a price to pay for conservatism?" NBER working paper, No w12491, August 2022

Brown, Brendan "Monetary Chaos in Europe" Routledge 2011

Guex, Sebastian "The Origins of the Swiss Banking Secrecy Law and its Repercussions for Swiss Federal Policy"*The Business History Review* , Vol.*74* , No. 2 Summer 2000 pp 237–66

Hildebrand, Philipp "From Monetarism to the Inflation Forecast: 30 years of Swiss Monetary Policy" *Public lecture, University of Berne*, November 23, 2004

Hillwood, Paul; Macdonald Ronald; Marsh Ian "Remilitarisation and the End of the Gold Bloc in 1936" De Economist, Vol. 159, pp. 305-321, April 23, 2011

Morubelli, Armando "The day UBS, the biggest Swiss bank, was saved" Swiss info.ch, October 16, 2018

Jenkins, Brian " The Six Fevrier 1934 and the "survival" of the French Republic"*French History* , Vol. *20*, Issue 3, August 2006, pp 333–51

Pedroza, David "Mountains of Cash" IMF*Finance and Development* , Vol. 53, no. 3 September 2016

Pierdzoch, Christian and Stadtmann, Georg "*The Effectiveness of the interventions of the Swiss National Bank*" Kiel Working Paper No. 1160, April 2003

Rathke, Alexander "Made in Frankfurt? The Monetary Policy of the Swiss National Bank since 1973" *Comparative Economic Studies* ,August 2, 2024

Rich, Georg "Swiss Monetary Targeting 1974-6: the role of internal policy analysis" ECB Working Paper, December 2003

Revill, John "Swiss deny drop in value of frozen Russian assets signals weak enforcement" Reuters, April 23, 2024

Revill, John and Koltravitz, Silke "Swiss national Bank exits negative rates with 0.75% hike" Reuters, September 22, 2022

Roth, Jean-Pierre "Seventy Years After -the final collapse of the gold standard in September 1936" Opening remarks to Conference "Seventy Years After" University of Zurich, December 15, 2006

Vital, Christian and Mengle, David "SIC: Switzerland's new electronic interbank payments system" *Richmond Federal Reserve Economic Review*, Nov/Dec 1988

Volcker Commission Report "Holocaust Restitution: the "Volcker Commission" investigation of Swiss banks, February 2000

Wasserfallen, Fabio "Switzerland and the European Union" Oxford Academic, December 2023

CHAPTER 18

Epilogue

A Great Inflation Without End

How will the latest great monetary inflation end?

Most likely, the Federal Reserve at some stage will confront another sustained run-up in consumer prices. The fault as before will lie with the bad money regime in which that institution plays a lead role.

At that future point, however, no supply side bonanza might be in sight to provide relief—different from in 2022 at the worst point of the pandemic consumer price inflation. Then, as we have shown in this volume (see Part C), the Fed moderated its response to CPI inflation "shock" in the expectation that the evident receding of the Covid-19 disease would foster a rapid mending of supply dislocations. That restoration would bear down on many goods prices. Moderation meant a continuation of monetary inflation.

An alternative scenario for the end of the actual great monetary inflation is that the Fed might implement disinflation by accident. As illustration, this central bank could have judged its chosen path for the policy interest rate to be neutral or accommodative. Then results—fading symptoms of inflation in goods and asset markets—reveal with notorious lags that in fact Fed policy has been restrictive.

Would there be an early sequel—another great monetary inflation after a few years' intermission—as has been the pattern ever since the international gold standard collapsed in August 1914? Or could sound money

B. Brown and P. Simonnot, *Bad Money*,
https://doi.org/10.1007/978-3-031-95425-2_18

advocacy yet emerge from its present comatose state in the political arena and vanquish the inflation mongers? Read on for the answer, which stems from earlier chapters in this volume.

The present great monetary inflation started in the recovery phase of the business cycle upturn subsequent to the last Great Recession (in the US 2007Q4-2009Q1). We can describe this as the post-Great Financial Crisis (GFC) inflation—already the longest in modern history. The GFC on its most comprehensive definition includes the mega-quakes in the US and globally during Summer 2007 and Autumn 2008 together with the aftershocks in Europe during 2010–12.

We measure length (of any given monetary inflation) as the distance in time from the initial powerful shots (injection) of monetary inflation to when significant and sustained monetary disinflation occurs. Previous great monetary inflations on this definition include 1995/6–2005/6, 1962–73 and 1938/9–48. Shorter, yet severe, monetary inflations include 1915–19,1922–8, 1934–36, 1950–56, 1976–1980, 1985–9, and 1991/2–4. These dates are all based on evidence in the US. Similar dates apply to some key foreign countries, including Germany, Japan, and China, during episodes in which they came under the strong influence of the US monetary hegemon (see Brown and Simonnot, 2020).

The laboratory of monetary history is a fertile ground for clue-digging about the present and future, but it cannot yield predictions. The actual monetary regime—the 2% inflation standard—has had such a corrupting influence as to make laboratory use more challenging but not unproductive. In particular, monetary base has become so diluted in its provision of extreme moneyness that changes in its supply no longer have a high-powered influence on the wider economy (see chapter 3).

Hence, diagnosis of monetary inflation and comparison with previous episodes are now more difficult to make with significant confidence. Central banks, led by the Federal Reserve, in pursuing their policy objectives, now rely crucially on in-house assessments about whether a given level of their policy rate is restrictive, inflationary, or neutral. Yet we know from economics 101 that interest rates are a highly treacherous indicator of the underlying monetary stance.

So how can we recognize today the end of a great monetary inflation? There should be a fading away of inflation symptoms in both markets for goods/services and assets. In this volume, we have set out the principles for recognizing symptoms. These transcend simple CPI data or stock market trends (see chapter 15). As illustration, low reported CPI inflation might coincide with severe monetary inflation when there are coincident strong non-monetary disinflationary forces at work. Irrational exuberance including the illusions of financial engineering in their various forms may be present still even when asset prices have been stable or well below their latest high point for some time.

During the post-GFC inflation, there has been a non-stop sequence of stimulus shots (injections) administered by the Federal Reserve. Central banks of foreign countries (or groups of countries as for EMU) in Europe and Asia under the strong influence of the US monetary hegemon have taken similar action. These shots, with virtually no monetary disinflation in between, have occurred ostensibly in response to perceived near-term dangers of economic and financial weakness sometimes joined with incipient downward pressure on prices.

The concept of a super-long post-GFC inflation stretching from early in the second decade of the twenty-first century to at least the middle of the third decade is far from consensus. Many commentators by contrast take their measure of inflation for dating purposes as simply consumer prices without a theory-based focus on monetary conditions. The finding here of super-long monetary inflation continuing from the early 2010s turns to an important degree on the diagnosis of persistent asset inflation. Also there is the evidence that the Fed has brutally repressed non-monetary disinflationary forces whenever these have gathered power (see chapter 1). It does this by administering additional shots of monetary inflation or by failing to withdraw excess vaccine stimulant already in the system.

We note in this volume (see ter 5) that the asset market spasm of February/March 2020, at the eruption of the pandemic, does not qualify as an end to the post-GFC inflation. Nor does the series of half-point rate rises effected by the Powell Fed through summer and early autumn 2022 qualify as such (see chapter 6). Symptoms of asset inflation remained severe in 2023–4, even though the bubble burst in some darling pandemic start-up darling stocks. (see chapter 15). The fall in reported CPI inflation—still significantly above target—was due to powerful non-monetary disinflationary forces emitted by the receding of the pandemic and the related fading of supply dislocations rather than to any monetary disinflation. Opposing non-monetary inflationary forces emitted by the Russia-Ukraine War via energy supply disruption turned out to be much less substantial than widely feared at its start.

The non-monetary disinflationary forces earlier in the post-GFC inflation, specifically during the first decade of the post-GFC great inflation (say 2010–20), had featured prominently "globalization". International supply chains were built to take advantage of new scope for sourcing cheaper manufactured goods from the emerging market world. Important factors strengthening globalization included China's entry into the WTO at the end of the 1990s and also the IT revolution. This latter made possible the essential management control and marketing processes alongside the resourcing away from advanced to emerging market economies.

As the central banks around the world, led by the US monetary hegemon (the Federal Reserve), pursued their target of 2% inflation despite the circumstances of powerful non-monetary disinflation, virulent asset inflation took hold. China was one epicentre of asset inflation, as driven by the combination of Fed monetary policy and Chinese exchange rate policy (which officially aimed for stability of the yuan despite huge upward pressure from trade and capital flows). Alongside the bubble in domestic real estate was the boom of foreign direct investment into China. A hunt for yield generally across the globe, as driven by super low policy rates in the US, Europe, and Japan, fed huge demand for emerging market corporate (financial and non-financial) credit paper including Chinese.

Globalization most likely became excessive—a form of mal-investment (see chapter 14). The standard of measurement here is the pattern of capital spending which would have occurred under sound money where sober-rational expectations remained dominant. In fact, though, speculative excitement reigned in asset markets about businesses pursuing the opportunities of cheap sourcing in emerging market economies. In that climate wealth managers who considered carefully all the possible snags in global supply chains would have found that their performance became sub-standard compared to peers who applied no such rational caution.

Asset inflations can come to an end sometimes in ways which accelerate a transition already in process from monetary inflation to monetary disinflation. For example, the pilots of Federal Reserve policy in plotting the path for the policy interest rate might not realize that speculative cooling is already well underway and setting the stage for sudden economic weakening. The Fed may have taken rate action with the intent of disinflating gradually. The economic and financial scene which emerges, especially allowing for such feedback loops, turns out to be much more sombre than its policy-making committee had expected.

As of the time of writing (summer 2025), the last episode of substantially disinflationary Fed monetary policy whether by design or unintended was 2006–8. There has not been a period of severe or even modest monetary disinflation since. Instead, a sequence of monetary shots (or injections) has occurred, four to five in just the course of the Powell Fed. This followed earlier sometimes mega-shots under the Bernanke and then the Yellen Fed.

There has been periodic chatter about disinflation in the 13 years to 2025. In 2013, there was all the pseudo-drama as reported in the financial media about a "tapering" of quantitative easing (QE). In 2018 the subject was the Powell "normalization" of Fed funds rate as this rose from around zero to just above 2%. There was then the noisy speculation of Summer 2022 about the Fed pivoting to a Volcker-style monetary crackdown to deal with the eruption of high-CPI inflation. In all cases, monetary inflation once again picked up momentum after only at most a gentle tap on the brakes.

The long absence of monetary disinflation may well have encouraged many investors to assume this will not occur in the future. If indeed CPI inflation again headed much higher, there are grounds for doubting the strenuousness, conscientiousness and competence with which the authorities would respond. The Inflation mongers are now prominent throughout the corridors of power (see chapter 7). Even so popular resentment about loss of purchasing power could stimulate a political backlash against those perceived as responsible. Accordingly pressures for monetary disinflation would build up. The inflation mongers are then likely to go silent for a while.

Take an alternative way in which the post-GFC inflation could end—monetary policy turning out to have been much tighter than the policy rate setters intended. Asset markets as subject to irrational exuberance may well underestimate this possible future scenario. Its likelihood of realization is enhanced by the long duration of the present asset inflation. Malinvestment and high leverage have accumulated to mean much more than normal economic fragility. Growth of general prosperity across the population as a whole in the advanced economies (considered in aggregate) has become at best mediocre in consequence—creating political fodder for populism and its pursuit of sometimes illiberal solutions (see chapter 14).

The fiscal situation can play an important role in how this great inflation ends. Governments have seemingly broad access under the present monetary regime to cheap funding for a bonanza in expenditures. Government programs ostensibly compensate voters for cramped real income growth—for which the culprit is malinvestment. Ultimately, however, the underlying insolvency of the state could show up in a crisis of high inflation as the government and its central bankers resort to the punitive levying of inflation tax. A shock rise in consumer prices - together with a related jump in long-term interest rates - radically reduces the real value of outstanding government debt. Political forces might catapult into power a new government and different central bankers who would terminate the inflation.

Transition to sound money should help towards healing malinvestment and its blight on the essential process of innovation in the economy. The invisible hands under ideal sound money and competitive conditions guide the journey into the forest of the unknown in a rationally cautious way allowing for the accumulation of knowledge. Under monetary inflation however these hands might become super-powered—as huge speculation and monopolies take control, overturning the natural brakes on the process of implementing new technology. The journey into the unknown and the adaptation of business to the new technology might occur at a grippingly rapid speed. That would be well in excess of the slower and measured pace under the ideal monetary conditions. This pace would be well-calibrated, allowing time for possibly serious negative aspects of the new technology to emerge before network or other effects make it too late to feasible walk back (see chapter 14).

Biologists study how bad innovation ultimately handicaps or even dooms a particular species. Malinvestment in innovation lies within that purview.

Malinvestment in this great post-GFC inflation has also crucially taken a form which we could describe at the build-up of monopoly capital. Digitalization has spawned the potential for monopoly or oligopoly formation, most of all in provision of the digital platforms but also more broadly. The combination of speculative storytelling and the hunt for yield has meant that enterprises which potentially could obtain s long stream of giant and growing monopoly revenues became the darlings of the asset markets. Their access to high-priced equity inflows in turn expanded their capacity to engage in predatory and killer-zone (against new entrants) strategies. Monopolization and curtailment of free entry are burdens on the long-run growth of prosperity across the population as a whole, albeit there are some obvious big gainers.

It is hard to find in the laboratory of history any great recession or overall market crash which was obviously precipitated solely by failing prosperity due to mal investment, although this may have been an unprovable seriously contributing factor. That generalization excludes crashes due to obvious exogenous events—for example outbreak of the Great War in July 1914 or arrival of pandemic as in February 2020.

If the Fed is indeed programmed to extend massive potential support to all "systemically important" financial institutions, then perhaps a financial crisis will not reach the intensity which we have seen historically. Potential bailouts are now so huge and predictable that we could describe the US financial system as having become subject to Sinicization (Chinese-style bailouts amidst severe financial repression).

Sample sizes in the laboratory of history are typically small. No, we cannot yet point definitively to a great recession which has unfolded in a setting where the Fed had not already for some time gone down the path of implementing intended monetary disinflation. But there is not sufficient evidence to rule out that sequence as being significantly possible in the future. And as to the proposition that bailouts in their various forms will be most probably sufficient to prevent crisis in our present world, this is just too large and heterogeneous to endorse this. It could be true in the US for some time, but in all of Europe and Asia? Doubtful. And we have to consider the possible fall-out from mania formation and ultimate dispersal (see chapter 15).

The emergence of manias historically has always coincided with powerful monetary inflations including as a symptom virulent asset inflation. Manias do not occur in isolation from the monetary environment. Real-time diagnosis of these phenomena is always troublesome in some degree. There are just not the empirical test-kits which flash a warning signal when speculative temperatures exceed a certain degree or when sober-rationality at large in a market descends below a given danger point. This is all the more so in today's world where monetary aggregates—and in particular monetary base—have lost significance. Sky-high moves of the gold price may be in such circumstances useful evidence about whether the disease of monetary inflation is present or widely feared.

Another episode of monetary stimulus leading on eventually to a spike of CPI inflation might be under way at the time or writing (August 2025). Symptoms of monetary inflation in asset markets are cause for increased concern - the mal-signalling of long-term interest rates, the compressed credit spreads, the hot speculative narratives, the suspected manias, in sum the degree of exuberance. There is much controversy about whether and how the Fed should respond to the implementation of the Trump Administration's trade policy. The implementation is emitting a supply shock, albeit of largely unknown dimension, with respect to the US economy. The suspected actual revving up of monetary inflation would be in the context of this supply shock. The inflation mongers tell us that any possible blip in the CPI in the next year or so due to tariffs should be regarded as "one-off". Sound money advocates view this differently. The new trade policy is unleashing a supply shock whose impact effect on prices goes well beyond just goods subject to tariff, including domestic goods which are substitutes for these. A fundamental characteristic of a good monetary regime is its in-built resistance to supply shocks now or in the future becoming the catalyst to monetary inflation. Yes it is possible that one of these supply shocks will erupt coincidentally with a gathering of recessionary forces or a coincidental good supply shock (such as a big increase in energy supplies). A good monetary system, solidly anchored, provides a flexible response to these possible actualities without allowing combustion into monetary inflation to take place (see chapter 3). Beware of the arguments for an exception just this time - cutting loose the anchor - in the face of supply shock. If not now, when? A present exception means less grounds for confidence regarding this money's soundness in the future. Bad money in the future as in the past surely means a continuing series of supply shocks - war,trade conflict, pandemic, famine - triggering episodes of aggravated monetary inflation. These episodes are likely to include a serious late phase where monetary inflation is applied to repressing a fall in prices once the original supply shock goes into reverse (see chapter 1).

Would a new spell of high CPI inflation under the present bad money regime, whether triggered by supply shock or anything else, cause the case for monetary reform to become prominent in the political arena? Arguably, monetary reform in a sound direction has never before (in the US election history since 1890 summarized in this volume—see part F) been such a dead subject as now. By contrast, the great monetary inflation of 1962–73 (the first instalment of the so-called "greatest peacetime inflation" which includes also the shorter monetary inflation of 1976–80 (this followed the intermission of the Great Crash of 73–4 and the Great Recession of 73–5) did catalyse the cause of sound monetary reform both in the US and Europe. The main strand of reform at that time was practical monetarism, present most strongly in Germany and Switzerland.

The case for a "return to gold" could also be heard then in the political arena. In the mid-1960s, President de Gaulle and his economic adviser Jacques Rueff had campaigned for gold. In 1980, President Carter had signed into law a mandate from Congress for a Gold Commission to consider a return to gold. President Reagan in 1981 appointed an anti-gold majority of experts in the Commission who were monetarists in the main. Its recommendation as to be expected was against gold and broadly in favour of practical monetarism (see Schwartz 1987).

Two main flaws characterized these monetarist prescriptions as applied in practice (see "A Guide to Good Money", Brown and Pringle 2022).

First, they failed to acknowledge that an essential condition of success was that monetary base (otherwise described as high-powered money) should render widely sought after super qualities of extreme moneyness (whether as medium of exchange or store of value). In consequence there would be a large, strong and stable demand for the components of monetary base—cash and reserve deposits in the case of fiat money.

Second, they did not secure a slow growing but flexible increase in the supply of the actual fiat monetary base. There was the Friedman formula of an arbitrary low x% p.a. increase in supply. Or alternatively constitutional rules could be drawn up which would allow the monetary authority to adapt the supply in line with perceived sea-changes in demand for real monetary base balances.

We argue in this volume that the success of a sound money regime depends crucially on addressing these two main flaws (see chapter 3). That is true whether advocacy is for fiat money or gold money (see Brown 2023).

Addressing flaws is itself a dry subject unlikely to cause stir in the emotions of the political arena. Rather, a fundamental message of the reformers should recite the ills of the present monetary regime—disappointing growth in overall living standards, great financial crisis and ensuing great recession, monopoly, episodes of high CPI inflation as during the pandemic and continuing into its aftermath. These ills are all set to continue and recur as long as the actual regime remains in power.

The reformers have to make the case that their alternative monetary regime will cure those ills. Their package of reforms should stand out as promoting competitive capitalism and freedom. Indeed, as we show in this volume, a competitive financial system and roll-back of regulations which impede the market delivering forms of money which individuals would choose ideally, are pre-conditions for the success of a new sound money regime. At the time of writing there is much excitement about US legislation - the "Genius Act" - which provides a new regulatory framework for US dollar stablecoins. The excitement is apparent in the soaring valuations of firms which might well become the leaders in this space. None of this so far is cause for big celebration amongst the advocates of sound money and should be viewed instead as evidence of the present severe asset inflation (see chapter 15). Dollar stablecoins subject to the regulations are to be backed by Treasury Bills as well as deposits at insured US banks. The regulations thwart rather than enhances the potential intense monetary services of base money. A better framework would foster a strong and stable demand for base money (despite paying no interest as would be the case under a sound money regime). Development of base money's qualities is essential to sound money reform. Instead, the Genius Act promotes Treasury Bills as a near substitute for base money. The main cause for optimism is that the structure of stable coin could be adjusted and extended to gold, boosting the yellow metal's potential to eventually become a key component of a new sound money order. A hopeful sign in that direction has been the passing of a law in Texas (2025) which makes gold a form of legal tender from 2026 and provides a legal framework for electronic payments in gold backed by gold in specified state vaults from 2027.

Should sound money advocates stop their prevaricating and announce that their proposed monetary regime is gold rather than fiat? In the conclusion to our earlier volume, "Europe's Century of Crisis Under Dollar Hegemony", Philippe Simonnot wrote, when discussing our proposal for an ultimate restoration of gold money in Europe:

> "The proposal here is not a return to a bygone past but the closure of the disastrous experience of the 20th century which resulted for humanity in millions of deaths and destruction.—We surely all realize that it is not sufficient to explain the chaos of the present global economic system by just going back to the mega crisis of autumn 2008. It is in that final European month of August 1914 where the traveller backwards through time gets to the bottom of the search for explanation. In a few hours the convertibility of paper money was abandoned, provisionally it was claimed, in the heart of Europe which in that era was the heart of the world"

Well now at the time of writing (summer 2025), substantial evidence from the new century of monetary chaos under the prevailing fiat money regime is now in. Europe's vaunted monetary union (EMU) is a creature of that regime built on the false canons of central bank "independence" and the 2% inflation standard. This further evidence surely adds to the case for cynicism on what future fiat monetary reform might bring. There is now a record of reform failure under the banners of first "practical" monetarism and then 2% inflation targeting.

The best and most plausible way forward to a better monetary regime is to start with planting the roots of a new sound money and nurturing their growth. This program means bolstering monetary competition—tackling for example credit and payment card oligopoly power whilst ending "too big to fail" assistance by government. Then free market forces would foster the supply of extreme moneyness as rendered by monetary base components. There should be new and hard constitutional guardrails against the monetary fuelling of Big Government. These should include tight limits on central bank balance sheet expansion, and also making clear that in a future government insolvency crisis "money printing" would not come to the rescue. In consequence, the cost of government borrowing would rise sharply if its debt profile worsened seriously, acting as a powerful discipline on public spending.

A near-term aim should be the withdrawal of the central bank from setting short-term interest rates as the monetary base regains sufficient power to become a key component of a solid anchoring mechanism. Deflation phobia would fade away as a new monetary reality dawned. Substantial stretches of price declines and price gains would be the norm; they would be expected to cancel each other out over the long run.

Supply shocks whether triggered by war or pandemic or any other cause could well mean prices on average at a substantially above-normal level. But monetary forces coupled with a possible reversal of the supply shock (peace or end of pandemic) would bring prices back down eventually. In recessions, prices would most likely fall well below their normal level on average, recovering and even rising above normal transitorily in a subsequent expansion and then boom phase.

Gold convertibility of the dollar provides a much stronger guardrail than is possible from fiat money constitutionalism around these same principles of good money. It may well be the case that gold, due to its physical characteristics, can offer a breadth and intensity of monetary services (as medium of exchange and store of value) in an exceptional fashion which cannot be matched by fiat money. Hence gold would be ideal as the base for a sound money system. Gold can sparkle in the imagination of voters in ways not possible for dry legal principles about good money on their own. US election history does provide rare examples of where a bad money regime—actual or potential—has been severely wounded, even terminally, at the ballot box. These wounds are sometimes less severe at second than first sight (think here of 1952 and 1980—see Part F). For gold to triumph, some lead campaigners in the political arena must consider gold money to be a winning theme. A forerunner of such success is an infectious excitement about principles of good money and its benefits.

References

Brown, Brendan "The Qualities of the Monetary Base Essential to Sound Money: Fiat and Gold" *Quarterly Journal of Austrian Economics*, Vol. *26*, Issue 4, 2023

Brown, Brendan and Pringle, Robet "*A Guide to Good Money*" Palgrave 2022

Brown, Brendan and Simonnot, Philippe "*Europe's Century of Crises under Dollar Hegemony*" Palgrave 2020

Schwartz, Anna J "Reflections on the Gold Commission Report" pp. 317–333 in NBER's "*Money in Historical Perspective*" University of Chicago Press 1987

Correction to: Bad Money

Correction to:
B. Brown and P. Simonnot, *Bad Money*,
https://doi.org/10.1007/978-3-031-95425-2

The original version of Chapter 9, 10, 12, 17 was previously published with small typographical error, which has now been corrected. The chapter has been updated with the change.

The updated version of this book can be found at
https://doi.org/10.1007/978-3-031-95425-2

B. Brown and P. Simonnot, *Bad Money*,
https://doi.org/10.1007/978-3-031-95425-2_19

Index

B. Brown and P. Simonnot, *Bad Money*,
https://doi.org/10.1007/978-3-031-95425-2

MIX
Papier | Fördert gute Waldnutzung
FSC® C083411

Kolibri 360 GmbH
Ferdinand-Jühlke-Straße 7
99095 Erfurt, Deutschland
produktsicherheit@kolibri360.de